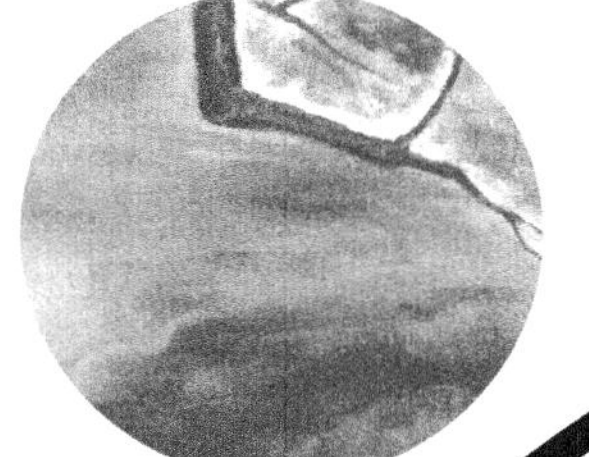

POLITICAL ECOSYSTEMS

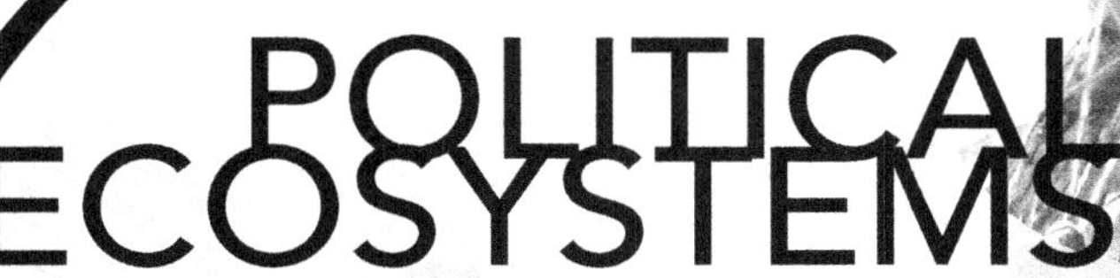

*Modernity, Complexity,
Fluidity and the Eco-Left*

J. P. HARPIGNIES

SPUYTEN DUYVIL

New York City

Spuyten Duyvil;

http://spuytenduyvil.net; 1-800-886-5304

Acknowledgements

To Kenny Ausubel, for all I have learned from him in 34 years about perseverance, discipline and loyalty; to the visionary poet André Spears for his support, life-long friendship and the use of his retreat in the Catskill Mountains where these ideas were honed; to that great unsung nurturer of struggling artists, poets, musicians, activists and thinkers, Anne Hemenway, for all her encouragement over the years; to Elizabeth Thompson, a few scintillating conversations with whom led to my deciding to write this book, and without whose help and encouragement it never would have come into being; to the Situationist Godfather of Grand Army Plaza, picnic master and translator sans pareil, Donald Nicholson-Smith, for his help and support; to Betsy Tompkins for her life-saving, invaluable research assistance; to Professor Tyler Volk for his important critique of a crucial section of this text; to that very different drummer and most multi-cultural and poly-linguistic of private investigators, Adam Raskin, for his valued feed-back; and to my friend and cyber-savior, Glenn Macura.

Library of Congress CIP Data

Harpignies, J. P.
Political ecosystems : modernity, complexity, fluidity, and the eco-Left / J.P. Harpignies.

    p. cm.

    Includes bibliographical references.

ISBN 0-9720662-9-2 1. Social movements. 2. Environmentalism.

3. Political ecology. 4. Political activists. 5. Right and left (Political science) I. Title.

HM881.H37 2004

303.48'4--dc22   2004003974

Contents

About this book ...
Why it was written, what it is not,
to whom it is addressed,
some definitions of key terms,
and an apology
for thematic repetitions in the text

I am a frustrated environmental activist with roots in the left to explore some largely unexamined rifts and unconscious assumptions that I feel may be hampering the effectiveness of environmental and social justice movements. There are many very worthy people and groups in these movements with sophisticated outlooks, doing excellent work, whom I admire, and this text is by no means an attempt to critique them to tout my own solutions. I have no ultimate solutions. I am very critical of a number of reflexes and underlying assumptions, but these are deep collective problems with complex historical roots, and I share many of them, so I am not out to attack individuals. I may be harsh at times, but my goal herein is simply to encourage more complex, less pat, more multi-perspectival ways of reading the socio-political landscape, especially that of the United States, which I argue, is sadly far more conservative and resistant to progressive agendas than most of us in our camp usually acknowledge.

I do not, for the most part, advocate specific positions, as I'm fairly pessimistic about the possibility of changing people's core ideas. I'm more interested in encouraging all of us within the broad swath of the eco and social justice movements, whatever our particular ideological bents may be, to be more open to political self-examination and more fluid in our thinking. This text is an attempt to unearth underlying contradictions and to bring them to conscious attention; it is not, for the most part, a prescriptive work. It also avoids as much as possible areas that have been extensively discussed by many others, such as class vs. race and "identity" politics or "deep" vs. "social" ecology, to focus on rarely discussed topics that may be as important. It does not offer any wondrous cures for our predicament or some revolutionary over-arching theory, just what the author hopes might be a few original approaches to broadening our political perspectives, and it tries to avoid ad hominem attacks to remain focused on larger issues.

The book is addressed to others who share eco-progressive world-views and assumes a fairly high degree of familiarity with left and eco-politics as well as a more general interest in history, politics and culture. People of other political persuasions may find some insights that apply across the ideological spectrum, and may find some other aspects of the text of interest, but they will have to suspend their distaste for my obvious biases. (Of course, they might also enjoy reading about their opponents' angst.) This book is intended for a fairly literate audience, but it is a subjective polemic, not an academic or scholarly work. To make it more reader-friendly, I have eschewed footnotes. References to works cited in the text and to some additional relevant books or articles, as well as some elaborations and explanations of specific points will be found in a separate section at the end of each chapter.

I have to admit that, while I usually advocate linguistic precision, I have found myself forced to be sloppy with regards to some of the key terms I use repeatedly. I use the terms "left" and "progressive" somewhat interchangeably, for example. I am not using the term "progressive" in its precise historical context (i.e., the post-populist early twentieth century reform movement and its heirs) but as a general, blanket term to cover a broad range of (non-Communist) left and left-liberal tendencies. Part of the reason for this is that I am not concerned in this book with touting any specific sectarian positions but, mostly, in addressing a wide wave of at least somewhat like-minded people, so I need broad, blanket terms. When I do deal with very specific groups, positions or ideologies, I then strive to be as precise as possible.

Also, "left" and "right" are obviously very hard to define. One frequently hears, for example, contemporary commentators refer to "hard-liners" in the post "fall of The Wall" Russian or Chinese Communist parties, who once would have been seen as far-left on the global scale, as "the right," and pro-market modernizers and reformers as "liberals." But this apparent contradiction does capture something essential in the right/left dynamic. People instinctively tend to think of the left as that part of the political spectrum/impulse that constantly challenges the status quo and entrenched power elites, that pushes for more egalitarian economic and social relationships and for global, universal standards in human rights. And they tend to think of the right as that part of society that tends to resist rapid social change; to distrust utopian, egalitarian impulses; to be more concerned with order than with justice, with the individual rather than the collective; and to be more comfortable with hierarchies of wealth and power and local "tribal" and national allegiances.

Obviously, though, nearly all significant movements have been hybrids of left and right impulses, and many of us contain elements of both general tendencies in our political make-up. At some historical moments rightists are the revolutionary rebels and the left in power, and movements can mutate into their opposites as power corrupts. And both left and right movements and regimes have trampled upon individuals' and groups' rights at different junctures. Furthermore one of my key points is that, while the left/right axis is still a relevant lens on a variety of issues, especially economic ones, on many other crucial questions other political divides, such as communitarian vs. libertarian or neo-Luddite vs. techno-utopian reflexes may be more relevant. So I wish I could do better, but for my purposes in this book, I'm just using the terms left and right very broadly, like that Supreme Court judge who couldn't define pornography but claimed he knew it when he saw it.

Also, some might object that I seem to be just assuming the environmental movement is a phenomenon of the left. I realize American conservationism has some of its roots in nineteenth century patrician, elitist (and not infrequently racist vis-á-vis Native Americans), nature Romanticism, but the situation is very different today. And while there are "red vs. green" disputes between environmentalists and unions over jobs and economic issues and disputes between enviros and social justice and other progressive activists over other questions, and disputes with Indian tribes over land use, I think it is fair, at this stage, to view these as mostly internecine conflicts within the broad swath of the panorama of what is today considered the "left." It is a somewhat confusing situation as there are environmentalists across the political spectrum, but the vast preponderance of committed eco-activists are part of the continuum of the "left." And anyway these are only a few examples of the divisions and confusions that make the political landscape harder and harder to decipher and that are, in fact, some of the major topics of this book.

A note on repetition in this text

This book was not written as separate essays that were then cobbled together into a book. Nonetheless quite a few of my main themes are repeated or rather revisited in different chapters. Part of that is due to the fact that an author tends to have a few key obsessions that keep reappearing, and I apologize for that, though, obviously, I think my pet obsessions are worthy of repeated examination or I wouldn't have bothered writing about them. But much of the repetition is intentional in that I use a few principal themes as the main lenses through which I examine the different topics I am exploring, and so felt the need to keep reintroducing them in different permutations, a bit like exploring an object from several different angles to get a better sense of it. And the book does follow a logical order, but is also somewhat holographic in that someone could probably read the chapters in any order or just read at random and still get some sense of my approach and key concepts.

INTRODUCTION

I have found myself for a very long time depressed by the relative failures (or at least lack of deep enough success) of most of the environmental and left/progressive movements I have participated in or to which I feel some kinship. Of course those failures are not always the fault of activists. Sometimes the winds of history just aren't blowing your way. But very often I also find myself irked by some of the tenor and substance of the discourse prevalent within the left and, more seriously, by many unexamined assumptions and glossed-over contradictions underlying that discourse. So I began to attempt to analyze those logical inconsistencies and dubious pre-suppositions that were pushing my buttons and to seek as well to understand the reasons for the so frequent shrill and hysterical tone found on the left. I am not naïve. I realize political rhetoric rarely has any claims to literary elegance, and that politics throughout history has almost invariably involved exaggeration, deception and manipulation (not to mention betrayal, murder, etc.). This actually poses special problems for the left because it is, by and large, the most utopian part of the political spectrum with the most exalted aspirations, so its failures to live up to high moral, intellectual and aesthetic standards are, perhaps unfairly, harder to forgive.

I also realize frustration is a constant in political activism of all stripes. The collision of the harsh realities of the world and the need for distasteful compromises with the idealism that initially motivates most activists makes political engagement a painful affair, with at best short-lived victories. And this sense of perpetual anger and dissatisfaction is as true on the right as it is on the left. Some fundamentalist Christian activists seethe when, for example, despite their impressive political gains, they feel powerless to stanch the growing acceptance of homosexuality or the amorality of Hollywood, or to roll back totally access to abortion. But I would argue that because the left has historically been concerned with righting injustices and fighting for universal standards and a more egalitarian social order (thankless, never-ending tasks), and because its followers are in general less soothed by communal cohesiveness and religious belief (and deep-pocketed support) than folks on the right, its adherents live in a particularly exacerbated, near constant state of heartbreak and impotent rage.

Those of us in the environmental movement also experience a particularly acute sense of angst. The overwhelming majority of the scientific community accepts our core concerns and analyses about the dire state of the biosphere: plummeting biodiversity, fraying and degraded ecosystems, increased global toxicity of water and land, topsoil loss, climatic destabilization, rising sea levels, collapsing fisheries, looming water shortages, and so forth. And yet, despite small victories here and there, the political will to address genuinely and meaningfully the very real impending disasters facing our entire planetary ecology is clearly lacking. This cognitive dissonance between a near universal acknowledgement of the scope of our environmental crisis and the refusal to engage it in any authentic manner drives many of us to despair. A convincing case could after all be made that, while injustices and human suffering are worth fighting to remedy, they always have been with us and will always continue to arise, while the unraveling or radical impoverishment of the natural world, the matrix of all past and future life on this planet, has to take precedence over all other concerns.

As I continued to probe the sources of my irritation, I began to feel that the problems went much deeper and had far longer historical antecedents than I had initially suspected. Those annoying contradictions and histrionic speeches were only the tip of the iceberg, akin to (forgive the old-fashioned Freudian and then Jungian metaphors) the behavioral tics of an individual that may reveal a more serious underlying mental disorder. Perhaps too many unresolved contradictions had been buried in the left/progressive collective unconscious and were manifesting themselves in inappropriate behavioral reflexes.

Politics' fundamental concern is power and the steering of social bodies, so its primary attention is on the mobilization of social forces sufficient to take and hold power, and to obtain tangible policy results. It therefore tends not to be particularly self-reflective. It may study history and sociology for very practical lessons on tactical decisions, and psychology for clues on how to manipulate masses of people, but it invokes these disciplines very selectively for precise goals. Political movements tend to assume, by definition, that their worldviews are correct. They are concerned with convincing others to join them in their assumptions, so political ideologies aren't interested in psycho-social-aesthetic archeological excavations of themselves. But that is part of what I'm proposing we try to do with our own political ideas and movements, because I don't think we will have much chance of achieving most of our objectives unless we undertake some sort of rigorous self-examination.

The Main Themes

One of my key themes is the need to develop less linear political mindsets. I invoke the metaphor of looking at the political landscape less as a chessboard and more as an ecosystem in which different groups can be both competitive and symbiotic and find productive niches. One hears a great deal in sophisticated eco-circles about getting beyond antiquated nineteenth century mechanistic/positivistic worldviews and applying insights drawn from systems theory, "complexity" mathematics, ecology, and holistic thinking to solve environmental and social problems, and yet our political reflexes remain rigidly linear. The few attempts at new holistic political theory have usually been marred by utopian wishful thinking. What might an authentically rigorous, non-linear approach to politics entail? This discussion explores how political ideas spread and mutate; laws of unintended consequences; the unpredictable and complex relationship of culture and time to politics; an awareness of the role of cycles and the changing "winds" of history, and the crucial importance of those breakthrough periods of sudden eruptions from the collective id; and some thoughts on how best to approach surfing these waves of culture and history.

Another of the "big ideas" I'm putting forth is that it would behoove us to borrow some of the tools of philosophical and psychological self-analysis and to apply them to our political ideas and lives, both personally and collectively, to seek to "know ourselves" politically as well as psycho-spiritually. What are the sources and roots of our ideas? Do we accept them blindly or periodically hold them up to rigorous scrutiny? I also draw from the ancient Chinese classic *The Art of War* and from Taoist martial arts study the idea that one must understand one's opponents nearly as well as one knows oneself, and study the terrain of the conflict with exacting precision to enhance one's chances of success. This must involve, I argue, deep, visceral attempts to get inside our opponents' minds and emotions, as well as a cold look at the harsh facts of the American political landscape as they really are, not as we wish them to be. A deep appreciation of self, opponents and terrain in a dazzlingly complex society necessitates new, more refined analytical tools, so my contention here is that the post-modern era demands of us the ability to see the world through multiple lenses, to get beyond our knee-jerk political reflexes and expand our capacities of observation and our creativity. We must learn the admittedly difficult skill of being appropriately multi-perspectival without losing our center or ethical essence.

I also explore why the tone of the left is so often more shrill and aesthetically jarring than that of the center and right, arguing that the left has certain historical disadvantages. The left is the part of the political spectrum whose historical mission is to struggle for greater equality and access for the disenfranchised, so it is constantly embattled and repressed. Furthermore it emerged in its modern form from a mix of Enlightenment rationality and Romantic utopianism, which consistently seeks to appeal to the most idealistic and generous aspects of human nature: to global solidarity, equality, justice, compassion, and so forth. This is asking far more from people than the historical agenda of the traditional center-right, the preservation of a stable, "natural" (and often divinely ordained) status quo and of national and "tribal" norms. Cultural change and the long arc of time have favored the left in the last few centuries, but year-in-year-out progress is painfully slow, defeats more common than victories, and gains often largely (though never completely) rolled back in periods of reaction.

I come to the conclusion that this asymmetry is inescapable, but that by being more conscious of its origins we can decide to accept that we do indeed have a greater degree of responsibility, higher peaks to climb than our opponents do. And instead of whining about it, we can decide to strive for higher standards of political honesty, linguistic precision and aesthetic elegance to compensate for the bigger political burden that is ours. This discussion involves an exploration of the difficult relationship between art and truth seeking and politics, and the special problems of the left in this regard, as well as its Enlightenment-inherited tendencies to intellectual arrogance.

I delve into many largely unexamined fault-lines that divide our movements (communitarians vs. libertarians, secular vs. spiritual traditions of resistance, "deep ecologists" vs. utilitarians, techno-utopians vs. neo-Luddites, anti-essentialist vs. neo-pagan feminists, utopians vs. pragmatists, etc.) and examine how the confrontation with modernity, new life-altering technologies and globalization fracture left and eco-movements. But these various fault-lines also often apply to other parts of the political spectrum and offer us new ideological typologies, new lenses through which to analyze the political landscape so that we can build coalitions across usual right-left divides. We have recently seen these in ad hoc alliances of left civil liberties advocates with right libertarians on reining in excessive government domestic surveillance, and between left and right local community defenders against corporate media consolidation.

Finally, in the end, though this book is more an attempt to broaden perspectives and to trigger reflection and discussion than to tout positions, and doesn't claim to offer any definitive solutions to any political problems, I do, in the last section, propose a few possible tactical and strategic tacks and approaches that flow from what has been said earlier.

Notes

Examples of wishful/naïve "holistic" socio-political thinking on the eco-left include over-enthusiasm for concepts such as Paul Ray's "Cultural Creatives" (the supposed millions of people with less materialistic values who represent an emerging force for positive change) or the "Tipping Point," popularized by Malcolm Gladwell's eponymous bestseller. Fritjof Capra's 1982 book *The Turning Point* (an early effort—this sophisticated thinker has evolved a lot since then) offers another example, of, in my view, overly optimistic social analyses that draw from newly emerging holistic scientific ideas.

The Art of War, attributed to "Sun Tzu" but of unknown authorship, was probably written in the fourth century BCE during China's "Warring States" period, and is widely considered the most profound text on warfare ever written. It has been translated countless times. A few recent translations include: Roger T. Ames (Ballantine Books, 1993); Denma Translation Group (Shambhala Publications, 2002); and John Minford (Viking Press, 2002.)

Section I:
Beyond Linear Politics

Toward More Sinuously Sophisticated Political Perspectives

There has been a great deal written about how the emergence of new holistic scientific disciplines such as ecology and "complexity" mathematics has been paralleled by new, less linear and more sophisticated approaches to fields such as biology, medicine and economics. There is no doubt that we are slowly evolving far better models of how complex living systems and human societies actually function than the mechanistic templates we inherited from nineteenth century positivism, but this is a nascent transition which hasn't yet begun to influence how our decision-makers approach problems. We still have genetic manipulators convinced they can tweak and alter a specific gene in immensely complex, dynamic genomes we haven't begun to understand, and achieve controllable, predictable results, with no unforeseen side effects, for example. Or we have politicians and military and intelligence leaders eternally confident a surgical coup or military intervention won't result in any messy "blowback." These unsophisticated linear worldviews combine with the greed for fast profits in a hyper-competitive global economy, generalized hubris, and megalomania to cloud the judgments of our ruling elites.

Nothing illustrates this more vividly than the late 2003 situation in Iraq, which is seeming, in certain aspects, like a Hollywood remake of "Vietnam" with Donald Rumsfeld starring as Robert McNamara, Syria and Iran as North Vietnam, sand as jungle, and the Islamic world as the commie menace. That earlier conflict was so counter-productive (even from a perspective sympathetic to U.S. empire maintenance) it managed to keep the then extensive, entire Communist world (and most world opinion) united, allied against the U.S., and probably kept the Communist system alive longer that its natural lifespan. Not long after it ended, former allies North Vietnam and China reverted to their ancestral rivalry and fought a war, Vietnam invaded Cambodia, China and the then Soviet Union suffered a serious chill in their relationship, and so forth. It is now clear that many of the leaders and planners of the current U.S. adventure are veterans of that earlier war and want to exorcise that humiliating historical failure, which dared limit America's omnipotence, wounded its pride, and contributed to fracturing its internal consensus. In Max Planck's oft-cited phrase: "Science changes one funeral at a time." Unfortunately, too many of those old cold warriors are still with us, unrepentant and eager to get it "right" the second time.

This new *enlisement* seems like an almost ideal way to radicalize and unify disparate anti-American, anti-Western and anti-modern tendencies in the Islamic world, and offers them a crack at crippling the other overconfident veteran of the Cold War after seriously wounding the Russians in Afghanistan. This is a wet dream for passionate jihadists. They get to experience not one but (so far) two radical Islamic equivalents of what the Spanish Civil War had been for lefty idealists some seventy years ago. It is hard to know how this situation will play itself out, but it is not hard to envisage a worst-case scenario. A fluid front, extending nearly half way around the world, from, west to east, North Africa and Egypt; Israel and Palestine; through Syria, Jordan, Iraq, Saudi Arabia and the Gulf states; Iran; some of the Balkans and Caucasus and Georgia and the Armenian-Azeri conflict; Afghanistan and Pakistan and Kashmir and all the other "stans" across the old silk route to western China; and parts of Southeast Asia into Indonesia and the Philippines, and so forth, could bog down the empire and its cast of hesitant allies in an unbelievably costly and ruinous sand pit, which would make the old northern frontier of the Roman empire seem like Euro-Disney.

This nightmarish scenario may, of course, turn out to be an exaggeration or inaccurate. I don't claim to be psychic. But this type of linear approach, which includes an overconfidence in one's moral superiority and historical mandate, and a failure to understand one's opponents and the terrain of engagement, is something we on the left also suffer from, though, obviously, we are currently not in a position to do as much damage as the present U.S. leadership. I would argue that we who keep talking about "paradigm shifts" haven't really, when it comes to socio-political and cultural thinking, practiced what we preach. We too are overly arrogant and confident about the rectitude of our worldviews and need to engage in far better self-analysis. This might be a good time to begin such a process because we are, for the moment, to some extent sidelined (at least as principal players) in this major military confrontation between two worldviews that are not ours.

If we look at the writings of the most noted thinkers who are influential on the eco-left, the majority of these most pointed critics of reductionism, who most vigorously tout the emergence of a "new holistic paradigm," are themselves often remarkably linear in their thinking when it comes to socio-political matters. It is an implicit assumption in many eco-left circles that the concomitance of various emerging cultural movements such as heightened environmental sensitivity, the struggles for women's and minority rights, and the rejection of consumerism and the spread of non-sectarian spirituality, will lead to the dawning of a new more conscious and sustainable era. Now I might share those values and would be happy to see a more enlightened, humane, eco-conscious civilization emerge, but it is wishful thinking to pick those particular socio-cultural trends one approves of and assume they will combine in precisely the way one hopes they will. It is, in fact, remarkably *linear* wishful thinking.

Cultures and societies are extraordinarily complex organisms and are fundamentally unpredictable. Social movements and ideological tendencies ebb and flow and combine and re-combine in often surprising (and not always pleasant) ways just as artistic and musical styles (and bacteria) do. And things can mutate into their opposites or change stripes: utopian populist movements can become fascistic; the Catholic Church has been a reactionary force and a progressive one at different historical moments in different regions of the globe; a few notable right-wing politicians and judges have moved to far more compassionate positions as they have aged; and the youthful radical intellectual who turns into a grumpy old conservative is so common as to be an archetypal cliché.

The timing of radical social transformations usually catches everyone off guard as well, as the fall of the Berlin Wall and the Soviet Union and the ferment of the 1960s illustrate. Socialist labor organizers can hand out flyers at factory gates for twenty-five years with little to show for it, and suddenly a spontaneous national strike can surprise them as much as everyone else. The Bolsheviks were at first opposed to the labor unrest that began the Russian Revolution because they had no control of it. The C.I.A. can wage the Cold War for forty years with enormous resources but wind up being clueless about the sudden demise of its Soviet archenemy (not to mention the fall of its clients the Shah of Iran and Nicaragua's Somoza, or most of the other significant sudden events of the last fifty years).

In recent years the world's elites and the anti-globalization movement were both surprised by the size and militancy of the Seattle anti-World Trade Organization (WTO) protests, and that very ebullient and decentralized movement has continued internationally, greeting nearly every global trade meeting with large demonstrations (most recently in Cancun). It has developed an international network of resistance to corporate globalization with its own institutions such as the World Social Forum and the International Forum on Globalization think tank, and its own large gatherings (Porto Allegre, José Bové's summer 2003 "festival" on the Larzac plateau in France, and the like.).

But this very diverse movement has to be careful not to get locked into a sterile, linear strategy of seeking to recreate the "magic" of the Seattle protests over and over. Political organizing must go on, of course, but spontaneous eruptions of energy can't be mechanically reproduced. New cultural and political energies will continuously emerge in novel forms outside of anyone's conscious control. The Rainbow Gatherings, for example, have been trying to reproduce the Woodstock festival for decades in a what strikes me as an obsessive-compulsive cultural nostalgia repetition reflex, while, for now (but most likely not much longer as a tone of messianic, pompous self-importance has emerged), the Burning Man festivals have a fresher edge. Holding on to one's essential values is integrity, but clinging to outmoded forms can be among the most pathetic of behaviors in political as well as cultural and artistic movements.

Clinging to a sense of certainty about the shape of the future is also a problem behavior. Yes, one can probably identify with a fair degree of confidence some very long-term trends that are likely to continue: the increasing complexity of technology and socio-economic organization; global urbanization; continuing battles between the forces of economic globalization and local resistance; the slow evolution of a more universal and inclusive morality; the radical impoverishment of biodiversity; the devastation of global ecosystems, global climate destabilization, and so on. But the details will always be surprising. These positive and negative dynamic trends occur over centuries, and there are periods during which some of them may slow down or seem to change directions. Nothing guarantees they will all continue indefinitely in a linear progression and any of them can dramatically intensify or dissipate or suddenly bifurcate. Of course we must try to nudge them in positive directions, but the outcome of colliding variables in any very complex system is ultimately unknowable.

Also, these days we are sailing in truly uncharted waters. While all empires have ultimately collapsed or lost their dominance, we don't know what the collapse of a fully globalized economy or the unraveling of planetary climatic patterns and the radical impoverishment of an entire biosphere would look like, since we have no real *historical* parallels with events on that scale to look to. So let's curb our arrogance and remember that history is unpredictable, especially in the short and medium term, and very long term prognostications are not all that helpful. The death of the sun in a few billion years seems a pretty safe bet, but not of immense practical political use.

There may be no area of life in which people are more linear than in politics, even those who should know better. We look to support a political figure or movement that most closely reflects our views, even though it is common knowledge that politicians who accede to power invariably betray some or all of their core supporters to broaden their base, co-opt their opponents, or fulfill a historical imperative. Everyone knows only a Richard Nixon with his rabid anti-communist past could go to China when no Democrat could have. No Republican could have succeeded as easily as Bill Clinton at "reforming" welfare. Now the socialists Schroeder and Lula push through pension reductions rightists would find much harder to achieve. Only a rightist national military hero like Charles De Gaulle could get colonial France out of Algeria, to the horror of his army. Most likely only a politician on the right with no links whatsoever to the counterculture could ever decriminalize "soft" drugs (probably on fiscal grounds). Politicians of the center-left often saber-rattle as much or more than rightists to prove they are not weak. It was the Reagan administration's FBI that violently pursued and destroyed the Posse Comitatus, the Ark and Covenant of the Lord, the Order, and other ultra-right, rurally based armed groups in the 1980s. Often the first thing a left-wing regime does is crush its extreme left and a right wing one its far right.

Unfortunately there is no easy way to avoid being betrayed. It is hard to avoid supporting leaders with whom we share at least some common ground, as it usually makes no sense to support political figures who are anathema to us in some convoluted attempt to be non-linear. (Though there is a noteworthy science-fiction book, *Agent of Chaos* by Norman Spinrad, which is precisely about a non-linear revolutionary group that worships chaos as the guiding principle of the universe and commits a variety of seemingly incomprehensible acts, and in the real world some of the Russian nihilists came close to that model.) There are radicals whose goal is the ultimate destruction of the social order who sometimes argue it is better to "intensify the contradictions" and let the true nature of a society reveal itself. They encourage a visibly repressive regime's accession to power rather than support a more subtle, less heavy-handed but still "enemy" administration. This is a very dangerous gamble, of course, and might only make any sense at very rare historical junctures when a broad-based revolution seems distinctly possible, if ever. And we are certainly not in such a situation nor will be in the foreseeable future anywhere in the West.

Yet continuously engaging in wishful thinking and becoming naïvely optimistic about a candidate's promises, blindly supporting political actors who take our support for granted and routinely sell out our interests upon acceding to power is certainly not a pleasant alternative. It is at least helpful to keep these dynamics in mind instead of being shocked over and over by political betrayals. They are the norm, not the exception, and if we are at least realistic going in, we may on occasion be able to devise clever strategies to further our goals in specific situations. And it may be necessary on occasion to vengefully punish a political figure for a specific betrayal to make a point, even if the alternative is unpalatable. But such a tactic must be very carefully weighed, not stumbled into unconsciously. There is no facile answer to these dilemmas, but there may be ways to be more creative and subtle in whom we support and how. Certainly it would help if we could keep this non-linear aspect of politics firmly in mind rather than getting lost in the reactive emotion of each struggle and campaign.

Another aspect to linear political thinking is our relationship to our adversaries. We seek to triumph completely over them, but don't seem to register that most of them represent real constituencies and aren't going to disappear, and that on some occasions crushing them too convincingly could eventually make them re-emerge in a more virulent form, like antibiotic-resistant bacteria. Some historians view the post WWI Versailles treaty, which humiliated Germany, as one causative factor in the rise of Hitler, for example. We must learn to be as magnanimous as possible when we triumph (without ever compromising on our core values), thinking ahead to the next turn in the cycle when we will be weaker. Unless we are certain we can really annihilate an opposing political tendency, something exceedingly rare, it might be best if we can avoid rubbing salt in our opponents' wounds unnecessarily. If we can find ways to soften their pain in defeat, we have a much better chance of weakening their unity and muting their rage. In the same vein, when we are weak we should always look to forge coalitions on very specific issues to achieve some gains.

We have to develop not only an intellectual but a visceral understanding of the fact that history and culture move in cyclic yet also jagged patterns, with long periods of relative stasis punctuated by bursts of novelty or crisis, invariably followed by retrenchment and reaction. If we can hold to this long view, we will be more prepared to make greater gains during the historical openings and less likely to be depressed during the lulls and reactionary years. This doesn't mean one shouldn't continue to seek consistently to promote one's values and make one's arguments during all periods, but a monotone response, identical in all circumstances, is unimaginative and ineffectual. Just as ancient health wisdom advises us to tailor our behavior to the seasons and our expectations and goals with age and context, we must learn to be politically adaptive and ready to adjust to continuous change.

There are events that are completely predictable though their exact timing is never knowable. It is a very safe bet there will be a dramatic oil spill fouling a coast somewhere in the next few years, for example. The entire environmental movement should be ready to swing into well-coordinated, well orchestrated high-gear at a moment's notice to press its arguments to reduce reliance on fossil fuels when this occurs. The same is true for the sadly as likely nuclear accidents or dramatic lethal incidents involving toxic chemicals à la Bhopal or Seveso. There is no excuse for being caught off guard by events almost certain to transpire. There are crucial moments when the world's attention is focused on a question, and the gains one makes during those "window" episodes are likely to be as or more determinant of one's success than the long, patient work of linear organizing. The patient work is important to pursue, of course, but how nimbly a movement makes its case and advances at those points of crisis will make it or break it.

Unfortunately the very mentality that is best suited to patient, long-term organizing is uncomfortable with sudden change and the need to rapidly shift tactics. Often, in fact, established groups in leftist movements have been threatened by spontaneous eruptions of protest, as the aforementioned Bolsheviks were in 1917 or the French Communist Party was in France during the 1968 rebellion. And conversely, leaders who emerge in periods of high intensity and crisis are rarely temperamentally suited to leading effectively during those times when patient consolidation or tactical retreat is required. Those who thrive in crisis usually think radical action is called for, and those who are more suited to slow movement-building resist sudden shifts in strategy. To a hammer the world looks like a nail. The ideal would be if we all had a good sense of our temperaments, our strengths and weaknesses as well as a good barometer of the tone of each political moment, but if most people or even activists had that level of self-awareness, the world would already be an altogether different place.

Developing a less linear view of politics is no panacea. It doesn't necessarily lead to immediately more effective organizing strategies or guarantee better results. It may even make it more difficult in the short term to come up with the simplistic positions or slogans to which most people are accustomed to responding. Still, I can't help but feel that a more nuanced understanding of how the world really functions and how complex societies and ideas change and evolve has to wind up being beneficial. Staying more acutely aware of socio-political and cultural phenomena's propensity for sinuous cycles and periodic surprising twists and turns has to make us more sophisticated, and ultimately more effective, agents of change.

Notes

The quote from Max Planck (1858-1947), the German physicist who invented Planck's Constant in 1899, commenting about the controversy surrounding quantum physics around the turn of the century, is also sometimes translated as "Science changes funeral by funeral."

A very good book on the 1917 Russian Revolution from a non-Communist left perspective by a participant in the events is Voline's *The Unknown Revolution, 1917-1921* (Montreal: Black Rose Books, 1975), published earlier in France in 1947 as *La Révolution Inconnue, 1917-1921*.

The most important and impressive counter-institution to economic globalization is the World Social Forum. First held in Porto Allegre, Brazil, in 2001 with 100,000 participants from all over the world, it was established as a counter-meeting to the World Economic Forum, the annual ruling elite gathering usually held at Davos in Switzerland. The World Social Forum is an open meeting space for civil society groups and social movements opposed to what the rest of the world calls "neo-liberal," i.e., unfettered "free market" capitalism.

Norman Spinrad's 1960s classic *Agent of Chaos* was last re-issued by Pulpless.Com, Inc. in 1999.

The Seveso, Italy, industrial accident of July 10, 1976, exposed thousands of people to high levels of dioxin. For more information, see the European Commission's Environment Directorate-General's report http://europa.eu.int/ comm/environment/ seveso/; or Corliss, Mick. "Dioxin: Seveso disaster testament to effects of dioxin" in the *Japan Times* of May 6, 1999, http://www.chem.unep.ch/pops/POPs_Inc/press_releases/pressrel-99/pr32.htm.

Ideological Ecosystems
and Multi-Perspectival Politics

A metaphorical tool I have found helpful in trying to undermine my own political rigidity consists of looking at political and cultural "landscapes" as though they were ecosystems, entertaining the possibility that even bitterly competing viewpoints can serve vital functions in maintaining a certain dynamic equilibrium in the larger body politic, and that a variety of ideological tendencies can productively occupy different niches. I really want to be clear, though, that I am not going new-age and soft and claiming this idea in any way obviates the need for opposition or confrontation or resolves real ideological differences or real disparities of power. One has to be careful not to get too literal and overdo the metaphor. It may not necessarily change our immediate situation as we, say, struggle against specific human rights abuses or civil liberty erosions or more privatization of the commons, but, nonetheless, I have found this approach very useful both in looking at the overall political panorama and at the political spectrum within specific movements.

If one looks at the dynamic tension between the impulse to preserve traditions and norms (the archetypal right) and the urge for novelty and transformation (the archetypal left), it is evident all humans and cultures contain both these impulses. We consider individuals who find a happy balance between these two poles to be well adjusted, and, to some extent, we can say the same about social structures. Granted, things are never as simple as facile archetypal models. I hear the impatient reader think: "So get real. How would one apply this metaphorical lens to real politics?"

There are primarily two ways in which I find it most practically useful. The first is that when I look at major opponents from this perspective, I realize the tendencies they represent are a major part of the political ecosystem. They may represent a competing species, yes, but most likely a cornerstone one. They have been around a long time and aren't going away. When I think this way, I find that my strategies have to change, because the concept of "winning" changes. One doesn't want to be like the U.S. leaders I just discussed in the last chapter who conquered Iraq but had no sense of the forces they were stirring up or the realities of the alien ecosystem they were embedding themselves in.

Understanding I am going to have to co-exist in some way with my opponents for a very long time doesn't mean I can necessarily accommodate them or they me as our goals may be too radically mutually exclusive. It might not mean I have to fight them any less forcefully, but it does force me to think very long-term and very precisely. I can't only think about "defeating" the adversary in a simplistic and linear way, but must consider the possible long-term repercussions of each "victory" or "defeat." I have to understand fully that I will be living in the same landscape as that other creature for the foreseeable future, and I shouldn't delude myself about that. The odds are I won't be able to drive a stake through the adversary's heart and be done with it. So is there any way to be clever and creative so that my freedom of action is as great as possible, without constantly having my enemy hyper-mobilized against me? What other unusual allies have I not thought of who could be helpful? Are there ways of distracting my opponent for a long period? Are there ways of giving it some of what it wants when it doesn't threaten my core habitat?

But, one might object, some political movements and tendencies do in fact suffer total defeat. After all, authentic Nazis or hard-core Marxist-Leninists are now endangered species as are shameless Southern segregationists. True enough, but those ideologies were powerful for a very long time. It took a hundred more, bitter, brutal years even after the Civil War to really start to push overt institutionally-ensconced southern racism back, and modern Communism was a vital force for some one hundred and fifty years. So, at some point in the middle of that cycle, those fighting one of the above ideologies would have been quite wrong to expect their opponents to be defeated in their lifetimes, or even those of their children, which just illustrates my point that one must think very long-term. Furthermore (and more central to my argument), those specific ideological strains may be now on the verge of extinction, but the underlying impulses that generated them certainly aren't. Racism and "tribal" politics are still very common around the globe, and anti-capitalist resistance has simply taken a slew of new forms. Major tendencies reflect deep parts of the human psyche and real social contradictions, so they may retreat for periods or go dormant for a while, but the odds are the yearnings or fears they represent are too deep-seated not to emerge in new forms. Yes, the goalposts may move as cultures and global politics shift, but core impulses—anger at inequality, fear of change—will find political expression.

Most political activists of all stripes are so embattled in immediate struggles, and so passionately convinced of the moral rectitude of their positions and the evil of their opponents, that they don't think this way. Even those who do think strategically (as sectors of the U.S. right very effectively did from the late 1960s on) think obsessively about how to succeed in their aims. They may study their opponents carefully to probe for weaknesses and points of vulnerability, but they don't really think about their opponents as a permanent feature of the landscape. Most activists are motivated on some level (consciously or not) by a sort of messianic impulse to see their ideals of perfection achieved in the world. So even the most far-seeing who plan ahead and build movements and institutions with patience and stamina, on some level believe that once they achieve power and have their way, history will stop. They may be too intelligent to believe this intellectually, but that is the emotional goal that most activists, who are nearly all closet utopians, live for—the success of their cause and the disappearance of their enemies' ideologies.

In this regard, evangelical Christians who believe in "the rapture," end times and so on; old school Marxists who believe in the historical inevitability of a workers' utopia; purist free-marketeers who swear by the infallibility of the "invisible hand;" bioregionalists who believe in the inevitability of ecotopia; or spiritual seekers who believe in Enlightenment as an absolute state of perfected cognition, are all alike. But what if there's ultimately no such thing as a neat end-point, only more cycles of action and reaction, rebellion and resistance, a succession of periods of radical novelty and conservative reaction and ever-new mutant hybrids? That doesn't mean I should use that as an excuse to be passive and not work for what I view as positive values and outcomes. But political engagement is so frustrating by its very nature that most who engage in it, on whatever level, tend to need a utopian crutch of some kind to sustain them. And while I think utopian traditions have much to contribute to political thought and life and am not advocating pessimistic centrist pragmatism, I would argue that if some of us can get beyond these sorts of unexamined and unconscious utopian reflexes, we may be able to fashion more sophisticated and effective long-term strategies.

The second way I find this ecosystemic view of politics helpful is when looking at the spectrum of groups within a specific movement, within, say, the environmental or women's or anti-globalization movements or within the coalitions that bolster the right. If we use this tool to analyze the landscape of a movement we are involved in or broadly sympathetic to, one goal could be to look at how different groups or ideological tendencies fit into specific niches, how their work could be more symbiotic, where there are unnecessary redundancies, and so on. Far too often many groups within a larger movement are hyper-competitive with each other and bitterly divided over what might seem like minor points of doctrine to outsiders, and are fighting over a limited base of support and a finite funding pie. There is no easy solution to this. Preaching unity is usually a pointless exercise (and one not infrequently engaged in by competing megalomaniacs who want everyone to unify behind them, and do nothing but engender further divisiveness!). Different groups have their own leaders, histories, cultures and traditions and are jealous of their turf.

That said, activists need to understand that important social change nearly always involves very broad movements with very different people working in a wide range of settings. Trying to look at a whole social movement with this ecosystemic analogy in mind can perhaps help us to engage in less internecine combat over who within the wide wave we are all riding has the correct analysis, and to look instead at how people with different temperaments and from different milieus might be able to serve complementary functions. You may be a tough street protester, but you will be glad your lawyer was willing to stay straight enough to get through law school and years of drudgery, and she might be glad someone is more temperamentally suited to getting arrested for an important cause. And you might both be cynical about politicians but glad if one of them takes a stand on an issue you feel strongly about. And high-ranking military or intelligence officials who have a *satori* experience and realize the folly of a policy and turn against it, can be extraordinarily effective figures, garnering far more attention for a cause at times than a whole movement, even though one might have thought of such people as one's unredeemable adversaries.

My little metaphor is certainly no miraculous, movement-healing cure-all, but a slight perceptual shift can sometimes stimulate more creative explorations of new approaches to coalition building and organizing. How could we make the environmental movement's competing parts function more symbiotically without seeking to lessen its diversity? Is there some way to create institutions that would not seek to dominate the movement but gently, homeopathically, nudge its various parts into more efficient, symphonic resonance? Can we develop mechanisms to contain strong disagreements amongst ourselves so we don't expend enormous energy, depress our supporters and baffle the mainstream with public infighting? These are the types of questions to which we can use an ecosystemic approach to seek answers.

When studying movements that are usually our adversaries, this ecosystemic gaze can help us get beyond looking at them as evil monoliths and help us highlight the range of opinions and social groups that compose them. This is invaluable, first just to understand them better, and then to help us probe for fault-lines, for possible divisions in their ranks we could exacerbate, and for possible areas of common concern—issues on which we and some groups of our usual enemies might benefit from building limited ad-hoc coalitions to achieve very specific goals.

But in order to study both our own and our opponents' political ecosystems with any degree of sophistication, we need a wide range of sharp analytical tools. We can't just look with our habitual political eyes, with pre-existing, rigid mindsets. We need a more varied set of lenses through which to interpret the political landscape. The left/right lens is not obsolete. It still describes divisions over economic issues fairly reliably. The further to the left one is, the more likely one is to advocate redistributive and egalitarian economic policies; the further to the right unfettered "free markets" and low taxes on the rich. But when one looks at a slew of other issues: environmental conservation, civil liberties, the impact of new technologies and globalization, military interventions abroad, and so forth, things get far more complicated.

Looking at political divides through a "communitarian vs. libertarian" lens on issues such as drug use and privacy rights is far more useful than the usual right/left dichotomy, for example. Two of the states that voted recently to legalize the use of medical-marijuana in referenda, Alaska and Arizona, have very conservative electorates, but they have strong libertarian streaks. And hard-core conservatives have a historical distrust of central government, which makes them more concerned about the federal government's attempts to increase its policing prerogatives than nearly any other part of the political spectrum. Some communitarian moralists on the left are as hostile to Hollywood's vulgarity as conservatives and willing to support bans on pornography, and few left politicians are willing to expend any capital on pushing meaningfully for drug policy reform.

Economic globalization is perhaps the most significant political phenomenon of our epoch and left/right divides are only marginally useful in analyzing reactions to it. Yes, labor unions in advanced economies tend to view globalization with alarm as manufacturing jobs move to lower-wage regions, but local capitalist classes and small business owners who are swept aside by multi-nationals are even more rabid in their opposition to it. Some European leftists, such as the 1968 Franco-German anarchist leader and current European parliamentarian Daniel Cohn-Bendit, now advocate a strong Europe with a unified currency as the only possible counterweight to American hegemony, while the late billionaire corporate raider Sir James Goldsmith railed against globalization and the European Union (albeit as a Franco-British bilingual, bi-national bigamist member of the same European parliament!).

The dizzying developments in biotechnology and cybernetics may ultimately be the most important factors that will have the greatest impacts on the shape of future human life, and attitudes toward these new directions in technology also don't reflect any neat right/left divides. A "neo-Luddite/techno-utopian" axis is a far more instructive analytic tool on this topic, as is the aforementioned "communitarian/libertarian" polarity. Techno-utopian libertarians argue, for example, that families should have the right to genetically enhance their offspring if that becomes feasible, while communitarians, more distrustful of technological "progress" as an invariable good, reply that all rights are socially negotiated and that the global impact on the whole society has to be considered before plunging into large scale eugenic experiments. These issues find some fundamentalist Christians and radical left-environmentalist critics of modernity arrayed against pro high-tech business boosters and historically pro-progress, secular liberals and socialists.

Even economic issues are not always clear-cut. A "populist vs. elitist" divide also confuses any pat right-left classificatory scheme. The best recent critique of the U.S.' current plutocratic economics, *Wealth and Democracy*, came from the pen of Kevin Phillips, a centrist but disgruntled populist Republican, and the prescient author decades ago of *The Coming Republican Majority*. There is a strain of populism on the right that hates left-liberals more for their perceived elitism and their sympathy for minorities than for their economic ideas, and has no great love for the business elites either. And many left-populist movements have also, in the past, unfortunately combined nativist and racist attitudes and rigid anti-modernity with their redistributive economic demands.

I urge us to look at our own movements and our own political psyches through these and other lenses. Some are very obvious: all movements have moderate to militant gradations, for example. But other lenses are less frequently invoked. In another chapter I look at a "utopian/realpolitik" axis within individuals and within movements as another very revelatory tool of self-examination. Individually and in our movements and organizations, we all contain a range of political reflexes, ideas and impulses that are somewhat contradictory. I think this is inevitable. Life is complex and fraught with paradox. Why would politics be any different? What is problematic, however, is when these inconsistencies are unconscious, unexplored and denied.

In other sections of this book I look at a range of insufficiently discussed cleavages or fault-lines in left and other movements exacerbated by our collective collision with modernity: the secular vs. the spiritual left, "anti-essentialist" vs. neo-pagan or "Gaian" feminists, holists vs. reductionists, prudes vs. libertines, and the like. My goal is to attempt to bring to light these often underlying but latent or brushed-aside divisions so that we can face them more honestly and build more realistic and solid alliances. We need first to examine our own ideological make-ups with more rigor, to see where we fit into the larger political ecosystem on different issues. The more of these "lenses" we can look through the deeper and richer our understanding of our own political reflexes and of the larger universe of political attitudes is likely to be.

The purpose of such an exercise in political self-analysis is not necessarily to change our views, but rather to help place them in context and clarify them in relationship to a larger landscape. Nearly all of us who are passionate about political questions tend to be emotional and reactive in our political responses, conditioned to be sure of our views and filled with righteous indignation toward our opponents—and as a result very linear in our approach. Looking at the political landscape as a dynamic ideological ecosystem and placing ourselves within it can be very helpful in giving us a more nuanced view of our positions, and even perhaps insight into how to be more effective in building coalitions across the political spectrum to achieve specific goals.

But I hear objections. Why highlight and exacerbate all these divisions in our ranks? Aren't we weak enough? Might not looking through such a multiplicity of "lenses" only confuse us further—yet another post-modern, overly cerebral exercise in moral relativism and mental masturbation? Perhaps, but I would argue that these underlying, latent or un-excavated divides are already actively hindering and confusing us and limiting our effectiveness. I wrote this text because I kept noticing these usually unarticulated cleavages clouding judgments. Not everyone needs to be a political junkie fascinated by the endless subtleties of ideological variations, but at least our leaderships and movement theoreticians, in my view, need to have richer understandings of the complexities of current socio-political realities. We do live in an increasingly complex and very rapidly mutating society. I don't rejoice at our predicament, but this post-modern condition does demand of those of us who are cursed with the necessary analytic/intellectual background and skills that we at least attempt to decipher civilizational trends with more sophisticated, multi-faceted approaches. Those of us who advocate more holistic approaches to medicine, ecology, biology and technology, design and architecture surely realize we have to practice what we preach in our political analysis, and with real rigor and open-mindedness, not wishful thinking. That said, one must also then come back and synthesize what one has learned by looking through all these various ideological microscopes, which are, after all, just tools. I'm arguing for more fluid and creative thinking and better tools. I'm not advocating we abandon core values or moral compasses.

Notes

Cohn-Bendit, Daniel and Duhamel, Olivier. *Petit Dictionnaire de L'Euro* (Paris: Seuil, 1998).

The late Sir James Goldsmith's critique of globalization is to be found in *The Trap*, in french (Fixot, Paris, 1993) and in english (Carroll & Graf, 1994).

Phillips, Kevin P. *Wealth and Democracy: a political history of the American rich* (Broadway Books, 2002). Other, older classics on class divisions and the American wealth pyramid include C. Wright Mills' *The Power Elite* (Oxford University Press, 1956), Gabriel Kolko's *Wealth and Power in America* (Praeger, 1962), and G. William Domhof's *Who Rules America?* (Prentice-Hall, 1967).

Time, Culture and Politics

Progressive grassroots movements that achieve some traction are nearly always fueled by outrage over specific governmental or corporate actions and by passion for a more just and sane social order. This type of motivation can be very powerful in the short run, especially during crises, but these "hot" emotional states cannot be sustained by most people for too long. And many on the left respond hyper-emotionally to injustice and suffering, which is understandable yet unsustainable because suffering and injustice are a permanent feature of the human landscape and will be for the foreseeable future. I bemoan it as much as anyone, and of course one should try to change that reality, but children are always starving somewhere, and that won't stop anytime soon. It is not healthy to live in an over-adrenalized state in perpetuity nor is it politically productive because it scares people away.

It is certainly understandable that in the midst of a campaign which is gathering momentum one would seek to stoke people's anger to keep the movement's energy level high. But that can't be kept up indefinitely, and very few campaigns succeed or see all their demands met, so a high percentage of participants become frustrated, then disillusioned and finally disengaged, especially young, less experienced activists whose expectations may have been unrealistic. Too often those who have been around and should know better are so happy to get energetic young recruits on board and perhaps hopeful a cause they're involved in might finally succeed, they fail to prepare the newly enthusiastic for the long haul. And unfortunately, most important ideological struggles are very long-term affairs.

The most important issues we face, those that will define the shape of societies and the condition of the biosphere—our relationship to our technologies (especially to fossil fuels, nukes and persistent toxic chemicals in industry and agriculture, hyper-destructive weaponry, genetic manipulation, electronic information systems, artificial intelligence, soon nano-technology); our attitudes toward the natural world and population control; how we cope with the often violent centripetal/centrifugal tension between globalization and cultural, ethnic, national and regional resistance movements; the success or failure of nascent global governance bodies; the fate of the American empire; the gradual spread (or not) of more inclusive, universal ethics trumping "tribal" or nationalistic reflexes; how "progress" and "growth" will be defined—have been part of centuries-long battles for the soul of civilization. Balancing the productive canalization of short term passions during specific campaigns with a less excitable long-term strategic view is not easy, but we had better learn how, because many of these questions will most likely still be the ones haunting us, albeit in novel forms, for decades and probably centuries to come.

Grassroots movements are at a tremendous disadvantage because they have far fewer resources than entrenched institutions (which Aldous Huxley once quipped are all quite mad, because, unlike even the craziest human, they never sleep) and have to rely on the passions of concerned citizens. When those passions are aroused to a high pitch, the results can be dramatic. But inertia is an awesome force as well, as the longevity of an institution such as the Catholic Church can attest. Even after revolutions or the fall of regimes, the old bureaucratic networks and economic elites usually re-emerge minus a few sacrificial scapegoats, and re-assert their control in some modified configuration. This certainly happened in much of Europe after the defeat of the Third Reich, or in Russia after the fall of the Soviet Union, or earlier after the French Revolution, when a character such as Joseph Fouché, the J. Edgar Hoover of his day, managed to remain the head of the powerful secret police during countless regime changes between the revolution, Napoleon's rule, and the restoration of the monarchy.

But, lest we get too depressed, let us remind ourselves that changes do occur, and major ones at that. We live in far more egalitarian and less socially-Darwinian times than our great grandparents did, at least in the industrialized world. We may face a raft of global perils they couldn't have envisaged, but the values one could associate with a "left/progressive" agenda have spread and had a powerful impact over the centuries. To the struggles of the left we owe: universal education; finite work weeks; those social safety nets that exist; the principles (if not yet the full reality) of racial and gender equality and equal treatment in the eyes of the law; and some limits on the privileges of wealth; and so forth. This moral evolution and the pace of social change are not linear and predictable, and there are periods of regression and reaction, but a long view clearly reveals that concepts such as inalienable, universal human rights, the protection of the weakest and disenfranchised, full ethnic and gender equality, and ecological sensitivity, have made enormous strides in acceptance. There does seem to have been real moral progress (at least in attitudes): people around the world embrace far more humane, compassionate, universal ethics than in previous centuries. To paraphrase Martin Luther King: The arc of history is long, but it bends toward justice. This has not prevented outbreaks of extraordinary brutality, nor does it guarantee such progress will continue, or that, even if it did, our most dire ecological predicaments would necessarily be solved. But it does give us some basis for long-term hope, even if we seem to lose most of the skirmishes most of the time.

In producing lasting change, it is the slow but inexorable tide of cultural transformation which is most significant. It comes before, sometimes long before political change. Institutions are very resistant to real novelty, and whole generations of bureaucrats and leaders often have to die off before already widespread new values can finally penetrate the corridors of power. The power of vibrant grassroots cultural ferment is what terrifies defenders of the status quo and moral conservatives most. Today, as I write this, the U.S. is being governed by the most right wing, culturally conservative politicians in a century (or, arguably, ever). And yet, to the anguish and fury of their most fervent supporters, these politicians seem powerless to staunch the progress of the rights and the social acceptance of homosexuals, the mutation of the traditional nuclear family into novel forms, an increasingly multicultural society, overt hyper-sexualized imagery everywhere, the legality of abortion, the constant popularity of defiant, transgressive adolescent musical genres, and so forth. And, though they are succeeding in other aspects of their agenda: asserting global American hegemony, rolling back environmental safeguards, curtailing some civil liberties, transferring resources away from their historical enemies (unions, artists, teachers, the helping professions, the poor) to their allies (corporate elites in defense/aerospace, petroleum and finance, the military-police sector), and so on—ironically the cultural battles are the ones many of them care about most passionately.

When significant numbers of white youth began passionately to embrace black music, starting with swing and ultimately exploding in the rock'n roll phenomenon; and some gutsy rockabilly women such as Wanda Jackson (who even had an integrated band in the early 1950s country circuit!) dared to express themselves as women with sensual passions and aggressive charisma, as black women R&B singers long had, it was only a matter of time before the civil rights movement and then feminism would make major gains. It would take decades, but those waves of creative, explosive Dyonisian energy that first manifested in the culture were the harbingers of the coming political storms. So "culture wars" are ultimately even more important than political ones. But culture is a strange animal. As convoluted and irrational as politics can get, culture is a far murkier, more complex and unpredictable realm. The collective unconscious throws its waking dreams onto the canvas of reality in a totally mysterious process, outside of anyone's ultimate control, and it produces phenomena that are more Rorschach collages various groups project their desires and fears upon than straightforward narratives.

The political role of culture is infinitely complex, and it is very hard to make any generalizations about it, but I would argue (with many caveats) that, by and large, popular culture, especially youthful popular culture, is a domain that favors the aspirations of the (non-authoritarian) left. At the very least it is the source of trends that scare and threaten the conservative right. This is because cultural movements are the manifestations of unconscious desires, not the will of the super-ego. And it is in those periods when long dormant, repressed or neglected desires and aspirations erupt suddenly that the left often makes its greatest pushes forward, whether it is in the England of the

1640s and 1650s with the extraordinary radical political and religious creativity of groups such as the Levellers, Ranters and Muggletonians; or the surge of the *sans-culottes* in the Parisian streets in the French Revolution, or later their equivalent in the Paris Commune; or more recently the ferment in the 1960s all over the world. This phenomenon can begin in one place and spread, as in the late 1970s/early 1980s South Bronx where artistic movements involving novel forms of the spoken word, dance and music coalesced into what became the hip-hop/rap tsunami, or it can erupt simultaneously in multiple locales, but it is characterized by wild contagion. The form and timing of these periodic eruptions, however, are impossible to predict. Conservatives see them as akin to periodic global viral pandemics that threaten social order; to left-bohemians they're golden ages (or moments).

These periods of explosive novelty and utopian aspiration are always followed by (have to be followed by!) periods of repression, reaction and cultural digestion as the mainstream "recuperates" those fragments of these surges from the id its stomach can handle, the classic thesis/antithesis/synthesis cycle (or in the mytho-poetic language of astrology, the Saturn/Uranus polarity). Cycles of waking and sleeping, expansion and contraction, excitement and stasis, and so forth, seem as embedded in cultures' lives as in biological life. Generally, the more extreme and vigorous such a great surge in popular ferment and utopian aspiration is, the longer and more intense the period of reaction. But usually, that reaction is unable to fully roll back the clock culturally, even if it can politically. Hence the impossibility for current Christian conservatives, with the strongest position they have enjoyed in recent memory in American politics, to stop, say, open discussion in respectable media of the necessary precautions required in anal penetration to avoid the transmission of HIV, or the extraordinarily enormous landscape (and mainstream acceptability) of pornography on the web, or the inevitability of the working mother, or the perpetually high divorce rate, and so forth.

These changes also highlight the problems the left confronts in dealing with culture. Not all these trends are clearly positive or pretty. Cultural phenomena are ultimately uncontrollable, though they are certainly at times manipulable and obviously constantly prone to exploitation (or the entertainment industry wouldn't exist). Some of the more strictly communitarian sectors of the left also exhibit culturally conservative reflexes and can be nearly as uncomfortable with phenomena such as pornography and transgressive adolescent music as conservative Christians. Segments of the right and left share a revulsion to the most vulgar aspects of capitalism, such as the commercial exploitation of children and of sexual imagery, and the commodification and de-sacralization of just about everything. Both have profound ambivalence toward many aspects of modernity and yearn for a return to smaller-scale, community and family based living patterns. On the other hand some free-market worshiping libertarian capitalists may be largely unconcerned with many of these questions as long as taxes are low and profits high. Communist regimes have been notoriously prudish, as were the anarchists during the Spanish Civil War period, at least in the rural areas.

So cultural novelty and rebellion are not unambiguously favorable to the left. Eruptions of deep-seated rage are as likely to be bizarre or xenophobic or racist as espousing of universal liberation. Neo-Nazi skin-heads; militia movements; survivalists; the Hell's Angels; and rabid "angry white male" radio talk jocks are as authentically grassroots socio-cultural phenomena as the Crips and Bloods; anorexia; the Stonewall riots; the Rainbow or Starwood gatherings; punk rock; or the Harmonic Convergence. At best most movements are multi-faceted. Take, say, populism in the nineteenth and early twentieth centuries in the U.S. Populism was both an authentic and inspiring broad-based anti robber-baron workers' and farmers' movement, but was also capable of horrific racist violence (the New York draft riots during the Civil War, the pogroms of Chinese laborers during the building of the railroads, and the like) and of very old-fashioned morality as manifested in William Jennings Bryan's campaigns for the presidency. The novel (and the film based on it) *Fight Club* captures how the rage against the emasculation corporate capitalism, consumerism and a tame, regimented life inflict on modern men; can, when released, be extraordinarily cathartic, but can be easily canalized into fascistic cults and mass violence as well.

Rebellions by groups that feel neglected or oppressed or suppressed or humiliated all have a similar emotional fuel, but they take very different ideological forms depending on where they occur. An angry white man in rural Kansas might find resonance with the apocalyptic ideas of "black helicopter" fearing Christian groups; a pissed-off guy in Bedford-Stuyvesant, Brooklyn might find resonance with Five-percenters or Louis Farrakhan. Pre-existing chreodes and attractors canalize rage into ideological patterns that already have a history and resonance in regions and communities. Novel forms erupt, but they do not arise out of thin air. They have roots.

So, clearly, nothing guarantees that eruptions from the id of the collective unconscious will be all sweetness and light. The suppressed rage of humiliated and oppressed groups needs to be tapped if they are to liberate themselves, but is sometimes hard to contain once it arises. Often it can't help but be excessive initially as a severely disenfranchised group finally achieves a realization of its condition and senses the possibilities of liberation, as, say, in the early days of the "Black Power" or 1970s militant feminist movements. Then it achieves some success and social acceptance and is able to tone down its most strident aspects as it moves into a different phase of its struggle. This is the positive scenario. But at other historical moments an explosion of deep-seated social rage can wind up being canalized into an ultimately authoritarian and oppressive regime as problematic (or even, on occasion, worse) than the one it toppled.

Movements (and people) can sometimes mutate into their opposite, or, to use Jungian jargon, be swallowed by their shadow. Many workers who joined fascist movements in Germany and Italy had been socialists, just as many voters in France who in recent elections have been voting for the far-right candidate Jean-Marie Le Pen used to vote for the Communist Party. Yesterday's radical youth is today's grumpy old conservative, and, on occasion yesterday's right wing fanatic can be today's mellow old man. Victimized groups often later become cruel oppressors. One time shocking bad-boy, bisexual, drug-addled rockers are knighted and listed on the stock exchange in middle age.

One thing is for sure: eruptions of social rage will arise, and on occasion massive outbreaks will topple or shake up social orders, but it is never easy to know where they wind up. Rage is an understandable impulse, and one that must be acknowledged and at times ridden; but by itself it rarely leads to anything positive and, at any rate, it is most often appropriated by ruling elites who manage to channel it into violent mass spectacles, rituals, patriotic fervor and wars.

Fortunately, rage is not the only suppressed force that demands periodic release. Authentic mammalian/primate/human needs for affection, play, pleasure, bonding and social solidarity are usually unmet in industrial culture. Among our closest kin, bonobos are lovers not fighters and even the more martial chimps like watching sunsets. Nature may be "red in tooth and claw" but it is also green with fertile creativity, mutual aid and symbiosis, and pink with love, warmth and the pleasure of swollen erogenous zones. The large scale of modern society demands uniform standards of production and consumption and prizes "efficiency" above all. Humans who have been free-wheeling, tree swinging, small-pack primates for nearly all their evolutionary journey are not yet fully adapted to living regimented, disembodied, overcrowded, yet lonely lives in dwellings similar to insect hives or robot dwellings. If there is even a shred of truth in E.O. Wilson's Biophilia Hypothesis, our severance of contact with the natural world must inevitably lead to neurosis, anomie, disassociation and high rates of dysfunction and psychosis.

I'm not saying that early human life wasn't also violent, or denying that chimps and gibbons (and even dolphins!) fight wars, but rather that the desires for love, play, pleasure, creative expression, and even for some sort of aesthetic or spiritual transcendence or ecstatic joy are as central and vital to the human make-up. And the periods of socio-cultural upheaval that are most associated with advances of left/progressive thought contain strong elements of this desire for human connection and the refusal to ignore the need for ecstasy. The 1960s was a time of great anger but also of remarkable quests for beauty, authenticity, and transcendent experience.

I don't deny these impulses are fraught with problems, and that history has witnessed many tragedies resulting from utopian social and religious eruptions. But the suppression of those urges is co-creative of the carnage caused by the excesses of the movements that finally erupt when they have too long been dormant. So, what good does culture do us, politically, if it is so unpredictable, complex and fraught with risks? That may be the wrong question. For one thing, as with nature, we aren't outside culture; we're all embedded in it, so we have no choice but to be actors in it.

Crude attempts at manipulating cultural trends for political advantage are certainly laughable, and decrying this or that cultural expression is usually pointless, as the so predictable periodic denunciations of popular music's (or other youthful cultural vehicles') corrosive effect on the young remind us over and over: masturbation ("self abuse!"), comic books, jitterbug, rock n' roll, drugs, video games, and so forth. From "Reefer Madness" to Elvis to "The Wild One" to "Dancing in the Streets" to "Street Fighting Man" to Bob Marley, Public Enemy, NWA, Ice-T and Eminem. From Anthony Comstock to Harry Anslinger to Tipper Gore and William Bennett, the cyclical attack on pop cultural icons of the moment by the prim and proper has surely become one of the most tiresome and predictable rituals in American life.

But the left doesn't acquit itself much better when it comes to pop culture. There is a very different (but strangely parallel to the anti-ecstatic right) tradition of serious left-leaning philosophers attacking pop culture, from Walter Benjamin, Theodor Adorno and Max Horkheimer agonizing over Mickey Mouse and Donald Duck's fascistic potential in the 1930s to William Irwin Thompson's more recent takes on EPCOT. Nowadays it is more fashionable among left academics to ironically embrace pop kitsch, with Jean Baudrillard's bizarre ramblings about Las Vegas a prime example; there is a virtual industry of left "cultural studies" academics searching for profound significance by dissecting the most obscure recesses of cultural detritus; and rock music criticism has become astonishingly pompous, self-referential and self-important. Some contemporary pop culture analysis can certainly be interesting. Los Angeles art critic Ralph Rugoff's takes on Sea World, Bodybuilding and the L.A. County Sheriff's Museum, to name only a few topics, in *Circus Americanus* are brilliant, highly readable, insightful (and hysterically funny), for example. In my view, while "deconstruction" may on occasion offer valuable insights, and its role in promoting "identity" politics, is a complex phenomenon with real value as well as pitfalls, it has also lured quite a few budding young intellectuals of recent decades into a somewhat nihilistic ideological black hole. Fortunately, these people's work is frequently incomprehensible, so the damage it can do is somewhat self-limiting. In general, the intellectual left's grappling with pop culture, while it has produced some fascinating texts and artifacts, has, with the exceptions of more visceral artistic movements such as Dadaism, the Mexican muralists and many of the artists associated with the Works Progress Administration in the 1930s and 1940s, in general been so distancing and aloof as to be almost irrelevant in terms of tangible social-cultural-political impact.

But culture is profoundly politically significant because it is where the battle for "hearts and minds" really occurs. It is a more subtle domain than the short and medium term allocation of resources and power, but ultimately the more determinant of a society's direction—though I'm not denying there is a feedback loop: the concentration of power and resources certainly has a major influence on ideas and culture. I just don't think power can ever fully control culture, at least not indefinitely. A big problem the left faces is that hearts and minds are easier to canalize in habitual, reflexive responses, especially in times of perceived threat or crisis. And though an important aspect of left politics is rooted in economic self-interest for its core supporters (labor, the historically disenfranchised, the helping professions and government employees, for example), the left is also usually asking people to change, to reach beyond a self-protective stance to a more generous one. So it is often frustrated by people's fundamentally conservative impulses, which, let's face it, predominate most of the time. Periods of explosive creativity which inspire leaps forward are extremely important because they are seed periods during which old reflexes weaken and new values can make major inroads. Reaction and repression inevitably follow, but they are never able to eradicate some forms of the new ideas which, over time, continue to percolate and subvert and are finally accepted by the broader culture in a watered-down form.

These are history's rhythms. Understanding that doesn't give us any magical pre-cognitive ability to predict when these periods of heightened possibility will occur or what to do when they do, but it should help wean us away from plodding, linear political expectations and responses. Understanding that there are winds of history that blow steadily for long periods and then suddenly form into typhoons that no one will really be ready for is not helpful in a specific, tactical way, but it can help us psycho-spiritually and aesthetically. The ancient Greeks attributed this fundamental mystery of history's ebbs and flows to the fact that the affairs of humans were pale reflections of battles among the gods. Jungian historians would see potent archetypal forces competing in the collective unconscious. However we choose to look at the winds of history, it is probably wise to accept we can never control them, but we have no choice but to navigate our way through them, so we had better have a more accurate sense of their patterns.

The periods of intense change and the far more frequent periods of seeming stasis or regression each present pitfalls. In the long novelty droughts it is hard not to become depressed, pessimistic and cynical. In those years it is important to remind ourselves that our most important battles are over profound values, and to keep looking for creative ways to further those core worldviews (including artistic and personal ones), even as we pursue mundane political work that often leads to defeat. We must take the long view and seek solace in the personal, aesthetic and spiritual dimensions of life, and remain flexible and available to whatever new forms the next breakthrough might take. We must also do far better at patiently building institutions that embody our values, so that we are poised to make greater gains when the tide turns.

The right has been much better at this in recent decades as the think tanks and institutes it set up in Washington, D.C. since the 1970s, have emerged as key players in the triumph of the "far center-right" in recent years. Of course they do have a key advantage in that they are heavily funded by among the richest and most powerful vested interests, whose interests they largely further. Still, that is not the whole story. They planned ahead and thought strategically. The left and environmental movements do have worthy institutes and activist organizations, but the left has a terrible long-time tradition of chronic infighting and a lack of coordination between its various strains and groups. This might arguably be understandable if one were actually in power, fighting over real spoils, but is pretty pathetic for a weak and divided movement with no real power at all.

In any case, during both types of eras, it is useful to remember that "this too shall pass." In the most intense of the eruptive periods, it is the manic rather than the depressive impulse that needs to be reined in. It is hard not to get over-enthusiastic and utopian at those eruptive moments, and there are those whose function is to test the furthest limits of the envelope. But it can also really help to have some game but centered folks on hand to keep movements tethered to earth. In retrospect, those who manage to enunciate reasoned positions in the midst of whirlwinds can add a lot of credibility to a movement down the line. It is particularly important to remember that the state of frenzied enthusiasm, as refreshing as it is, won't last too long, and that the more exalted the vision, the more challenging its shadow. It is not fair to expect the young who have no experience of past historical cycles to be capable of such judgment in the throes of an exciting storm. And the more experienced will be ignored if they are scolds or wet blankets, so it is a tough line to walk.

These tidal waves tend to be excessive and to look silly in hindsight, but they are vital and need to be ridden. Some inevitably soar too high, Icarus-like, and fall; the more experienced, good-natured surfers there are on hand who appreciate big waves and like to ride, but know the risks (and have cautionary tales to tell), the better the odds of keeping the casualties down. The most intense exploratory and eruptive times can be very similar to serious journeys into altered states of consciousness, which are best attempted by the most stable and grounded personalities among us. In midst of the most demonic or ecstatic visions and wild hypothesizing it is vitally important to somehow retain a calm observer in a corner of the psyche to remind us with a still, small voice to take good notes and enjoy the ride, but not to race to conclusions. Many of us in our children's crusade who thought we were on the verge of a revolution in the late 1960s certainly later wished we had had better internal bullshit detectors, but it's hard to explain the intoxication of such periods when everything seems possible to those who haven't participated in such a moment.

Obviously, there aren't only two types of historical moments, wild and reactionary. As with most somewhat cyclic phenomena (there are big ice-ages and mini ice-ages for example), there are micro patterns and endless variations within the macro trends: periods that combine qualities of stasis and novelty, purely local or regional eruptions of novelty, and so on. 1848, for example, exhibited European-wide upheaval; 1968 a nearly global one; the emergence of the anti-globalization movement at the Seattle WTO meetings and for a while thereafter an important but smaller scale version of this type of suddenly dynamic global movement. There are also very localized periods of hyper-creativity in small artistic or intellectual circles, even on athletic teams. These patterns of short creative breakthrough followed by long recuperative periods seem to be archetypal rhythms.

Perhaps a somewhat Taoist attitude to history's dance is what is called for: press your advantage but don't get too crazy in the wild times, and don't get down in the bad times because our enemies may seem like massive, impregnable boulders, but the flow of cool water will grind them down with time and, one day, overflow once again with life-giving fresh nutrients, so try to find clever ways to keep at least some of the water flowing all the time.

Notes

For a fascinating portrait of Fouché, see Stefan Zweig's *Joseph Fouché, the portrait of a politician,* trans. Eden and Cedar Paul trans. (The Viking Press, 1930).

Martin Luther King Jr. used the following quote often, "...the arc of the moral universe is long, but it bends toward justice" in his writings and talks, most famously at the National Cathedral in Washington, D.C., in March 1968. But the origin of the quote is actually Theodore Parker (1810-1860), an American theologian and social reformer, pastor (1837-46) of the Spring Street Unitarian Church in West Roxbury, Mass. He said, "Look at the facts of the world. You see a continual and progressive triumph of the right. I do not pretend to understand the *moral universe; the arc is a long one,* my eye reaches but little ways; I cannot calculate the curve and complete the figure by the experience of sight; I can divine it by conscience. And from what I see I am sure it *bends towards justice.* Things refuse to be mismanaged long."

For the story of the women pioneers of rockabilly, see Bob Garbutt's *Rockabilly Queens: the careers and recordings of Wanda Jackson, Janis Martin, Brenda Lee* (Toronto: Ducktail Press, 1979); and the excellent PBS documentary based on the research of Robert Oermann and Julie Clay, "The Women of Rockabilly," which aired in March 2002 (http://www.pbs.org/itvs/welcometotheclub/index.html).

The classic on the Ranters, Levelers, and the like, is the great Marxist historian Christopher Hill's *The World Turned Upside Down; radical ideas during the English Revolution* (Viking Press, 1972).

Some of the cultural phenomena I refer to are: the originally Los Angeles-based rival gangs, now nation-wide, the Crips and Bloods; the 1969 Greenwich Village Stonewall gay riots against police harassment that launched the modern gay rights movement into national prominence; the Rainbow Gatherings, an annual utopian counter-cultural event often held in national forests; Starwood, the biggest annual neo-pagan gathering; and the 1987 Harmonic Convergence, initiated by Jose Arguelles, the author of books such as *The Transformative Vision*, *The Mayan Factor* and *Earth Ascending*, involving hundreds of simultaneous gatherings throughout the world held at a supposedly mystically-charged moment to influence world history.

There are many books on populism in the U.S. Here are a few: Ashby, Le Roy, *William Jennings Bryan: Champion of Democracy* (G. K. Hall, 1987); Goodwyn, Lawrence. *Democratic Promise: The Populist Moment in America* (Oxford University Press, 1976); Hicks, John. *The Populist Revolt* (University of Minnesota Press, 1931): Hofstadter, Richard. *The Age of Reform: From Bryan to F.D.R* (Alfred A. Knopf, 1955); Holmes, William, ed. *American Populism* (Hill and Wang, 1994); Kazin, Michael. *The Populist Persuasion: An American History* (Basic Books, 1995); McMath, Robert C., Jr. *American Populism: A Social History 1877-1898* (American Century Series, Hill and Wang, 1993); Ostler, Jeffrey. Prairie *Populism: The Fate of Agrarian Radicalism in Kansas, Nebraska, and Iowa, 1880-1892* (University Press of Kansas, 1993). See also: William Jennings Bryan recognition project: http://www.agribusinesscouncil.org/bryan.htm

Palahniuk, Chuck. *Fight Club* (W. W. Norton & Company, 1996).

"Black helicopters" are an object of paranoia among right-wing conspiracy afficionados who claim mysterious black helicopters affiliated with secret, covert U.N. forces spy on them. These reports are reminiscent of and most likely derived from the tales of "men in black," a staple among U.F.O. enthusiasts in the 1970s and 1980s.

"Five Percenters" are an esoteric group of African American Muslims with a strong black-nationalist ideology. See "The Five Percenters: A Teenage Nation of Gods and Earths," by Yusuf Nuruddin," chapter 5 in *Muslim Communities in North America* (SUNY Press, 1994).

"Chreode" and "attractor" are terms I'm borrowing from "complexity" mathematics. I'm using "chreodes" here metaphorically to describe different pre-existing social or ideological patterns in different locales or nations, and "attractors" as the powerful mythic ideas that tend to shape political impulses in specific communities. Some basic books for lay people on "complexity" and "chaos" from the 1980s are: *Order Out Of Chaos* by the Nobelist chemist Ilya Prigogine; *Chaos* by James Gleick; and *Complexity* by M. Mitchell Waldrop.

"Nature red in tooth and claw" is often cited to illustrate the idea of natural selection, as described by Darwin, but Darwin published his theory of evolution in 1859. The actual quote comes from Alfred Lord Tennyson (1809-1892) in section 56 of "In Memoriam A.H.H" written nine years earlier:

"Man, her last work, who seemed so fair,

Such splendid purpose in his eyes,
Who rolled the psalm to wintry skies,
Who built him fanes of fruitless prayer,

Who trusted God was love indeed
And love Creation's final law —
Though Nature, red in tooth and claw
With ravine, shrieked against his creed –"

Wilson, Edward O. *Biophilia* (Harvard University Press, 1984).

Some of my references to pop culture artefacts that have come under attack over the decades for decadence or immorality or subversion include the films *Reefer Madness* (1936; aka: *Tell Your Children*), and *The Wild One* with Marlon Brando (1954); the mid-60s Motown song "Dancing in the Streets" by Martha and the Vandellas that was denounced in the U.S. Congress for being an incitement to urban insurrection; the Rolling Stones' ode to 1960s political militancy, "Streetfighting Man;" and a list of controversial rappers and rap groups—Public Enemy, NWA, Eminem, and Ice-T (who was a target of police campaigns against his song "Cop Killer" but now plays a cop on television!).

My quick list of culturally conservative scolds who have attacked popular culture at one time or another includes the nineteenth century anti-smut campaigner Anthony Comstock (see James Morone's *Hellfire Nation: The Politics of Sin in American History*, Yale, 2003, for more on Comstock and the strong strain of Puritanism in our culture); the infamous Harry Jacob Anslinger (1892-1975), the first commissioner of the Narcotics Bureau (1930-1962); former Vice-President Al Gore's wife Tipper Gore who led a campaign against "obscene" rock music; and the former "Drug Czar" and current right wing ideologue and author, William Bennett, recently exposed as a habitual gambler.

The left intellectuals I mention who made famous critiques of popular culture include: Walter Benjamin: his oft-cited essay "The Work of Art in the Age of Mechanical Reproduction" can be found in *Walter Benjamin, Illuminations* (Trans. Harry Zohn, with introduction by Hannah Arendt; Schocken Books, 1969); Theodor Adorno and Max Horkheimer, see their famous: *Dialectic of enlightenment* (Herder and Herder, 1972) or, for a more recent edition *Dialectic of enlightenment: philosophical fragments* Gunzelin Schmid Noerr, Ed., Edmund Jephcott, Trans. (Stanford University Press, 2002); the text was originally published as *Philosophische Fragmente, von Max Horkheimer und Theodor W. Adorno* (New York Institute of Social Research, 1944); more recently, cultural historian William Irwin Thompson (*The American Replacement of Nature*, Doubleday/Currency, 1991); and Jean Baudrillard (*America*. Trans. Chris Turner, Verso Books, 1989).

An interesting recent book on one aspect of the historical left-intellectual critique of U.S. pop culture is: *Hollywood Flatlands: Animation, Critical Theory and the Avant Garde*, by Esther Leslie (Verso, 2002). It contains a fascinating account of a meeting between Walt Disney and Leni Riefenstahl in the 1930s,

Ralph Rugoff's *Circus Americanus* (Verso, 1995) is a brilliant look at the weirdness of Southern California.

The WPA was set up during the Great Depression by the Roosevelt administration to put people to work. It included some arts projects and hired many artists whose work later became famous.

SECTION II:

SOME SPECIAL PROBLEMS OF THE LEFT

Ethics, Rationality
and the Handicaps of the Left

People rarely acquire political beliefs by a deliberate, rational process of consciously choosing an ideology after having carefully weighed all the alternatives. And yet, while this is common knowledge, sincere political activists, especially left/progressives, continuously try to drive home the correctness of their views with logical argumentation as their central method. One might argue, reasonably, that that is inevitable, since politics, by definition, involves attempts to mobilize social groups to act (or acquiesce) as a result of their adherence to a set of beliefs or assumptions. But it is at least ironic and most likely futile to keep simple-mindedly hammering away at a highly complex stew of largely unconscious, non-rational factors with relentless attempts at reasoned persuasion.

Before proceeding any further, I want to emphasize that I am absolutely not advocating the abandonment of rationality in political life. It is obvious that the more deeply informed, intellectually rigorous, and nimble and capable of articulate argument activists are, the better. I am not advocating that progressives adopt the hypno-trance subliminal techniques of advertisers or the manipulation of the basest emotions so gleefully adopted by governments and major political party operatives.

I am also not claiming that reason is absent from the struggles for power and spoils that underlie most political battles at all levels. Self-interest can be very rational, and many political allegiances are based on real or perceived self-interest. In fact, the left is often accused of being naïve in failing to appreciate the power of self-interest in politics because it often assumes its brand of universal ethics should trump selfish greed. (To be fair, the left and environmental movements do often offer strong arguments that suggest short-term self-interest is not necessarily always beneficial to communities down the road, but unfortunately most people's political time horizons are restricted to the near-term.)

The great geo-political machinations of states and corporations to assure global dominance and maximum profit are certainly highly rational *realpolitik* hardball, though even at these highest levels of political and economic power, individuals and groups are also subject to a slew of subjective, a-rational influences and beliefs. Probably the same proportion of CEOs or high level bureaucrats believe in UFOs or Satan or are into various non-mainstream sexual practices as in the general population, and esoteric ideas about numbers and cycles are very common on Wall Street.

What I *am* saying is that a fundamental, largely unexamined, misunderstanding of the roles of rationality and ethics in politics and in individual and collective psychology is a serious problem for progressives. A one-dimensional, linear approach to a complex ideological ecosystem is doomed to fail, again and again. If one has a flawed conception of how political ideas rise and spread, one's chances of success are dim. And the relentless mechanical repetition of unsuccessful behavior is a hallmark of mental dysfunction, akin to the limited worldview of test animals who keep bumping up to a glass partition with food behind it.

Almost all of us who have a strong interest in politics would reactively insist, if challenged, that our political opinions are based on reason and choice. And yet it's no secret (especially to pollsters) that most people's political beliefs are largely determined, or at least heavily colored by, familial, historico-cultural, ethnic, class and regional factors. In other words, as with religious identification, core political ideas are most often, to one extent or another, inherited. Many of us on the left are, of course, no different, as the prevalence of "red diaper babies" among the militants of the New Left of the 1960s illustrated. In electoral politics the degree of dominance of these "inherited" factors may vary from election to election and change with time as "swing voters" may increase or decrease for a variety of reasons, but that doesn't change the fundamental reality. The U.S' Civil War still has an enormous impact on the country's voting patterns one hundred and thirty-seven years (as I write this) after its end, for example, as Southern whites are the most consistently right-wing voters in the nation and their bloc of votes is often determinant in national politics. And this in a country with enormous population mobility and very little conscious historical memory!

It is also common knowledge, especially among political campaign professionals, that swaying the majority of undecided voters has as much or more to do with imagery, gut impressions and quasi-hypnotic slogans than with a clear analysis of a candidate's positions on substantive issues. In the U.S. a major factor in winning elections seems to be what I call a candidate's "perceived amiability." Very frequently the candidate who seems most relaxed, accessible and friendly wins (within the bounds of big party support, sufficient financial backing and no transgressions of narrow American political taboos, of course).

This is perhaps more true in the U.S. than in most places because it is, arguably, for a range of historical reasons, the most apolitical, least ideological nation on earth. It is considered rude and unpleasant to discuss politics at dinner in many mainstream American homes, and even those who actually bother to vote prefer to ignore politics, if possible, until very shortly prior to an election. But while political discourse may be more sophisticated almost anywhere compared to the U.S., socio-political and economic ideas are no less influenced by non-rational factors elsewhere. The Nazis, the Khmer Rouge, the Boxer Rebellion, the Tulip craze bubble, to cite only a few, are obvious if extreme examples that illustrate this point.

Most serious commentators decry the ever-more superficial, slogan-based, short attention span, sound-byte style of politics now prevalent in the U.S., and they are, of course, right to do so. The unholy combination of corrupting big money, viciously cynical political manipulation professionals, and the explosion of new electronic media are oft-cited culprits. Obviously all that and more is true. How can a thinking person not wish the fate of the common good were determined by more serious, substantive discussions of political questions than what our devolved political process now offers us? But wishing something were different doesn't change the facts on the ground.

Nostalgia for a caliber of political discourse akin to that of the orators of the Athenian elite in the agora or Cicero in the early Roman Senate is understandable but pointless in the face of the immense scale of our jacked-up mass electronic society.

Crucial issues do of course get debated by professionals in academia and in think tanks. Progressive scholars, sadly too few in number and influence (and rarely agreeing with each other in any case), do engage in jousting in this arena, as they should, and this world can on occasion be important in the corridors of power. But these debates reach very few people in the larger population outside of the handful of political junkies and insomniacs who watch C-Span at 3 a.m. And even in this arena the parameters of discussion are largely confined to views well within mainstream acceptability. This universe has also been dominated in recent years by right-wing think tanks. These rarefied "policy wonk" domains can be real loci of power, as often, especially as regards the detailed strategies of U.S. foreign policy, the public plays virtually no role and the entire debate takes place in these elite fora but this is obviously not where grassroots movements get activated.

Sincere activists of all stripes are obviously, by definition, firmly convinced of the absolute correctness of their positions. That's after all the reason one is an activist in the first place. It comes with the territory. It is therefore natural for activists to assume that anyone who can be brought to see things as they do ("correctly" or "more clearly") will be won over to their cause. But it is an error to assume others would see things in the same light as you if only they weren't poorly informed, brainwashed, manipulated or simply deluded or dumb. Of course, quite a few people are manipulated and/or dumb (and some of them are on our side!), but most may be unreceptive to our arguments for other reasons. The people one could hypothetically actually convince with reasoned discourse on most issues represent a very small wedge of the population.

The majority of people, in the U.S. at least, are far more focused on personal concerns than collective ones and are authentically and profoundly uninterested in politics (and I am not unequivocally willing to say they are wrong to feel that way) unless a political issue very visibly and tangibly dramatically impinges on their daily lives and their political attention span lasts only as long as that issue is biting hard on their ass. Many other folks who do have slightly more interest in political questions have inherited worldviews and allegiances that can make them largely immune to another line of argumentation. Finally there are some people who are highly intelligent and deeply informed but simply philosophically aligned with an opposing ideology.

This may be the hardest thing for activists to grasp fully. We make a very serious mistake if we assume, consciously or unconsciously, that our position is the only one at which an intelligent person could arrive. There happen to be very smart, articulate, well-read people with vastly different political views than ours. Sometimes, it is true, these people have more of an economic stake in preserving the status quo than most, but that is not invariably true nor does it automatically invalidate their arguments. If we fail to understand this in a very deep way, we will most certainly project an arrogance that will immediately alienate most people, who respond instinctively to visceral/aesthetic impressions far more than to arguments. Also, as *The Art of War* advocated long ago, a deep, intimate understanding of your opponents is key in fashioning successful strategies. And an unflinching appraisal of yourself is as important: "*Know the enemy and know yourself; in a hundred battles you will never be in peril.*"

Unfortunately the left suffers far more from a blind faith in the power of its logical arguments than the right. The main reason for this is that the left's modern form is rooted in the Enlightenment's embrace of reason, science, democracy and egalitarianism, in movements that arose in the "age of reason," to overthrow the irrational mystical creeds of the church as well as the privileges of the aristocracy. From this tradition the left has inherited a tendency to conflate reason and ethics. The extraordinary advances of science and the discovery of objective laws governing the natural world in the eighteenth and nineteenth centuries were linked to the social impulses that produced egalitarian revolutionary movements. Some revolutionaries, children of their positivistic and utopian age, began to think of their heady new political creeds as akin to scientific truth.

This revolutionary worldview calls for an enormous effort to rebel against very entrenched unjust authority and to build a radically new society and "new" humans. From the get-go this is a very ambitious, tall order, and as many of the rebel writers and poets of the Romantic era described it, it is heroic but often a tragic Sisyphean struggle. The overwhelming majority of people during most periods in history really can't be bothered. Change is a daunting task. And that creates a strange and uneasy tension which has been evident throughout the history of the left: you feel your ethics are rational and just, based on intrinsic universal rights, akin to universal scientific laws, but your struggle is poetically tragic as you face the deadly duo of ruthless entrenched power and inertia. You feel you are absolutely right, but you keep losing (or gaining ground excruciatingly slowly).

Often those on the right seem inherently more relaxed and comfortable in their positions. They tend to feel their worldview is realistic, based on natural law and hierarchy, life's fundamental competitiveness, man's imperfect nature, and so forth, a view at least as old as the Stoic philosophers of ancient Greece, and updated by Thomas Hobbes. (I am, of course, oversimplifying a very complicated picture.) These antecedents of the modern right/left divide in the debate between Jean-Jacques Rousseau's utopian optimism and Hobbes' pessimism are well-known to any political science student. But it is surprising to what extent these ideological ancestries still color the tone and flavor of political debate, even though there have been so many political realignments and historical changes, and present-day activists are largely ignorant of these ancient arguments. It still feels those on the left always have to make a case for big efforts to make big socio-economic changes and the right can sit back and argue they're unrealistic and go against the nature of things. (Though these days sometimes the business sectors of the right seem more radical than the left in that they embrace rapid, unrestrained, market-driven transformation of the technological and social landscapes, but the populist, cultural right does not share that enthusiasm.)

It is true many on the left believe that a more compassionate social order is, in fact, a more "natural state" than Hobbes' dog eat dog, "nasty, brutish and short" model of primitive life. They invoke Pyotr Kropotkin's observations and more recent studies on "mutual aid" and cooperation in the animal kingdom, findings about the importance of symbiosis in the evolution of life, and research showing hunter-gatherers were actually far healthier and worked less than farmers, and so on, to buttress their arguments. But, whatever the merits of the argument that cooperation and symbiosis are more "natural" than brutal competition, it's a tougher sell. Even if people had more intrinsic good in them than Hobbes thought when a few million people walked the planet, billions living more like insects than the small-pack primates we are have a hard time being noble, and are easier to manipulate en masse. Hard-nosed "realism" is easier to peddle to people who have to survive day in/day out in society as it is. Sadly perhaps, rightly or wrongly, Machiavelli's statement that *"a man who wants to act virtuously in every way necessarily comes to grief among so many who are not virtuous"* seems more readily believable than Rousseau's view of people as fundamentally good.

So the left, I would argue, is starting the game at a disadvantage because it is constantly urging people to live up to higher and more noble ethical standards, and universal ones at that. Major religions do this as well, but the most successful adapt more organically to specific cultures, make far better use of mythic elements, leave a fair amount of room for hypocrisy, and usually find mutually beneficial accommodation with established power. Religions may to some degree make utopian moral/spiritual demands on the private individual's psyche but (with the exception of left religious movements such as Liberation Theology) they usually share the pessimism of the right about *this* world.

Another big disadvantage for the left (and other genuine grassroots movements) is that most political organizing work is boring and depressing. Professional political operatives, well paid by powerful, moneyed interests lobbying for lucrative contracts or favorable legislation, do it for a living. But it's much harder for unpaid (or barely paid) citizens to maintain the high level of enthusiasm and commitment for political work over the long period of time required to make gains. As a result of all this it is no surprise the left suffers from chronic stridency. The left was almost always fighting from below and outside the halls of power to demand more social justice, democracy, expanded freedoms and rights, more equitable distribution of wealth, and so forth, while the right was defending the status quo and the rights of elites, usually confident that the rule of the rabble went against the laws of nature and the will of God. People yelling outside the palace walls tend to be more strident than the lords or burghers within. The left has accomplished a great deal in a few centuries: social safety nets, saner work weeks, the abolition of child labor, woman's suffrage, the decline of official/institutionalized racism and blatant apartheid, and so on, but it had to bite and claw and scream and march and die a lot. That tends to make you strident by reflex. And it really, really doesn't help that on those occasions in which radical leftists did come to power in the twentieth century, the most authoritarian strains of the movement took the helm and committed some of the worst atrocities of the age.

The negative impact of stridency has been vividly driven home to me when I have attended, and on a few occasions moderated, debates between progressives and corporate or government representatives. On several of those occasions the defenders of the status quo fared far better in the debate because they appeared reasonable and relaxed and less confrontational. Granted, it's easier to be relaxed and feel good about the system when you're earning considerable sums of money and have the backing of powerful, wealthy and entrenched institutions. You have all the confidence of, in Mark Twain's phrase, "a good Christian holding four aces." Fortunately representatives of dominant institutions do get in trouble when they are *too* smug and confident, or in situations in which the greed and elitism of their employers simply can't be hidden or fudged.

On the side of the social critic and protester, one has no choice but to be somewhat confrontational when one's calling is precisely to challenge abuses of power, so there is again that built-in disadvantage from the get-go (all the more reason not to compound the handicap by being an asshole!). Very aggressive rhetoric can work in certain situations in which public outrage is already at a high pitch (an oil spill, corporate deceit exposed, and so forth), but, in general, being perceived as strident is particularly problematic in the U.S., where naïveté about class issues, mythologies about social harmony, and can-do, feel-good optimism are so endemic. I too have often found my stomach turning even if I largely agree with speakers if their tone is harsh or humorlessly pompous and self-righteous.

One major reason this tone occurs so frequently is that those of us whose informed analysis leads us to believe, for example, that the earth's ecosystems are being perilously degraded, or that corporate and government policies are causing massive suffering in poorer regions of the world, feel a dramatic sense of urgency and frustration when our appeals for action are met by indifference and opposition. And for those of us who are passionate environmentalists, frustration is particularly acute. One can argue there has always been and always will be injustice, pain and suffering, but the crippling of an entire planet's biospheric resilience transcends all other questions. If we are right in our analysis (and most of the reputable science seems to support us) our species is indeed severely and perhaps irreversibly impoverishing and damaging the matrix on which all life depends, so our movements are characterized by a sort of permanent, crisis-mode consciousness that can often verge on the hysterical.

This hysterical edge is of course typical of most political movements not in the center of the spectrum. The "pro-lifers" on the right are as outraged by the daily "killing" of embryos, and nativists are outraged about being "overrun" by foreigners, and their stridency can hurt their causes as well. Movements outside the mainstream do tend to attract a high proportion of individuals who are either unhappier, or more enraged, or more psychologically fragile or sensitive than the norm. This certainly includes spiritual groups as well. This situation in no way implies that these groups' beliefs are less valid than more conventional ones. It stands to reason that those who are more or less content with their lot or simply not sufficiently motivated to rock the boat are not activist or spiritual seeker material, something that usually requires a more restless or searching temperament. But there are certain types of slightly unhinged, paranoid or very anal or borderline or obsessive "busy-body" personalities more willing to slog through endless meetings than normal humans, and they do seem to be present in many grassroots organizations in fairly large numbers.

Also, because movements of the left have historically been very concerned with fairness, solidarity with those of other groups, and the vanquishing of poverty and oppression, they attract many sensitive souls who are more anguished by the suffering of strangers than the average citizen. This is laudable compassion certainly, but it often engenders a whiny, preachy tone. The concern with "the other," rooted in Enlightenment values of universal rights and egalitarian impulses often runs counter to most people's knee-jerk solidarity with their "own kind," the tribal impulse that is especially strong in periods of real or perceived threat from an outside source. This is milk and honey to governments and military/police establishments, of course, which is why they have nearly always been eager throughout history to keep up the specter of outside threats. This is also the natural turf of the right: patriotism, nationalistic exceptionalism, a fetishistic fondness for things military, nativistic instincts, and so on. In periods of perceived crisis, tribal solidarity usually trumps utopian, universal ethics.

Fortunately Enlightenment values have increasingly penetrated deeply into the collective consciousness so the types of overt unapologetic racism or tribalism or discrimination so prevalent even a few decades ago are no longer acceptable in their blatant forms even on the far right (they still are on the extreme far right, of course, by definition). The right can resist reforms and changes tooth and nail, and then eventually accept those that simply have too much momentum behind them and move the goal posts. So the equivalent wedge of the political spectrum which once viewed the demand for broad suffrage rights for African Americans in the U.S.' south as insanely radical, or which supported apartheid in South Africa, now has no problems with (conservative) black Supreme Court judges or Secretaries of State, for example, and are shocked, shocked when they are accused of racism.

Many Western nations' populations have become far more heterogeneous, which creates tensions, but also makes blatant, official racism difficult. But in periods of heightened fear or when the nation engages in warfare, concern for "the other" is widely perceived as hopelessly naïve at best, treasonous at worst, though who "the other" is, of course, keeps changing. At these times the left is vulnerable to accusations of being an alien fifth column, or a dupe of "the enemy." And all the rational explanations about the government's manipulation of facts, the sorry, cynical history of U.S. foreign policy, as true as they may be, don't help. And if the policy fails spectacularly, then there's always the risk of being scapegoated.

To be fair, it is true that segments of the right do suffer from some of the same types of ideological problems. The far right is, in its own way, every bit as utopian as the radical left (it's just that theirs is a more tribal and less universal utopianism), and hard-core worshipers of the free market as an engine of perfection are as caught up in a nineteenth century positivistic mindset as Marxists who think the classless society is scientifically fore-ordained (if there are any left who do). Even the establishment center-right does have some handicaps of its own. Its rule is based on concentrated power and wealth, and in periods when the discrepancy between the condition of the elites and the rest of the population becomes too extreme or more fully transparent, a natural resentment by the large majority can lead to a tilt to the left and a slightly more equitable redistribution of resources, under the right sets of conditions.

With its roots in Stoic pessimism, conservative religious movements, and bourgeois stuffiness, much of the right can be dour and pompously moralistic. Even those "hip" modern rightists who are economic conservatives or libertarians and not prudish scolds currently depend on their alliance with aggressive religious moralists to maintain their ruling coalitions. While the Marxist left also has a rich history of puritanical repressiveness, Dionysian impulses and explosions of creative cultural ferment have most often had strong (if at times uneasy) associations with the left. In periods such as the 1960s when vivid ingressions of novelty burst to the fore, the left seems exciting, more attuned to the spirit of the age. When these supernova moments burn out, and the more frequent and longer periods of reaction, normalization (and assimilation/"co-optation") arrive, the left once again seems pedantic and shrill, and flashy CEOs in three-piece suits are the sexy stars of the moment. This is a cyclic, spiral dance. The winds of history can change directions when we least expect it, and it is ecstatic to ride a great wave but hard to fight the weather when it turns on you.

Notes

For more on irrational economic behavior and investor "bubbles," including the legendary Dutch "tulip bubble" I mention in passing, see Dash, Mike. *Tulipomania: the story of the world's most coveted flower and the extraordinary passions it aroused* (Crown Publishers, 1999); Garber, Peter M. *Famous First Bubbles: the fundamentals of early manias* (MIT Press, 2000); Balen, Malcolm. *A Very English Deceit: the secret history of the South Sea Bubble and the first great financial scandal* (Fourth Estate, 2002); Bierman, Harold. *The Causes of the 1929 Stock Market Crash: a speculative orgy or a new era?* (Greenwood Press, 1998); Chancellor, Edward, *Devil Take the Hindmost: a history of financial speculation* (Farrar, Straus, Giroux, 1999); Kindleberger, Charles Poor. *Manias, Panics, and Crashes: a history of financial crises* (Wiley, 2000); Shiller, Robert J. *Irrational Exuberance* (Princeton University Press, 2000). Link to Rotterdam School of Economics site about investment bubbles: http://www.few.eur.nl/few/people/smant/m-economics/bubbles.htm

Some of the most influential right-wing think tanks in Washington at the moment are the big business backed American Enterprise Institute, Heritage Foundation and Competitive Enterprise Institute, and the more libertarian Cato Institute, but there are several others both in Washington and in other cities, such as the Manhattan Institute in New York. There are also a few very influential groups that serve less as think tanks than as activist, coordinating and mobilizing organizations for hard-line anti-tax, cultural conservatives. The most significant of these are currently Grover Norquist's Americans for Tax Reform, Paul Weyrich's Free Congress Foundation and, of course, the Christian Coalition.

There has been a lot written about Romanticism's influence on environmentalism in academic books, most of it disparaging. A good recent (though still very academic), more nuanced view of the matter can be found in: *Romanticism and the Materiality of Nature* by Onno Oerlemans (University of Toronto Press, 2002).

Stoicism is a school of philosophy organized at Athens in the third century BCE by Zeno of Citium and Chrysippus and later adopted by Romans such as Cicero, Seneca, Marcus Aurelius and Epictetus. They emphasized living in harmony with a natural world over which one has no direct control. See Long, A. A. and D. N. Sedley, D. N. *The Hellenistic Philosophers* (Cambridge, 1987).

Thomas Hobbes (1588-1679) is one of the most important ancestors of modern conservative ideology and a was a defender of a strong "secular monarchy." In his masterwork, *Leviathan* (1651), he offers a pessimistic vision of human nature, and argues for strong laws and firm state authority to protect men from their own rapaciousness.

Jean-Jacques Rousseau (1712-1778) offered the most famous counterpoint to Hobbes' social pessimism, arguing for man's fundamental goodness in the "natural state" and for democracy in, among other works, *Du Contrat Social* (The Social Contract) (1762).

"nasty, brutish and short" is a quotation from Hobbes, in a passage that sums up his basic political perspective quite nicely:

"'Good' and 'evil' are inconstant names applied haphazardly by different men to what attracts or repels them. This egotistical psychology makes the life of man in a pre-social state of nature, 'nasty, brutish and short,' a constant war of everyman with everyman. Rational, enlightened self-interest makes men want to escape such a predicament by the establishment of a contract in which they surrender the right of aggression, but not that of self-defense, to an absolute sovereign, whose commands are the law, freedom being relegated to the spheres not covered by the sovereign's commands. The social contract is binding only so long as the sovereign has power to enforce it. Sovereignty may be vested in a person or an assembly, but it must be indivisible, not a division of powers between King and Parliament, church and state."

Prince Kropotkin was a brilliant naturalist and anarcho-pacifist thinker. His observations of what he called "mutual aid" among animals in the wild led him to challenge the dominant, simplistic neo-Darwinian ideas that argued nature was only about brutal competition and "survival of the fittest." Original English edition of his great work: Kropotkin, Petr Alekseevich Kniaz. *Mutual Aid: a factor of evolution* (London, William Heinemann, 1902). A more recent edition was published by NYU Press in 1972.

The then heretical theory that hunter/gatherers were, in general, healthier and worked less than agriculturalists was most notably put forth by the anthropologist Marshall Sahlins in *Stone Age Economics* (Aldine Publishing, 1972).

There are many translations of Machiavelli's *The Prince*, but I pulled this famous quote from page 91 of my old (1961) Penguin Classic paperback of it translated by George Bull.

Liberation theology was a movement within Catholicism, strongest in South America, that argued that the church should be involved in the struggle for economic and political justice, especially in the Third World. Starting mostly after the Second Vatican Council (1962–65) and the Second Latin American Bishops' Conference in Medellin, Colombia (1968), the movement brought poor people together in Christian-based communities to study the Bible and to struggle for social justice.

Mark Twain's exact phrase was "It is mighty regular about not raining, though, William. It will start in here in November and rain about four, and sometimes as much as seven days on a stretch; after that you may loan out your umbrella for twelve months, with the serene confidence which a Christian feels in four aces." In *The Celebrated Jumping Frog of Calaveras County, and Other Sketches* (1867).

I'm using "positivistic" here to imply an arrogant overconfidence in scientific theories. Positivism was a philosophy of science whose main exponent was Auguste Comte (1798-1857).

Dionysian refers to the wild rites of the god Dionysus in ancient Greece. It is often used to describe exuberant, frenzied, perhaps violent bursts of expressiveness and attempts to achieve ecstasy, the opposite of social or artistic restraint.

Modernity and the Left

(Note: By modernity, in the context of this chapter, I am for the most part referring to a mass society with very large institutions with economic "efficiency," the desirability of constant growth and expansion, and unfettered technological progress at the core of its worldview.)

Looking Back

Shaping the type of modernity we wind up with may ultimately be the most important political struggle of our time, and the left and the right are both being torn by internal conflicts over how to address the issue. The bulk of contemporary right and left movements, or at least their leaderships, agree that a modernity dominated by large-scale industrialism is inevitable and that there are no realistic alternatives to it. In fact, at the height of the "Cold War" one of the few areas of complete agreement between Soviet-style state socialism and American "free enterprise" was the embrace of techno-utopian progress as a liberating force. In that sense Ayn Rand's hero-architect and the mythic Soviet "hero worker" Aleksey Stakhanov have a lot more in common with each other's worldviews than with those of, say, Gary Snyder or Wendell Berry. In the eighteenth and nineteenth centuries it was mostly the left that was enamored of science and progress as the fervor of the French Revolution to systematize standards of measurement and measure just about everything illustrates. As scientific discoveries undermined religious authority and the assumed superiority of aristocracies or specific ethnic/racial groups, the largely secular, anti-clerical European left viewed scientific progress as a force for overcoming class privilege and religious superstition.

Some of the most pointed ideological resistance to industrialism and modernity in the nineteenth century emanated from conservative aristocratic intellectuals, especially in Germany, who were seeing their world collapse around them. They, of course, resented their loss of privilege and yearned for a return to a sort of Goethean worldview, but also quite prophetically anticipated the very real problems with the coming of, as one put it, "an asphalt cosmos." Many of the texts of these thinkers, in fact, bear a startling kinship to writings by recent "deep ecologists." So the right became associated with an often rural or at least traditional perspective that sought to resist what it perceived as the destruction of long-lived social structures and allegiances, "natural" hierarchies, and smaller-scale communitarian values, while the left, by and large, supported modernity and progress as vehicles of reform and promoters of egalitarianism.

As always, however, it is not that simple, in that robber-baron capitalists, not left intellectuals, provided the major motor of rapid technological change, and pro- and anti-modern currents have run through both right and left movements since the earliest stirrings of the Industrial Revolution. An agrarian/urban split is already present in the earliest days of the founding of the U.S. in the conflict between Thomas Jefferson and Alexander Hamilton, for example. One of Romanticism's major themes was a revulsion with industrialism (William Blake's "satanic mills") and Romanticism had a powerful effect on both left and right, though each tended to highlight different aspects of the Romantic impulse. The right highlighted tribal/nationalistic love of one's *volk* and ancestral turf and the left highlighted mystical nature-rapture and a more universal love of humanity, especially the oppressed "other". On the extreme left grassroots workers' movements such as the Luddites and the early *"saboteurs"* in French factories challenged technological society in their own very direct ways.

Later, among scientific figures supporting the Third Reich (itself a weird amalgam of traditional reaction and futuristic fervor) there were conflicts between holistic aristocrats interested, for example, in areas such as traditional herbology (one of the biggest medicinal herb gardens ever was at Dachau!), homeopathy and nutrition, and the more modernist, technocratic, linear pragmatists interested above all in advanced weaponry and dynamic industrial output, who congregated in parts of the SS and fairly quickly succeeded in weeding out the old holists. But many leftist intellectuals who experienced the Nazi period, and their intellectual heirs, continued, quite unfairly, to view anyone who expressed interest in alternative medicine or holistic scientific ideas (or pre-Christian mythology) in subsequent decades as tainted by Nazi ideology. This was particularly unfair because there was a whole strain of left-leaning progressive neo-Goethean holists (some Jewish), figures such as the neurologist Kurt Goldstein and the father of "Gestalt Therapy," Fritz Perls, some of whom managed to flee the Nazis and come to America, who were the early antecedents of what became the "human potentials movement" and other holistic ideas and initiatives in the last four decades of the millennium. In any case rejecting something simply because dubious people were also interested in it is immature. The same logic had most left intellectuals and artistic types until the last two decades or so ridicule physical fitness because of its association in their eyes with the archetypal Nazi propaganda of *Triumph of the Will*, as though only a self-destructive, romantic film-noirish lifestyle of nicotine, caffeine and alcohol could confer ideological and artistic credibility!

In the last few decades of the millennium the divides surrounding modernity became even more confusing. The great cultural upheaval of the 1960s, largely a left-leaning phenomenon, had a very strong anti-modern component. One can look for antecedents of this "counterculture" as far back as one wants, to Dionysian orgiastic rites or the Eleusinian mysteries; to Muggletonians and Ranters and William Blake, Lord Byron and Mary Wollstonecraft and Percy Bysshe Shelley and their cohorts; to nineteenth century Paris bohemians; to the Paris Commune; to John Muir, Ralph Waldo Emerson and Henry David Thoreau; to the Dadaists; to the experimental expatriate circles in Los Angeles around Aldous Huxley in the 1940s and 1950s, and so forth. But let's start closer at hand, with the Beats, who were very critical of mass society, obsessed with the alienation it engendered, its crushing uniformity and sterility. Allen Ginsberg's *Moloch*, which describes skyscrapers, the very emblems of modernism, as flesh-devouring gods, offers a classic example of this very widespread sensibility.

Later, "I am not a number!" was the *cri de coeur* of Patrick

McGoohan in a quintessentially 1960s artifact, the surreal, high concept British TV show, *The Prisoner*, much beloved by libertarian anarcho-individualists. The crushing scale of modern institutions, be they socialist bureaucracies or mega-corporations, was already captured by Franz Kafka, and later discussed in books such as *The Organization Man* in the 1950s. But the 1960s generation expressed its resistance more viscerally and en masse in an endearing but ultimately usually unsuccessful effort to either "drop out" or form alternative, smaller-scale, community-based institutions. Though, to be fair, many initiatives begun during that period did productively endure in more sober permutations, from food co-ops and Community Supported Agriculture (CSA) groups to co-housing, alternative media and medicine, small music labels, "intentional communities," music and art festivals, and the like. As importantly, many individuals lastingly withdrew their *internal* allegiance from the giant social machinery they resented, and a countercultural attitude permeated much of the national consciousness.

The Techno-Utopian/neo-Luddite Divide in the Counter-culture

As the counterculture grew exponentially in the 1960s and early 1970s, it took myriad forms, but it manifested a fascinating split personality in its relationship to modernity. "Back to the land" movements, natural foods, rekindled interest in traditional herbology and holistic medical systems; neo-Luddite thinkers, folk music, permissive schooling, and the like, all pointed to a visceral rebellion against a soulless, de-sacralized machine age. But the popularity of science-fiction and the thrill at the possibilities of new technologies, electric guitars, 72-track studios, and animation made a certain segment of the counterculture the most techno-utopian group in the entire society, one that midwifed the personal computer and the polymerase chain reaction (the inventors of these technologies were LSD enthusiasts). This natural/technological dichotomy was/is even evident in the drugs of choice. LSD, the most widely available psychedelic, was certainly a product of advanced Swiss chemistry, but a whole movement of ethnobotany enthusiasts who prefer organic, herbal mind-altering substances with long histories of indigenous human use (peyote, psilocybin mushrooms, ayahuasca, and the like) also emerged (and continues to thrive).

While the often bitter divide in the counterculture between Students for a Democratic Society-type advocates of political change and the more spiritually inclined was very evident in the 1960s, no one really noticed this as dramatic cleavage regarding technology. I don't think I've ever even heard it discussed. Part of the reason is that the whole countercultural phenomenon was/is so multi-faceted, and that while some stake out clear positions (a vegan Luddite gardener versus a psychedelic junk-food-eating sci-fi/computer geek, say), some hipsters may like natural foods *and* computers, bluegrass *and* acid rock (or techno), Wendell Berry or Edward Abbey *and* cyber-punk, and so on. Most people don't require ideological consistency in their cultural interests. But this un-discussed bi-polarity vis-à-vis modernity is still worth noting. The counterculture was/is a strange, sometimes inspired, sometimes silly amalgam of impulses and tendencies, but it has been an enormously influential tsunami in whose wake we continue to bob and bounce.

Globalization and its Discontents

The question of modernity is critical because the most aggressive resistance to the economic globalization now conquering the globe has largely been from nationalist and tribalist movements that cling to their interpretation of traditions and ferociously resist assimilation to the "new world order." And this poses tremendous problems for the left. In major recent conflicts the choice seems to be between, as Benjamin Barber described it, "Jihad vs. McWorld" or the worldview of the International Monetary Fund (IMF) vs. ethnic nationalism à la Slobodan Milosevic. It is impossible to support violent, intolerant reactionaries, but the final consolidation of the unchallenged power of giant corporate empires seems to be the only other game in town. And if our only choice is really the culture of the veil or that of the mall, suicide increases in attractiveness.

Intelligent sectors of the progressive left of course tout reasonable alternatives, pointing out, quite correctly, that this Manichean dichotomy is absurd. It is somewhat silly to even frame it as modernity vs. reaction or Luddism when all of history is a dance between forces of novelty and those of tradition, and it is always a battle about the speed and ultimate form novelty takes and who gets to define its parameters. There is no such thing as "free trade," for example, but very complex sets of agreements that favor this or that economic interest, and, of course, always tend to screw the powerless—as the U.S.' massive agricultural subsidies to its richest farmers, its blatant protectionism favoring Cuban-American sugar barons despoiling and drying out the Everglades; its shameless policies favoring the Chiquita company and ruining small banana farmers; to cite only a few random examples, make painfully clear. Also, not all traditions resisting the worst aspects of modernity are violent and reactionary or hopelessly naïve, so why not ferret out and retain the most benign aspects of globalization and technology and proscribe the worst, try to hold on to the best ancient traditions can offer, and show more discernment and deliberation in charting our civilization's course?

Sounds great, and it is self-evident wisdom, but it is a position with no real traction because current global capitalism requires ever more rapid capital flows and rabid competition between immense predatory mercantile entities and their nation-state enforcers. Slowing things down to mitigate, say, social and environmental devastation and obscene income disparities goes against its very nature. Most attempts to "humanize" globalization have been, to date, mere band-aids on severed limbs. Even a nation such as Mexico which had attracted U.S. manufacturers to its *maquiladoras* with low wages and weak unions is now seeing plants move to Vietnam or China as the "race to the bottom" intensifies. And the U.S. and Europe are losing not only blue-collar manufacturing jobs but now service and technical white-collar jobs to places such as Bangalore and Indonesia. The more rapid and aggressive global capital's onslaught, the more extreme and reactive the resistance, so Manichean reflexes on both sides predominate, and people who refuse to pick a side can seem at best irrelevant, at worst traitorous.

Astute critics of globalization don't deny the dynamism of the market or the current lack of viable alternatives, but advocate much stricter limits to its prerogatives, and the shielding of some core values—ecosystem integrity/biodiversity, fairness, reasonable social safety nets and income disparities, (those zany Europeans even demand actual leisure time and universal health care!), and more wildlands (and seas and rivers) and social domains—from total commodification. Every society does this already of course; it is just a question of where to draw the lines, how much to rein in markets. And one's position about where these lines should be and how strictly enforced largely defines one's position on the left/right spectrum these days.

Unfortunately, a sane "middle way" position gets drowned out over and over in dramatic confrontations between the overpowering onslaught of markets and infuriated, humiliated defenders of threatened traditions. So, as during the Cold War when opposition to nuclear power or the war in Vietnam was equated to aiding the Soviet enemy, opposition to draconian IMF "structural adjustment plans" or to military adventures is dismissed by our ruling elites as playing into the hands of regressive, pre-modern, dictatorial forces (or, simply, of unmitigated "evil"!). And if you patiently try to articulate a complex, nuanced position, the cameras and microphones, capable only of digesting sound bytes, are long gone before your paragraph is complete.

But segments of the anti-globalization left also create terrible problems for themselves by romanticizing any resistance to modernity and glossing over the transgressions of brutal dictators or fanatical movements. Ironies of all types abound. Westernized professional women in Algeria, for example, were among the biggest supporters of the military when it suspended the results of free and fair elections because Islamic parties had won a majority. And, by and large, (at least educated) women had a far better shake under the brutal Shah than after the Iranian revolution (unless they had had the misfortune of running afoul of the Shah's dreaded secret police, the SAVAK). It is important to maintain an objective eye on all the players and not shirk from the complex truth even if it is inconvenient and makes simple slogans impossible. It makes political work harder in the short term, but builds one's credibility in the long run.

The Right

The right is as fractured in its stance vis-à-vis modernity as the left, but has recently not suffered as much for it, partly because it feels less constrained by the need to be rational or consistent. In the U.S. the capitalist, free-market right has proven quite apt at throwing enough crumbs to very dynamic grassroots fundamentalist religious groups and other conservative social moralists, and to a large subset of working-class white men enflamed by a type of chronic "populist" rage, to build coalitions in order to further their own policy goals. It's a strange alliance in that it brings together some of the most pro-modernity global entrepreneurs who care mostly about their wealth and power and anti-modernity "rural" moralists under the same tent. It's also a fairly cynical alignment, in that many of these capitalists have nothing but contempt for their un-cosmopolitan fundamentalist fellow Republicans, but that's politics.

It is somewhat mysterious that phony populist politicians who pose for photo-ops chopping wood on the ranch, or use "wise use" public relations campaigns to save "small family ranchers and farmers" by allowing environmental transgressions or abolishing inheritance taxes, succeed, when most rural Americans know only an idiot doesn't use a chain saw, and the ranchers and farmers who receive the lion's share of government aid are giant operators, often owned by distant corporations, some even foreign. It is unclear if this right wing alliance is sustainable in the long run. Business' need for cheap immigrant labor collides with nativist impulses. Dramatic increases in income disparities and the fact that corporate pay-structures and employment practices are the forces most destructive to traditional families in our society irritate right-wing populists and Christian conservatives. The expense of maintaining outposts of empire grates on isolationist reflexes.

So, under certain conditions, the right's current coalition could face major strains or fracture. In Europe center rightists are in crisis as far-right anti-immigration parties make major gains, but these groups also draw from some older, formerly Communist working-class voters, and the European right is a different animal than the more colorful and surreal American bible-belt-inflected variant. And the European left is in no better shape. The overarching forces of globalization are severely limiting governments' and political parties' room to maneuver everywhere.

Modernity and Limits

The left's wrestling match with modernity is even more complex. Church groups in the U.S. have certainly played an enormous and too often under-appreciated role in left movements from Abolitionism to civil and women's rights, and have even played a preponderant role in certain struggles such as the opposition to U.S. Central American policies in the 1980s. Recently some major leaders in the environmental community have begun to acknowledge the important contributions religious perspectives on the sacredness of creation have made to the movement. For example, figures such as the Eastern Orthodox "green" Patriarch Bartholomew, the National Religious Partnership for the Environment's Paul Gorman, the "redwood rabbis," even some fundamentalist ministers who interpret the Endangered Species Act as a contemporary equivalent to Noah's Ark, and other religious leaders have come forward with vibrant eco-conscious worldviews (and actions). But, still, the overall tone of the left remains rooted in the secular rationalist tradition.

Parts of the anti-globalization and environmental movements have to some extent changed the left's unabashed pro-progress tone. Obviously it is unfair to characterize the very broad amalgam of anti-globalization groups as uniformly anti-modernity, as, for the most part, they're merely asking for a less frenzied and more equitable global trading framework. But there is definitely a vital neo-Luddite element within the movement. And this wing cannot be discounted as a collection of romantic primitivists. From some of the intellectual leaders of this tendency come some of the most intelligent, systemic critiques of our civilization and of our species' relationship to our technologies. They are asking the deeper questions no one else is addressing, even if their main proposed solution—a return to local economic systems—is, in my view, not realistic in the current context.

Clearly, many of the assumptions underlying our techno-utopian, hyper-capitalist civilization do need to be looked at far more rigorously. There is no question the combination of industrialism and market dynamism has been an extraordinary force for wealth generation and for raising the standards of living of hundreds of millions of people. It did all this brutally and broke a lot of eggs (human beings, cultures, whole ecosystems) making the omelet, but it has ultimately brought with it remarkable improvements in literacy and life expectancy as well as the wide diffusion of more egalitarian social ideas, at least in the "North." Those neo-Luddite critics who fail to acknowledge the very real achievements and extraordinary seductive power of modernity and who overly-romanticize pre-modern eras hurt their own case. But one has to judge a civilization by its ultimate trajectory, and a very good case can be made that ours may turn out, when historians of the future look back, to have been unsustainable and catastrophic. First, it is predicated on the desirability of eternal growth and expansion (with an occasional "correction"). Nothing in nature operates according to such a principle, and vertiginous growth in a natural system invariably leads to a crash.

Our attitude toward population growth offers an interesting example. On the one hand everyone realizes (except perhaps the Vatican or those who expect Armageddon in the near future) the human population cannot expand ad infinitum. The United Nations has figures it adjusts periodically according to demographic trends (birth rates, etc.) that project global population stabilizing at some figure (say 9.2 billion in 50 years). Obviously this is an iffy proposition in that it makes a number of assumptions, including that the development paths of poorer nations will resemble the demographic patterns of northern ones, or that the planet's ecosystems can withstand global consumption patterns similar to those of industrialized nations. But the main point is that the global consensus among experts is that there will be population stability at some point. And yet when those nations which have arrived at a steady or declining population (Japan, Russia, Italy, Spain and much of western Europe) are discussed in economic terms, their situation is viewed as alarming. The fact that their populations have stopped growing means to economists that the tax burden to people of working age will become intolerable, that these nations' power and clout on the world stage will dissipate, that they will be forced to import more immigrant workers, raising all kinds of cultural and political problems, and so on.

For economists only growth is good. I've never seen a single article anywhere describing any possible advantage one of these countries might draw from a reduced population, though population pressures are obviously problematic environmentally in causing sprawl, pollution, habitat loss, and so on. No leading thinker in one of these countries, to my knowledge, has said, "Yes, population stability or reduction poses real economic problems, but if we deal with it with creativity and intelligence, we will be offering a model for the rest of the planet, which, after all, must also arrive at this point, and we may even improve our lives in many ways after we get over a few transitional generations, which may have to make some sacrifices." There is a complete disconnect between the idea of limits to growth, understood abstractly perhaps to be inevitable but pushed into some hypothetical point in the future, and the theories of continuous economic expansion which underlie nearly all policy. That nations such as China and India, for example, now seem en route to adding hundreds of millions of automobiles and burning astonishing amounts of coal and perhaps having to import unimaginable amounts of food and oil as they ape the industrialization path of Europe and the U.S., seems to make any thoughts of global ecological improvement laughable, but doesn't elicit much commentary outside of environmental circles.

Yes, Thomas Malthus was largely wrong, and when eco-Cassandras sound alarms, they sometimes overstate the case and make dire predictions about famines or resource depletions that don't pan out ("Club of Rome" or "Population Bomb" syndrome), but that doesn't change the over-arching point: the economic ideas that dominate our world fail to acknowledge the realities of limits. They are, in a sense, a form of faith in cornucopian limitlessness. This seems, ultimately, every bit as utopian as Communism or Fascism or as mystical a concept as paradise or a New Jerusalem. It may work somewhat efficiently for a while longer because our planet is fairly big, and greed is, sadly, a better motivator than nobility of purpose at our stage of human evolution, but it seems highly unlikely that it is sustainable.

The current globalization frenzy is very good at disguising limits to ecosystems by ever more efficiently exporting waste and devastation to the poor parts of the world and importing resources at bargain basement prices to the more privileged parts, thereby largely shielding the middle classes (whose sensibilities still matter a little) of the prosperous nations from the cyanide and oil spills, mud-slides of denuded hills onto shanty-towns, brutal mining accidents, toxic chemical releases, strip-mines, drying lakes, fished out oceans, clear-cuts, and so on, that are the epiphenomena of our economic system. And, yes, we've mostly avoided catastrophe with nuclear materials so far (with some notable, dramatic exceptions), but those have only been around a tad more than a half century, and plutonium, say, has a half-life of something like half a million years.

What type of hubris does it take to keep producing a basically eternal material that's lethal in even infinitesimal doses? And even the rich can't escape the measurable amounts of hundreds of very poorly understood new synthetic chemicals now found in the tissue of nearly every creature on earth; or the cancer epidemic that continues, with some exceptions, to defy medicine and seems also to be, in its scope, a companion to modernity; or the need to medicate themselves and even their children to be able to stand staying in the game; or the deep sadness of living in a paved-over, biologically impoverished, de-vitalized world.

All is not well with modernity, and these types of observations are nothing new. Similar points were made in the nineteenth century and were far more prevalent in the 1950s and 1960s and taken more seriously by mainstream thinkers than they are today. Real systems, be they environmental, social, digestive, immune or nervous, have real limits, but limits are un-American, simply unacceptable to a still adolescent nation that only likes happy endings in its films and fiction. Though limits to civil liberties, dissent and free speech are more easily embraced than limits to economic activity in a nation whose main ideological glue is the thirst for material success and gadgets. And, to be fair, while progressives despair when folks balk at limits on their guns or gas guzzling Sport Utility Vehicles or consumption levels, religious/moral conservatives also despair because Americans don't like limits on their pornography, gambling or trashy entertainments either.

Modernity Fractures the Left:
Secular/Spiritual; Holistic/Reductionistic
and other Splits

When some in the anti-globalization movement and some radical sectors of the environmental community present these types of critiques of modernity, they are accused by nearly all the sectors of the political spectrum of being regressive and Romantic. A preponderance of left and liberal leaders are firmly rooted in a pro-progress secular ethos that profoundly mistrusts anything spiritual or mythic or a-rational, and is still haunted by the ghosts of Nazi ideas it fears lurking behind any expressions of interest in anything pre-modern. But at the grassroots level, there is far less ideological consistency, and one finds the same types of conflicted attitudes toward modernity that I described in the counterculture.

Quite a few people who are left-leaning politically also have non-traditional spiritual interests ranging from Eastern philosophies to various Western esoteric paths to neo-pagan or eco-pantheistic outlooks, or to very liberal Judeo-Christian groups that push the permissive envelope. Obviously these spiritual tendencies include apolitical and conservative folks in their ranks as well. And to a large extent, esoteric spirituality, which often has a very hierarchical aspect, has had more affinity, historically, with the far right than the left, as the relationship of the Japanese military classes to Zen, to cite only one example, illustrates. But that is no longer as true. And while a few religious cults are frighteningly authoritarian and even dangerous at times, a great many intelligent people, most quite liberal these days, find value in non-traditional spirituality. Part of the attraction for many is that these paths often tout eco-conscious, earth and nature honoring ideas that offer alternatives to materialism and greed. They contain implicit eco-critiques of modernity and advocate harmony and balance rather than social Darwinism and growth at all costs.

In a similar vein many in the environmental community have a deep interest in the worldviews and ecological practices of indigenous cultures, and find in them an edifying contrast to Western attitudes toward the natural world. They realize it is impossible to return to hunting-gathering shamanic culture, but nonetheless feel there is wisdom in these traditions we can draw from in revisiting our relationship to nature. The holistic/integrative/alternative medicine movement is another example, perhaps the most striking and impressive, of an enormous grassroots movement that has successfully challenged one of the bunkers of modernity, the medical establishment.

Millions of people voted with their wallets and feet for modes of treatment that Western allopathic medicine ferociously denounced for a century and a half as irrational and primitive superstition, and they forced the system to blink and back down. It may be the most extraordinarily successful socio-cultural movement of our time. And, here too, there was a pre-Rachel Carson time when alternative medicine and natural foods and worries about toxics were thought by most sophisticated urbanites to be associated with crazed John Birchites in the hinterlands (and a glance at a grassroots ultra conservative journal such as the only recently defunct *Spotlight* reveals this right wing health-food tradition is still alive) as the caricature figure of the unhinged General Ripper in the 1963 Stanley Kubrick film *Dr. Strangelove* (who unleashes WWIII because he's convinced water fluoridation is a Communist plot) exemplifies. But today I'd argue far more left-leaning folks than conservatives embrace non-Western and holistic healthcare modalities and concerns about pollutants and toxins.

It is a fascinating ideological situation, unparalleled in any other discipline: the medical profession has been obliged by sheer public pressure to make room for (and even occasionally learn from!) disciplines such as acupuncture and homeopathy it still has no analytic paradigm to explain or justify. Many of these ancient medical traditions are based on treating the body-mind as an ecosystem requiring careful balancing more than as a machine that can be repaired by linear heroic repairs to one of its discrete segments, and many are vitalistic, an absolute taboo in modern biology.

Very few social scientists have taken these health and spiritual movements seriously, perhaps because they are so diffuse and multifaceted and grassroot. And the leadership of the left has, for the most part, either ignored them or been hostile to them because they don't, ideologically, fall within its secular/modernist parameters of acceptability. This is a mistake in that they constitute, in many ways, extremely broad-based, unconscious waves of defiance to the power of the ruling elites and the ideas that dominate our culture. One can see divisions between unabashed secular modernists and the more spiritually inclined or between a totally pro-progress orientation and a desire for a return to a human-scale commons in nearly every progressive movement. Sometimes these divides are openly acknowledged and fought over, but even more frequently they lie beneath the surface and are not directly addressed or understood. Also, very often, individuals are internally conflicted and hold paradoxical views that they wrestle with or that, for most of us, simply co-exist in the confusing biodiverse universe of our rarely consistent personal, internal ideological ecosystems.

Here are a few examples of movements in which these splits are evident. In the contemporary women's movement academic post-modern, "anti-essentialist" feminist intellectuals who have been fighting to challenge ideas about gender differences they view as social constructs are horrified by the enormous vitality of goddess worshipping and neo-pagan women's groups who embrace their biological and emotional differences from men as badges of honor. In the environmental movement the dominant tone of argumentation is still utilitarian (we need healthy ecosystems for clean water, air, sustainable resources, etc.) while a majority of grassroots environmental activists are, in all honesty, as or more motivated by strongly-felt spiritual bonds with nature, and most feel passionately that non-human nature and species have their own intrinsic right to live and prosper. This split, which goes back at least to that between John Muir and Gifford Pinchot, and has continued in debates between "deep" vs. "social" ecologists and utilitarians, is obviously nothing new but it affects a broader array of people than in Muir's time, and it is a largely unexamined split between the tone of the leadership and the emotional fuel of the base.

Ideological Perils

In the anti-globalization movement there is a gamut ranging from mainstream groups that simply want trading rules that are less purely skewed to the interests of large multinational enterprises to far more radical critics of the international economic architecture who advocate a return to localism and smaller scale production units in a variety of areas from food production to culture and currency. This is very tricky political territory for the left because the most vigorous local opponents of globalization have been cultural traditionalists who usually don't share the (non-authoritarian) left's egalitarianism or attachment to individual rights and freedoms. Also it can seem opportunistic for sectors of the left or the environmental movement to argue against economic globalization treaties because they undermine national sovereignty (historically a concern of the right) when these same groups often support curtailing nation-state sovereignty in environmental accords such as the Kyoto or Montreal Protocols, in weapons treaties, and in international human rights tribunals. The pro-localism wing of the anti-globalization movement raises many convincing arguments, especially in regards to agriculture and food self-sufficiency, the social and ecological ravages of the raw material and specialty-food export orientation of the World Bank and IMF, and the homogenization of cultures, but it needs to be very careful in maintaining its intellectual integrity as it desperately searches for any means to slow the juggernaut.

There is nothing wrong with building coalitions with groups on the right who have very different worldviews in order to jointly oppose a treaty or law or initiative you both dislike for different reasons. In fact, on many issues of great import, these temporary ad hoc alliances may offer the only hope of success; but it is critical to be crystal-clear about your own positions and not to fudge your arguments to achieve short-term advantages lest you get tainted by association with ultra-reactionary forces and suffer a serious loss of credibility later on. It is one thing to critique the very real ravages of the current form of globalization and to highlight some local or regional or national models as viable alternatives in some areas, but to tout localism or nationalism as a *fundamental* principle in opposition to globalism is a terrible error.

Most horrific episodes of genocide have been orchestrated by local or national governments *with* majority support claiming to be combating a foreign or alien threat or a global conspiracy that undermined the national identity. Supporting "local democracy" in the American South in the 1950s and 1960s, for example, would have meant permitting the continuation ad infinitum of lynchings and the denial of nearly all rights to African-Americans. Yes, the U.S. federal government is often a vehicle or facilitator of great harm and devastation at home and abroad, but it can also at times be the only force able to impose more universal norms of behavior on reactionary local cultures. It may do this for cynical reasons or because too much political pressure has built up, but its actions may, at times, whatever their motives, have an at least partly beneficial result. This level of paradox and complexity makes the quest for genuinely ethical and wise political stances hard and frustrating work, but the price one pays for sloppy thinking and facile sloganeering is almost always too costly in the end.

More on Largely Unexamined Rifts: Unearthing the Political Unconscious

Another major division among progressives exists in the cultural sphere. Family-oriented, peace-loving liberals, some feminists, and ex-hippie types are deeply offended by the vulgarity of mass culture and are horrified by violence in the media and the gratuitous use of sexual imagery to sell products. Free speech absolutists and cosmopolitan, irony-embracing, pop-culture surfing, edgy-art friendly intellectuals are more concerned with preserving freedom of expression at all costs.

The most extreme of the first group go so far as to home school their children (still most frequently done by right-leaning Christians, but not as preponderantly as at the outset of the trend) and to not allow TV in their homes, and have real cultural affinities with conservative moralists, though they tend to be more tolerant, less likely to oppose abortion rights, more likely to oppose the death penalty, and so forth. An inkling of these types of divides came to public attention a few years ago when a few anti-pornography feminists briefly found common cause with fundamentalist Christians. These differing attitudes reflect a deeper rift that cuts across both left and right and the entire society, one between libertarian and communitarian impulses. Archetypally, folks on the left tend to be culturally libertarian (in matters of sex, soft drug use, and the like) and economically communitarian (for constraints on big business, for a less skewed wealth pyramid, for tighter environmental laws, and so on), and those on the right tend to be exactly the opposite; but it's rarely that simple.

Obviously this tension, like the one between the urge for novelty and that for stability, runs across all societies and individuals, and all constitutions and legal codes wrestle with it. The U.S. seems to manifest both tendencies in highly accentuated form and in bizarre permutations, from the wildest gender-bending, outrageous performance artists to bible-thumping TV evangelists and Appalachian snake handling cults, and the caricature of Old West, John Wayne-ish self-sufficiency—which, strangely, winds up using the illusion of rabid individualism to enforce stifling conformity. Some thinkers trace the U.S.' split personality to its earliest days when some of the first colonists (from French fur trappers to Anglo-Irish indentured servants) went native and pagan and started dancing around maypoles with Indian lasses to the horror of Miles Standish and the Puritans who were trying to keep the uptight Christian morality of that time operative in the "new world." Whatever their origins, we're still fighting these battles today both inside ourselves and in larger culture wars.

Because my primary focus is on the left/progressive/environmental impulse, I've been trying to uncover a series of rifts in fundamental worldviews between different wings of these movements and often between the tone of the leadership and many in the grassroots, because

I think quite a few of these divisions are largely unconscious, unspoken and unanalyzed, or at least insufficiently aired, and this has real negative results. I'm not saying these tensions between communitarian/libertarian, neo-Luddite/techno-utopian, secular/spiritual, utilitarian/Romantic, anti-essentialist/"gender-nationalist," rational/mythopoetic, family-friendly/libertine impulses, or for that matter far more overtly debated divides I'm not dealing with here (class vs. race or "identity" politics), are easily resolved, or resolvable at all. But to have any hope of achieving some political gains, far more of our political unconscious has to be made conscious so it can be examined and integrated in some way.

There have been figures, such as Rabbi Michael Lerner, author of *The Politics of Meaning*, who have argued that part of the reason for the left's recent failures and the right's ascendancy is that the left stayed so focused on rational, quantitative issues such as economic fairness, while the right was far more willing to engage with the mythic/moral/emotional dimensions of life. These thinkers urge the left to re-engage with ethics and meaning and morality to try to formulate an attractive ethos of compassion, interdependence and responsibility. This is an interesting line of thought which has much merit, but the emotions the right appeals to (fear, nationalism, and so forth) are, sadly, far easier to access and to mobilize people around than compassion, most of the time. And eco-spiritual types who advocate more spirituality in politics make a big mistake if they chip away at the separation of "church and state," because if that door is cracked open, it is far more likely to be fundamentalist Christians rushing in than peace-loving Buddhists or new-agers.

It's also quite understandable that left and eco groups which already have so much trouble advancing their agendas and being taken seriously, don't want to be thought of as irrational and anti-modern, so there's no easy way for them to embrace the types of mythic/moral impulses I've been discussing. And some of these grassroots movements can have a "new age" flavor very easy to ridicule, and are often, indeed, laughably naïve. But, nonetheless, they are authentic cultural expressions. Behind at times silly facades lurk some of the most important and powerful challenges to dominant worldviews to have emerged in the recent collective unconscious, and they will continue to find expression in one form or another. Ignoring them because they're not ideologically easy to package means denying a weak movement that needs all the help it can muster (the progressive left) a vital source of energy and renewal, and, worse, perhaps having some of that vitality drift into enemy hands.

The Battle over Genetic Manipulation of Crops/Foods

A fascinating arena that highlights how techno-utopian/neo-Luddite and libertarian/communitarian divides can throw traditional left-right divisions into chaos is the battle over genetic modification, which may also point us to some interesting approaches to reformulating the modernity/anti-modernity debate. Genetic modification, though so far a vastly over-hyped field with few tangible successes, nonetheless could potentially be the most radical technology ever devised and dramatically alter life on Earth (nukes may be even more dramatic but their capacity is for destruction, not modification).

Controversies surrounding the genetic manipulation first of micro-organisms, then crops, then animals, and now people, have generally been portrayed as classic struggles between scientific progress and fearful Luddites clinging to old-fashioned ways. And it is true that opponents of agricultural biotechnology do tend to be advocates of smaller-scale, often organic, farming, of biodiversity and the preservation of heirloom crops; and they oppose the now dominant form of industrial agriculture that they argue is environmentally devastating, socially destructive to rural communities, and economically skewed to large producers and giant cartels. The industrial agriculture folks say small farms are inefficient and that a rural economy based on smaller producers would result in higher food costs to consumers. Perhaps, argue back the eco-ag folks, but that's just because the real costs of industrial food production are hidden. The *real cost* of nitrogen and chemical runoff toxifying waterways and killing fish; topsoil and biodiversity loss; the awful smell of huge pig shit lagoons that make life miserable for whole counties; the depletion and tainting of aquifers; the cascade of harm done as pesticides, herbicides, and fungicides travel through the food chain and poison the planet; the air pollution caused by a totally petroleum-based production and distribution system; the loss of rural livelihoods, and so forth, is all passed on to the larger society (and taxpayers) in other forms. And genetic manipulation with its corporate patents of crops and reliance on expensive high-tech, only exacerbates all these problems by further concentrating agricultural production in the hands of giant operations. And that concentration is extreme: half of the 30,000 or so products in an average supermarket are produced by 10 multinationals. A vice-president of the grain giant Cargill wrote the guiding draft of the WTO's Agreement on Agriculture.

The main opposition to the genetic alteration of crops has come from some sectors of the environmental and scientific communities extremely concerned with the unintended *long-term* ecological consequences of tampering with very complex and still very poorly understood ecosystems by releasing novel life forms into them; the rapidly growing organic farming and consuming subcultures; and sectors of the anti-globalization left opposed to the continued destruction of smaller-scale rural economies and communities throughout the "global south" and the resulting flood of billions of impoverished peasants into urban shanty-towns. But the rest of the left has opposed these groups or stayed out of the debate. Centrist, mainstream liberals in the U.S. are completely pro "progress," which they equate with corporate research and development and seem resigned to the dominance of mega-business. Even left-leaning church groups such as the Episcopalians have at times been convinced by corporate interests and well-intentioned researchers that genetic manipulation could help feed the hungry as the result of higher yielding/more nutritious crops. And aggressively secular, urban leftists distrust all this talk of rural traditions and opposing new technology, something they equate with old-fashioned conservatism.

Are they right? Isn't a concern with defending old ways and advocating localism and barriers to free trade an anti-progress, reactionary stance unworthy of good lefties? Certainly, this issue does upset some of the usual left/right political assumptions and leads to very strange realignments and alliances. But a closer examination reveals this movement is far from akin to rural right wing populism. First, this movement is one of international solidarity with the most disenfranchised—rural, often indigenous, peasant cultures—whose rights, wishes and ancestral lands are trampled in a race toward a global marketplace dominated by giant players. This is very different from a nativist, purely local reactionary rural impulse. Though a concern with maintaining some aspects of local traditions is an unusual stance for the left, the opposition to the exploitation and domination of the poor and the many by the powerful few is perfectly in line with its historical role.

And those sectors of the right that historically played the role of defenders of traditional community values and even of stewards of the land as mainstays of conservationism have all but disappeared. They certainly don't seem to have arisen with any vigor to challenge the disappearance of small farmers or the extinction of small towns as Wal-Marts have marched across the continent dooming thousands of business districts. Associations of small businesses have been successfully co-opted and duped by giant corporate interests who are actually their worst long-term enemies. It is fascinating to watch millions of jobs disappear in rural America and in the "rust belt" with wide acceptance that it is merely a necessary readjustment of the global economic architecture, but if a handful of logging jobs are threatened by environmental restrictions, screams of protest ring out, but I digress ....

Food is an interesting arena, one that highlights our bizarre ambivalence toward techno-utopian modernity. On the one hand a preponderance of Americans, almost totally severed from any contact with nature or food production, seem to have no problem with a totally bio-engineered food supply and Jetsons-like glow-in-the-dark cereals and beverages. Meanwhile a growing subculture, mostly (but not only) among the more affluent and educated, has, over a few decades, become more and more "French" (or a northern California version thereof), enamored of gourmet cuisine using organic and local ingredients. And yet in France (and in much of Europe), where many still have ties to their ancestral villages and the *terroir*, and the masses resist genetic manipulation of food, most among the very Cartesian elite intellectuals and scientific classes, many on the left, bemoan the populace's archaic resistance to science and progress, and fear that once again the Anglo-Saxons will get to the future first. And the resistance to genetically modified organisms (GMOs) in Europe brings together green parties on the left and right-leaning traditional farmers.

The Surreal Politics of Human Genetic Modification

The battle over human genetic issues, especially over preventing the cloning of humans and, most importantly, of "germ-line" modification—the introduction of novel traits into the species via heredity as reproductive cells are genetically altered (as distinct from "somatic" genetic intervention to alter non-reproductive cells in order to cure a specific illness, which has been so far almost completely ineffective but which virtually no one opposes)—has been even more bizarre in its upsetting of usual left-right alignments. Many of the environmentalists and anti-globalizers worried about genetically modified foods in the U.S. seem less focused on the modification of humans, or are worried that they will seem insensitive to human suffering since these technologies are always touted as somehow essential to curing diseases (far from always the case). Furthermore the issue has been framed in the U.S. as a battle between fundamentalist Christians, obsessed with abortion, who are eager to ban "juvenile stem-cell" research which requires the uses of cloned human embryos in their earliest stages in petri dishes, and patients' groups and scientists who hope these very plastic cells could potentially be used to repair many organs and systems in the body. The fundies seem far more concerned about the discarding of these microscopic blastocysts in petri dishes than about the potential cloning of whole humans (which they also oppose but with less fervor) or the eugenic enhancement of offspring.

On the left the preponderance of feminist groups and their allies are so worried about the Christian right's relentless efforts to ban abortions, they are loathe to support anything these Christians might approve of or might somehow use to covertly further their agenda. When the Germans and French introduced a historic proposal at the United Nations for an international treaty to ban human reproductive cloning (cloning an actual human being), they thought it would be a slam-dunk, in that cloning human beings is something there is no legitimate reason for and no one on earth other than a few demented fertility doctors, a few outlandish cults and some misguided couples want, and poses tremendous ethical and social problems. But they were shot down by a bizarre coalition led by a U.S. administration eager to please its ultra-right base, opposed to treaties on general principle and eager to undermine pesky "old Europe" at any opportunity; the Vatican (pressuring Catholic nations); and some fundamentalist Islamic nations—perhaps the most reactionary cultural alliance ever assembled at the UN, all elements of which preferred no treaty at all to one that did not also ban embryonic cloning for research. That treaty could truly have been a profoundly significant precedent: a global agreement to impose limits on a technology for the good of the whole species, and though no one in the media paid much attention to it, its failure could one day loom large as a tragic missed opportunity. The issue is supposed to be revisited at the UN in a year or two, but it is hard to envisage a different outcome with the current U.S. administration in power.

Those few on the left who are very concerned with the potential use of human genetic manipulation for eugenic enhancement of the rich and of a plunge into a consumer-driven, yuppie version of Brave New World (the Center for Genetics and Society, the feminist health-care leader Judy Norsigian, the eco-authors Bill McKibben and Andrew Kimbrell and a few others), have so far been unable to mobilize many others on the U.S. left. Techno-utopians argue it is impossible to stop the march of technology, and use libertarian arguments (a couple's "right" to genetically enhance their offspring as they see fit). Those on the left and right who oppose this use of technology make communitarian arguments: all rights are socially negotiated; there is no inherent right to birth a child who is, say, your daughter and your sister (à la Faye Dunaway in *Chinatown*; cloning is not exactly incest, but it's even less "natural"); and societies always regulate technologies (the banning of certain weapons and of performance-enhancing drugs, pollution controls, zoning laws, and so on).

But the young and the hip are so imbued with sci-fi's depictions of cool oppressed mutants (whose hypothetical suffering is equated with that of racial minorities!) fighting for their freedom, that one actually finds journalistic pieces worrying about how we will treat new generations of the genetically altered. The fact that commentators are worrying about the rights of social groups that don't yet exist (and may never exist) before considering whether society should cross a hubristic genetic Rubicon in the first place startlingly illustrates just how profoundly the techno-utopian worldview permeates our culture.

So those on the left who view germ-line genetic manipulation as a potentially species-altering technology that could very possibly lead to the division of the human race into the elite "gen-rich" and the "gen-poor" masses (a terminology that comes not from a critic but from an advocate of such a future, molecular biologist Lee Silver), a stratification far more extreme than anything in history, can't find many allies on the historically reflexively pro-technology left. And they can't find allies in what might seem like logical places. Buddhism, for example, very popular among Western artistic elites, views the "self," as most of us think of it, as a largely illusory construct, so there is really no core tenet in that faith that would lead it to reject the mixing and matching of genes. So, while many individual Buddhists may have reservations about it, it is no surprise that the Dalai Lama, for example, has refused to condemn it (Taoists are more inclined to honor nature's inherent wisdom, but there are far fewer of them).

Many of the young are, as discussed, permeated by sci-fi techno-enthusiasm, and eager to mutate as evidenced by their piercings and adornment. Even the dystopian gloss of dark sci-fi visions such as that of the "cyber-punk" literary movement turns out to mask a gee-whiz fascination for the mind-bending possibilities of cyber-genetically altered, prosthetically-enhanced humans and human-machine and human-animal hybrids.

And the most militant wings of feminism and the cutting-edge of performance art are fascinated by gender-bending and morphing; why would they be concerned by genetic alteration? Some feminists might welcome genetic alteration that conferred to women parity in physical strength with males, for example, or even a freedom from pregnancy if artificial wombs can be perfected. Even the suburban masses are rushing to plastic surgeons in staggering numbers, and enormous amounts of people are on mood-altering medications. Why would they be opposed to passing on altered genes to their offspring to attempt to make them pretty, long-lived, and buoyantly happy in perpetuity, not to mention brilliant and athletically gifted without recourse to surgery or drugs, were all these things one day possible?

The only sizeable groups in the population that would seem to have an absolutely clear ideological basis for questioning this potentially species-altering technology are religious fundamentalists, or, at the very least, those who interpret their traditions as placing some limit on human prerogatives vis-à-vis creation or the natural world. And perhaps these groups can play a valuable role in this instance as that part of the political ecosystem whose instinct it is to slow down and question hasty, half-baked, inflated human hubris. But religion has lost every major conflict with science since the Renaissance, and, as I mentioned, the abortion question obsesses many of these folks, so alliances with secular leftists seem very difficult. And the aforementioned critics on the left who are concerned about the technology's anti-egalitarian potential; the scientists who have grave doubts about the wisdom of altering complex living systems we haven't begun to understand; and the various and sundry nature-honoring environmentalists and pantheists, just don't have enough clout (even if they were unified and mobilized, which they're not) to slow the plunge into a "post-human" future.

The situation is somewhat different in Europe and Japan where the "precautionary principle" is being more readily accepted, but, sadly, the dominant empire of the day usually winds up setting the tone. Still, we have not yet crossed this Rubicon, and the stakes are too high not to try at least to engage in a broad debate and offer as much resistance as possible before stumbling into dystopia.

In my view those of us on the left who are deeply concerned about the repercussions of this and other technologies will lose the day if we come off as wet blankets who are afraid of progress. Those who proudly embrace the "neo-Luddite" label for example, whatever the often very valid content of their critiques, are making a big mistake in that they will be unable to reach the bulk of the young who are by definition enamored of novelty and creativity, and of most Americans who also worship at the altar of the new and shiny. But there may be a way to challenge techno-utopianism without recourse to Luddism.

Holism and Complexity: Redefining Progress and Technology

A very strong case has been made by a number of holistic thinkers (such as Fritjof Capra) that the guiding ideas that still dominate most contemporary fields and our entire culture are antiquated relics of nineteenth century linear thought. I realize the embrace of holism can have a pop, pseudo-scientific component, but it is a mistake to throw out the baby with the bathwater. Leading edge disciplines such as ecology, some schools of biology and the mathematics emanating from the study of turbulent phenomena (popularized as "chaos" or "complexity" studies) are all pointing us to a deeper understanding of how whole systems actually function, the intricate net of interdependence in which all parts of a system are embedded and the delicate dances of adaptation and response continually churning within them. So, in that light, the idea that introducing a lone gene into an immensely complex living system one hasn't begun to understand (even if its genome is "mapped"), itself nestled in a web of other, ever larger living ecosystems whose relationships have barely been studied, will result in a predictable, replicable, controllable, highly specific desirable trait (frost or pest resistance, or, for humans, strength or intelligence) without unforeseen "side effects," is extraordinarily unsophisticated. It's actually bad science and worse technology, and will wind up doing a lot of harm.

A good example of a linear versus a holistic approach to a problem is the controversy over "golden rice." Some admittedly altruistic and well-intentioned genetic engineers created a species of rice richer in vitamin A than current varieties in order to combat the health problems (including blindness) associated with vitamin A deficiencies in the poor regions of Asia where rice is the staple food. The genetic manipulation industry has touted this as proof of technology's capacity to address dire health problems and of its limitless benefic potential. Never mind that the bulk of genetic manipulations in agriculture have so far actually been to make crops more pesticide-resistant so they can tolerate a specific corporate weed or pest killer, so more of it can be sold, and to create crop species that are patented and owned by huge multinationals who police farmers' fields so they won't illegally trade seeds (now the "intellectual property" of the corporation). If one looks more deeply at the health problems of poor Asian peasants, it turns out most of these people used to grow a wide range of green and leafy vegetables rich in vitamin A to supplement their diets. It is loss of land and poverty, the concentration of land into fewer and fewer hands, and giant export-oriented mono-crop plantations supplanting small local food producers (the model aggressively pushed by the WTO, IMF and World Bank) that are the causes of the problem. Adding a little bit of vitamin A (which probably won't work in terms of dosage anyway) to a crop instead of considering the whole socio-economic and political context is a classic case of linear thinking.

And this same type of "bull in a china shop" approach is apparent in nearly all the spheres of decision making in our society, from medicine to urban planning and traffic control, to testing the toxicity of chemicals one by one instead of in the "cocktails" we are actually subjected to in real life, to clumsy foreign policy moves that "blow back" decades later in far worse permutations than the original problem, and so forth. Rather than wearing the Luddite mantle, one could very convincingly argue it is the dominant worldview which is old-fashioned, stuck, and blocking progress. Our elites may speak the language of progress, but their technologies are often clumsy, toxic and inefficient, and their policies ultimately disastrous. We can do better. Far from opposing science and technology, we must critique bad science and dumb technology and offer more creative, subtle, beautiful and satisfying alternatives. That type of discourse is far more likely to galvanize some of the young than preaching a return to some sort of pre-lapsarian, purely local, agrarian ideal, or some bioregional variant.

And better, far less toxic and destructive and often radically more efficient models exist in agriculture, industrial design and production, transportation, urban planning, architecture, energy production, and disease prevention. Many of these technologies/approaches can be economically competitive even when not factoring in the horrific true social costs of our current methods. Small and medium scale organic farming can actually be more productive per acre than massive industrial agriculture operations; wind and solar and geothermal energy are already beginning to be competitive with fossil and nuclear fuel despite the massive subsidies these awesomely harmful sectors receive; the engines of our vehicles are absurdly primitive and wasteful, and so on. "Soft tech" exponents such as Amory Lovins, the eco-think tank the Worldwatch Institute, economists such as Herman Daly, and many others have been making this case for decades. Visionary designers such as John Todd and researchers such as Janine Benyus (the author of *Biomimicry*) who come together with their peers in fora such as the annual "Bioneers" gathering of cutting-edge eco thinkers, have shown the limitless potential of human creativity to generate highly efficient, benign technologies when it approaches nature with respect and humility rather than an impulse to subjugate. Granted, a genuinely sustainable global economy would require fairly substantial life-style adjustments for the middle classes of the "global North," and a fairly radical restructuring of economic and social priorities and paradigms, and of power alignments. This is hard to envisage at the moment given the political power of the oil, automotive, chemical and industrial ag sectors.

Nonetheless, at its core the problem is not predominantly technological but political and philosophical. It is the will to shift to less harmful practices which is lacking. And we environmentalists and sustainability advocates will continue to lose the war if we let the powerful vested interests, who resist any threat to their short-term profit and dominance with ruthless tactics including highly sophisticated massive disinformation campaigns, paint us as anti-science, archaic Luddites. This battle is hard enough without providing our opponents with easy targets by actually calling ourselves Luddites or by being sloppy with our facts and figures or overstating our case. We must strive for clarity, integrity, honesty and precision to refute the propaganda of polluters, not wishful thinking and fuzzy pseudo-science.

This doesn't mean we can't draw inspiration from pre-industrial cultures and indigenous peoples who do offer us very resonant templates that can inform our approach to the natural world and to social relations. The Iroquois concept of making every big decision by taking its impact seven generations down the line into account would certainly serve us well, and is a powerfully sophisticated philosophical and stewardship model. The popularity of nature-loving phenomena from bird-watching to backpacking, of Chinese medicine with its Taoist reverence for nature's inherent capacity for self-regulation, of Buddhism and other traditions' profoundly sophisticated analyses of human psychology and consciousness, of Yoga and Ayurveda, of indigenous and shamanic worldviews, are all indicative of our collective thirst for a re-connection to the natural world, to more balanced, traditional approaches to life than our current linear race into post-humanity. And African music's conquest of the world in one form or another (blues, jazz, rock, rap, etc.) with its sensual vitality and drumming rooted in the beat of the human heart, is another manifestation of this burning desire to resist soulless modernity.

But we have to realize we can't go backward. Rather, we have to integrate the best of the archaic with the best of the post-modern to achieve a new synthesis that somehow combines the undeniable power and rigor of the scientific method with the reverence and eco-spiritual sophistication of our ancestors' long-lived, land-based cultures. Much of the best art of our era points in this direction, starting perhaps with Pablo Picasso's use of African art's inspiration to launch radical new experiments in modernity. Contemporary architects discover techniques for natural cooling in the design and material of Bedouin tents, for example, or computer scientists and mathematicians marvel at the binary logic of the I-Ching. The lines and designs of ancient art can look far more sleek and modern and futuristic to us than those of the Middle Ages, Renaissance or nineteenth century. It may turn out that in the classic Hegelian cycle of thesis/antithesis/synthesis modernity and industrialism represent the antithesis period, and it's now up to us to forge the best synthesis we can muster. It is my belief that the aforementioned emerging new paradigms of "complexity" and "whole systems" studies provide us with at least some of the tools we need to construct sophisticated new holistic approaches to science and society, the means to build the bridge to a post-modern but not post-human era. And they will have to include new forms of non-linear politics as well.

I realize it is not easy. One of the key problems is scale. Societies with hundreds of millions of people can't be run like small-town or rural democracies, yet it is the very crushing size and impersonality of our institutions that make many of us recoil at modernity's soulless-ness. Reconciling the need for large-scale and even eventually global institutions with the human-scale community needs of a very brainy but still essentially small-pack primate species is not easy. And in many cases we need to change the whole context of debates since our economic system is skewed in the very way it measures costs and efficiency and hides damage, and our opponents are deeply entrenched and utterly ruthless. The arguments we need to make are not always sound-byte friendly. Trying to explain that political and technological decisions need to be weighed holistically, with a careful look at their potential long-term ecological and social implications, is very tough in a short attention span era, especially with the immense machinery of clever public relations and right-wing think tanks generating a non-stop fog of obfuscation.

But we can also learn from our enemies. They use hypnotic mantras endlessly repeated to brainwash the public during campaigns: "tax and spend liberals," "double taxation," "environmental extremists," "class war," and the like. Why can't we accuse genetic manipulators of "simple-minded science," or certain industries of "poisoning the public and pocketing the profits," or, ideally, much catchier equivalents, and so on, and repeat the slogans till they sink in? We shouldn't stoop to the level of our opponents, but nothing is wrong with being clear and forceful if we are being true to our beliefs and honest.

In any case we are engaged in an ideological war over the soul of our civilization and the shaping of the post-modern world. Being right will not be enough, and we are losing badly in this struggle for the moment. The signs that many, many people are profoundly dissatisfied with modernity's current trajectory are visible in the arts, popular culture, and other grassroots phenomena, but an excessive zest for novelty and an enthusiasm for dizzying leaps into the unknown are also powerful urges. It ultimately comes down to which aesthetic response proves stronger. Will we accept a world of identical malls and fast food outlets selling shiny, genetically modified eating substances produced by industrial meat and grain factories, a world with three or four corporate empires owning nearly all news and entertainment outlets (with, of course, a few nature preserves, artsy "bohemian" ghettos, and gourmet restaurants for the rich), a world of extreme wealth disparities and a genetically-enhanced ruling elite? That's the one we've got and/or are heading toward. Or will we be able to forge ahead with a new holistic approach to science and governance and reactivate our species' innate love and reverence of a vital natural world, of timeless wisdom and of real variety? It will take a lot of creativity, wisdom, will, endurance and perhaps luck, but accepting the alternative without putting up relentless resistance is simply unthinkable.

Notes

Ayn Rand is one of the most famous apostles of libertarian, free-market individualism. Her novel, *The Fountainhead* (1943), is one of the biggest-selling books of all time.

Aleksey Stakhanov was an idealized "worker hero" used as a propaganda device under Stalinism to boost worker productivity. See Siegelbaum, Lewis H., *Stakhanovism and the Politics of Productivity in the USSR, 1935-1941* (Cambridge University Press, 1988).

Gary Snyder is one of America's leading poets. Originally one of the leading "beats" with a deep affinity for Japanese culture, he has become one of the most revered figures among environmentalists for his sublime appreciation of nature, especially his beloved Sierra Nevada mountains in California.

The poet and essayist Wendell Berry is an "agrarian" and a leading figure in the neo-Luddite world. His works include: *The Long-Legged House, That Distant Land, The Art of the Commonplace: Agrarian Essays of Wendell Berry,* and *A Continuous Harmony: essays cultural and agricultural.*

For a great story about the obsession to measure everything and to systematize standards of measurement after the French Revolution, see: Alder, Ken. *The Measure of All Things: the seven-year odyssey and hidden error that transformed the world* (Free Press, 2002).

An extraordinary book about the ideological battles between holists and reductionists in Germany is *Reenchanted Science: Holism in German Culture from Wilhelm II to Hitler,* by Anne Harrington (Princeton University Press, 1996). There is also some discussion of this in Robert Proctor's fascinating *The Nazi War on Cancer* (Princeton University, 1999).

"Goethean" refers to one of the greatest figures in German and world literature and thought, Johann Wolfgang von Goethe (1749-1832), who was also a botanist, zoologist and philosopher of science. Some of his theories (about optics, for example) have proven wrong, but his ideas about primary forms and metamorphosis in nature are still highly influential in certain holistic quarters (notably among followers of Rudolf Steiner).

For more on the "deep ecology" movement, see Sessions, George, ed. *Deep Ecology for the Twenty-first Century* (Shambhala, 1995).

The reference to nascent industrialism's "satanic mills" is from William Blake's (1757-1827) poem "Jerusalem" (1804):

"And did those feet in ancient time
Walk upon England's mountains green?
And was the holy Lamb of God
On England's pleasant pastures seen?

And did the Countenance Divine
Shine forth upon our clouded hills?
And was Jerusalem builded here
Among these dark satanic mills?

Bring me my bow of burning gold!
Bring me my arrows of desire!
Bring me my spear! O clouds, unfold!
Bring me my chariot of fire!

I will not cease from mental fight,
Nor shall my sword sleep in my hand,
Till we have built Jerusalem
In England's green and pleasant land."

Triumph of the Will (1934), by Leni Riefenstahl, made for the Nazis, is considered the archetypal propaganda film. Riefenstahl often highlighted super-fit, ideal "Aryan" specimens in her films.

Note: I make a number of references to ancestors of the counterculture. Here are a few of the less well known I haven't yet referenced:

The Eleusynian mysteries, sacred to Demeter, were an important initiatory rite in ancient Greece, and may have involved, according to some speculation (notably that of Gordon Wasson, the "discoverer" of the Mazatec mushroom healing cult in the 1950s), the ingestion of ergot-based hallucinogenic potions akin to LSD.

The Paris Commune was a popular urban rebellion in Paris in 1871, which ended tragically but has remained an inspiring episode for some sectors of the left.

John Muir (1838-1914) was a deeply influential naturalist, explorer and writer, a "nature mystic" who founded the Sierra Club. He was one of the great ancestors of the modern environmental movement.

A highly entertaining book about the extraordinary expatriate circles that included Aldous Huxley (and Garbo, Chaplin, Stravinsky, Krishnamurti, Mann, Brecht) in Los Angeles in the 1930s to the 1950s is David King Dunaway's *Huxley in Hollywood* (Harper and Row, 1989).

The section on "Moloch" appears in Part II of Allen Ginsberg's "Howl", Ginsberg, Allen, *Howl and other poems* (City Lights, 1956).

Whyte, William Hollingsworth, *The Organization Man* (Simon and Schuster, 1956).

Jobs and Wozniak, of Apple fame, leading figures in the invention of the home computer, were definitely countercultural types, and Kary Mullis, an avowed psychedelic enthusiast, won the Nobel Prize for chemistry in 1993 for his process for amplifying nucleic acid sequences, the "polymerase chain-reaction" (PCR).

The drug LSD was discovered by a remarkable Swiss chemist working for Sandoz, Albert Hoffman, in 1943. See his *LSD, My Problem Child* (English version, Tarcher, 1983).

Ayahuasca is a psychoactive brew used for millennia by several Amazonian shamanic traditions, which has now "crossed over" into certain counter-cultural milieus as a sacrament used in spiritual ceremonies.

Students for a Democratic Society was the leading student group of the "new left" in the 1960s.

The late writer Edward Abbey (co-founder or at least inspirer of the group "Earth First!") is an iconic figure among "deep ecologists." He is also controversial among environmentalists because of occasional lapses into racial insensitivity in his writings.

"Cyber-punk" was a literary movement of 1980s that originally included four science fiction writers: William Gibson, Bruce Sterling, Lewis Shiner and John Shirley.

Barber, Benjamin R. *Jihad vs. McWorld* (Times Books, 1995).

Manicheism was an intensely dualistic form of Gnosticism that originated in third century Persia. The adjective "Manichean" is often used, as I am using it here, to describe a simplistic view of absolute "good" and "evil."

The IMF's "Structural Adjustment Plans" are often draconian conditions economically troubled poorer nations are forced to accept to get further credit. They usually include terrible burdens on the poorest classes and favor foreign investors' interests.

For more on the dreaded Shah's secret police, see: Delannoy, Christian. *Savak* (Paris, Stock, 1990).

The "wise use" movement and "sagebrush rebellion" were (and are still, in new permutations) attempts in the western U.S. to return control of federal lands to individual states. They're profoundly anti-environmental movements, ostensibly anti-government populists, but actually manipulated by large corporate extractive industries. The Sagebrush Rebellion came first. Its most famous and controversial figure was Ronald Reagan's Secretary of the Interior, James Watt (the current Secretary is Gale Norton, one of his protégés). Another leading figure was one of Colorado's worst polluters, brewer Joseph Coors. "Wise Use" was a term first used by Tom Arnold, the Executive Vice President of the Center for the Defense of Free Enterprise (CDFE), a major figure in the anti-environmental backlash.

Bartholomew I, the Ecumenical Patriarch of roughly 250 million Orthodox Christians since 1991, has taken very strong positions on the environment and has been, on occasion, called the "green Patriarch."

Paul Gorman is the founder of a very effective and influential interfaith umbrella organization, The National Religious Partnership for the Environment.

 The "redwood rabbis" were a few rabbis and rabbinical students who led rituals in the forest for a group of environmentally concerned Jews who got involved in the struggle to save old growth forests in Northern California in 1997 ("Redwood Rabbis" by Seth Zuckerman, *Sierra* magazine November/December 1998).

For more on religion and the environment, see "Religion and the Conservation of Biodiversity" by Max Oelschaeger in *Wild Earth Journal*, fall 1996, and "The Second Creation Story: redefining the bond between religion and ecology" by Trebbe Johnson, in *Sierra's* November/December 1998 issue as well.

For a good short primer, to get a sense of the range of neo-Luddite critiques of technology's role in modern life, see: *Questioning Technology: Tool, Toy or Tyrant*, ed. Zerzan and Carnes (New Society, 1991), a collection of excerpts from thinkers such as Jacques Ellul, Lewis Mumford, Jerry Mander, and Langdon Winner). One of the most profound critiques remains Jacques Ellul's *The Technological Society* (*La Technique ou l'enjeu du siècle*), written in the 1950s. For a very radically neo-Luddite "Green" perspective, see Rudolf Bahro's *Building the Green Movement* (Trans. Mary Tyler; New Society, 1986).

Thomas Robert Malthus (1766-1834) argued that population expansion is geometric while food production increases arithmetically, so population expansion would bring famine. His dire prognostications proved inaccurate (or at least premature).

Paul Ehrlich's *The Population Bomb* (Ballantine Books, 1968) also made dire predictions about imminent crises and shortages due to population growth that didn't pan out in the time frame he anticipated.

The Club of Rome, a group of economists and thinkers, also made some overly pessimistic predictions about resource depletion and shortages in the early 1970s, most notably in Meadows, D. et al., *The Limits to Growth* (Universe Books, 1972).

For more on the relationship of Zen to militarism in Japan, see chapters 4, 5 and 6 in D.T Suzuki's *Zen and Japanese Culture* (Bollingen Foundation/Pantheon, 1959)—a revised and expanded version of his 1938 classic. See also "Yasutani Roshi: The Hardest Koan" in *Tricycle* magazine, fall 1999.

Rachel Carson is the mother of the modern environmental movement. Her book, *Silent Spring* (Houghton Mifflin, 1962) about the ravages of DDT and other pesticides on wildlife and ecosystems had an enormous impact. She was savagely attacked by industry.

The Spotlight, published by the Liberty Lobby, Inc., for decades until 2001, was an often zany (and sometimes anti-Semitic) journal of the far right.

Gifford Pinchot and the Making of Modern Environmentalism by Char Miller (Island Press/Shearwater Books, 2001) discusses the split between the utilitarian Gifford Pinchot and the more pantheistic John Muir.

For more on the debates between "deep" and "social" ecologists, a very profound, core dispute, see *Defending the Earth: a dialogue between Murray Bookchin and Dave Foreman* (South End Press, 1991); *Debating the Earth: The Environmental Politics Reader,* ed. Dryzeck and Schlosberg (Oxford, 1998); *Beyond Bookchin* by David Watson (Black and Red/Autonomedia, 1996). For a more recent example of a knee-jerk attack on conservationists by an academic socialist, see "Grizzly Conservation and the Nature of Essentialist Politics" by John Hintz in *Capitalism/Nature/Socialism: A Journal of Socialist Ecology*, December 2003. An excellent, sophisticated rebuke to this type of "postmodern" over-reaction and animosity to land conservation, so common among left academics, can be found in: "The Wilderness of History" by Donald Worster in *Wild Earth* journal, Fall 1997.

To be fair, one of the leading anti-globalization think-tanks, the International Forum on Globalization (IFG), has recently tried to resolve this contradiction regarding national sovereignty versus international treaties by advocating qualified support for the UN as a legitimate international body while rejecting the "Bretton Woods" institutions such as the World Bank and IMF as illegitimate. The IFG has also responded to criticism that the anti globalization movement has no credible alternatives by publishing position papers on alternative modes of international governance. See especially their report *Alternatives to Economic Globalization: a better world is possible* (Berrett-Koehler, 2002) and for more info: www.ifg.org.

The Kyoto Protocol is a proposed amendment to an international treaty on global warming—the United Nations Framework Convention on Climate Change (UNFCCC). Countries that ratify this protocol commit to reducing their emissions of carbon dioxide and other greenhouse gases linked to global warming.

The Montreal Protocol (officially the "Protocol on Substances That Deplete the Ozone Layer") treaty was signed on Sept. 16, 1987, at Montreal by 25 nations; 168 nations are now parties to the accord. The protocol set limits on the production of chlorofluorocarbons (CFCs), halons, and related substances that release chlorine or bromine to the ozone layer of the atmosphere.

Lerner, Michael. *The Politics of Meaning: restoring hope and possibility in an age of cynicism* (Addison-Wesley, 1997). He is also the editor of the left Jewish journal *Tikkun*.

There are many, many books on the ravages of industrial agriculture. Perhaps the best is the recent: *The Fatal Harvest Reader: the tragedy of industrial agriculture*, edited by Andrew Kimbrell (Deep Ecology/Island Press, 2002). *Fast Food Nation* by Eric Schlosser (Houghton Mifflin, 2002) is also a must-read.

There are countless books on the problems with genetically modified crops and organisms. A good primer is *Genetic Engineering, Food, and Our Environment*, by Luke Anderson (Chelsea Green, 1999). Another is my own short polemic, *Double Helix Hubris* (Cool Grove Press, 1997). A less polemical and longer, but very thoughtful book is Colin Tudge's *The Engineer in the Garden: Genes and Genetics from the Idea of Heredity to the Creation of Life* (Hill and Wang, 1993). For a deep theoretical critique see "Unraveling the DNA Myth: the spurious foundation of genetic engineering" by Barry Commoner in *Harper's*, February 2002.

The Episcopal Church, for example, has had an ambiguous set of positions on genetically modified crops. Most recently, after tentative support for some biotech methods the church felt could help address world hunger, it seems to be somewhat more hesitant. Episcopal Church Resolution A016 on Food Security passed at the 74th General Convention in Minneapolis in summer, 2003. Authored by the Subcommittee on Genetically Modified Foods, it urges Episcopalians to be aware of the broader food security context of GM foods, including concerns for environmental disruption and bio-safety, reduced diversity of wild and domesticated plants, displacement of small farmers in the U.S. and worldwide, and the concentrated control of commercial seed production within fewer and fewer corporations. Full text of the Resolution can be found at: http://home.earthlink.net/~smithmoran/FoodSecurityResolution.htm

For an insightful short piece on American attitudes toward food, see "The Futures of Food" by Michael Pollan in the *New York Times Magazine*, May 3, 2003.

The main group broadly on the left in the U.S. trying to organize resistance to inheritable genetic modification, human cloning and so on, is the Center for Genetics and Society (www.genetics-and-society.org). See their report "The New Technologies of Human Genetic Modification: A Threshold Challenge for Humanity." See also *World Watch* magazine of July/August 2002, "Beyond Cloning: the risks of rushing into human genetic engineering." A recent polemic on the topic is Bill McKibben's *Enough: staying human in an engineered age* (Times Books, 2003). An excellent earlier work is Andrew Kimbrell's *The Human Body Shop: the engineering and marketing of life* (Harper San Francisco, 1993).

Judy Norsigian is a founding member of the Boston Women's Health Book Collective, a non-profit organization committed to education about women and health. The collective was started by twelve women in a church basement in Watertown, Massachusetts in the late 1960s and is famous for its hugely popular and groundbreaking book, *Our Bodies, Ourselves*, originally published in 1973, and republished in a new version by Simon & Schuster in 1998, *Our Bodies, Ourselves for the New Century: a book by and for women*. Norsigian is one of the only major left-feminist figures to have come out strongly against "germ-line" genetic manipulation and to warn of the risks of new forms of eugenics. See "Some for Abortion Rights Lean Right in Cloning Fight: genetic duplication issue proves nuanced" by Sheryl Gay Stolberg in the Januray 24,

2002, *New York Times.*

Roman Polanski's film *Chinatown* (1974) about water and power politics in Los Angeles featured Faye Dunaway as an incest victim of a very powerful father. Her terrible secret is that her daughter is also her sister.

Molecular biologist Lee Silver says genetic enhancement of humans is inevitable and will make human society far more stratified but welcomes it. While many others on the fringes (such as the extreme techno-utopian cult, the "extropians") share this view, he is one of the main major scientific figures being that blunt and unapologetic about a techno-eugenic future. See Silver, Lee M. *Remaking Eden: cloning and beyond in a brave new world* (Avon Books, 1997).

One example of a (remarkably stupid) journalistic piece worrying about the future rights of genetically altered humans is "Cyborg Liberation Front: inside the movement for post-human rights" by Erik Baard in the August 5, 2003, *Village Voice.*

Genetically altered humans are now a totally routine feature of sci-fi. And part human/part animal hybrids ("chimeras"), an ancient mythological theme, have also become a common plot contrivance in sci-fi books, TV shows and movies (from "Manimal" to "Dark Angel" to "X Men"). A good sci-fi book with that theme is *Ribofunk* by Paul Di Filippo (Four Walls/Eight Windows, 1996). For the last few years, the biologist Stewart Newman, an opponent of genetic enhancement, has been fighting the U.S. patent office, demanding his right to patent the concept of a genetic chimera, to expose the absurdity of patenting life forms and the dangerous slope we are on.

The co-inventors of "golden rice" are Ingo Potrykus and Peter Beyer. Potrykus helped develop plant genetic engineering at the Friedrich Miescher-Institute, Basel, where he worked from the mid-1970s. He went on to become Professor of Plant Sciences at the Swiss Federal Institute of Technology, Zurich, from 1987 to April 1999, when he retired. Beyer is affiliated with Freiburg University.

For arguments against genetic, high-tech quick fixes to reduce hunger see "Ten Reasons Why Biotechnology Will Not Ensure Food Security, Protect the Environment and Reduce Poverty in the Developing World" by Miguel Altieri and Peter Rosset, available from Food First/The Institute for Food and Development Policy (www.food-first.org). And, from the same source, for a critique of "golden rice" see "Genetically Engineered Vitamin A Rice: a blind approach to blindness prevention" by Vandana Shiva (February 2000).

I list a number of individuals and organizations at the forefront of sustainable technology and economics in the U.S. These include the leading advocate for energy efficiency, Amory Lovins, co-founder the Rocky Mountain Institute (RMI) (for a good overview of his approach see Hawken. Paul, and Lovins, Amory, Lovins, L. Hunter, *Natural Capitalism: creating the next industrial revolution* (Little, Brown and Co., 1999) and the RMI website http://www.rmi.org/sitepages/pid385.php); the economist Herman E. Daly, author of several books, including *Beyond Growth: the economics of sustainable development* (Beacon Press, 1996); Janine Benyus, author of *Biomimicry: innovation inspired by nature* (Morrow, 1997); one of the two leading U.S.-based eco think tanks, The Worldwatch Institute, which produces a highly regarded annual "State of the World" report; the visionary biologist and bioremediation genius John Todd (see he and his wife's classic *From Eco-Cities to Living Machines: Principles of Ecological Design* (North Atlantic Books, 1994); and the annual Bioneers conference, the leading multi-disciplinary eco conclave which brings many of the greatest figures in this world together (www.bioneers.org), founded by Kenny Ausubel, author of, among other works, *Restoring the Earth* (H.J. Kramer, 1997). Also, a collection about pioneers in alternative technologies, *Nature's Operating Instructions*, Kenny Ausubel with J.P. Harpignies (Sierra Club Books, 2004).

Georg Wilhelm Friedrich Hegel (1770-1831), in his woks *Wissenschaft der Logik* (Science of Logic, 1816) and *Die Encyclopädie der philosophischen Wissenschaften im Grundrisse* (Encyclopedia of the Philosophical Sciences, 1817), described the pattern of dialectical reasoning (thesis — antithesis — synthesis) and its application to all areas of human knowledge. His work had a profound influence on Karl Marx.

A book of interviews with top scientists working on questions relevant to the health of the biosphere that tries to inspire by showing brilliant, positive uses of science is *Life Stories: World Renowned Scientists Reflect on their Lives and the Future of Life on Earth*, Heather Newbold (University of California Press, 2000). This approach seems to me a valuable corrective to excessive Luddism.

Art, Truth and Politics

Art, science and philosophy have throughout history all had uneasy relationships with politics. Science (at its best) pursues verifiable truth; philosophy seeks wisdom ; and while art's mission is harder to define and more varied, the most powerful art often involves a quest for an aesthetic or inner/subjective truth. An authentic quest for truth (of whatever type) involves a willingness to accept what one unearths, no matter how unpleasant or complicated. Politics, however, involves the pursuit and management of power or influence, so it is not a realm where open-ended uncertainty or inconvenient information is prized. This is widely understood. The trials of Socrates and Galileo (whatever the real details of their cases) are our culture's archetypal cautionary tales about the collision of political power and independent thought. Truth and beauty certainly usually are butchered in politics. The most renowned political leaders throughout history have most often exhibited a monomaniacal sense of certainty and mission. Candidates for high office who publicly admit to having nuanced and complex thoughts or of being engaged in a tortured quest for truth are usually doomed to defeat and/or ridicule.

And yet artists, thinkers and scientists have often been drawn to political struggles. This is not surprising since thoughtful, accomplished people are likely to want to weigh in on the great issues of their day, and are also likely to bemoan the usual shortcomings of governance and feel they could do better or offer alternatives. They are usually frustrated in that political reality can be very cruel to the naïve who quest for a perfect world, pristine truth, or perfect efficiency. Meanwhile, politicians and political movements are often eager to receive the support and imprimatur of well-known figures in creative fields to boost their own cachet and credibility, but become uncomfortable if these creative types exhibit too much independence or zaniness.

Even on the level of the everyday grassroots activist there can be jarring conflicts between aesthetic sensibilities and political involvement. Most political discourse is shrill and crudely simplistic. The rhetoric public speakers usually disgorge at events, rallies or demonstrations is at best predictable, often horribly dull, and not infrequently sickeningly manipulative. The obligatory chanting of silly slogans can be a painful exercise. Most political figures seem grotesquely insincere and/or manically inflated. Gifted orators are rare indeed, and gifted orators who offer something more than pat answers and party lines rarer still. Meetings are constant, interminable and stultifying. In other words political activism can be very depressing for anyone with any subtlety of mind and/or a modicum of aesthetic sensitivity. And most idealists (who are the ones who tend to gravitate to progressive activism) are sensitive souls.

Most overtly political art is painfully didactic. In no domain of human endeavor is the expression "the road to hell is paved with good intentions" more apt. We all know dystopian novels are much easier to write than descriptions of utopias, and bad guys a lot more fun to play for actors than saints. The history of the relationship between art and politics is an immensely complex subject I do not have the space, inclination, or ability to do justice to, but a few examples will help illustrate the specific tension I am interested in here: the difficulty for a thoughtful, aesthetically sensitive individual to reconcile her/his sense of truth and authenticity with the so prevalent pedestrian, or worse, dishonest, dull and ugly aspects of politics. Robinson Jeffers' memorable advice in "Not Man Apart" about not being seduced by utopian pipe-dreams but, if you had to get involved in politics in a time of upheaval, to "pick the least ugly faction" comes to mind.

I am mostly concerned here with the relationship of left/progressive movements to aesthetics, but obviously not all artists and intellectuals are or have been on the left. Art has many different functions. Official, monumental art seeks to portray a society's (or at least its ruling elite's) cosmology and worldview and inspire the populace to embrace them. This is "establishment art." Sacred art and much traditional "fine art" seek to express universal truth or some form of essential beauty. Transgressive or experimental art often seeks to explore taboo or unacknowledged truth. By and large experimental/transgressive art has tended to be more resonant with the political left, and more structured, traditional art with the right, but, of course, there are many other functions of art, and these distinctions are far from set in stone, and. As always, there are many exceptions. A piece of monumental, official art such as Maya Lin's Vietnam War Memorial also has populist and even subversive elements. Ancient "official" monuments such as pyramids or Gothic cathedrals were also apotheoses of spiritual/sacred art, and sacred art can be conservative or mystically radical and rebellious (William Blake for example); utopian artistic movements in the last few centuries in the West have been mostly linked to the left but there are important exceptions such as the Italian Futurists. So it's a very complicated picture, but, still, some of these distinctions can be helpful.

Just as there are periods of political turbulence and experimentation in politics, there are predominantly Dionysian or Apollonian (i.e., wild or conservative) periods in culture. And very often, cultural rebellions anticipate and then accompany socio-political movements. R&B's and later rockabilly's and rock'n'roll's popularity among white youth in the 1950s came before many young white kids in the next generation joined the civil rights movement in the 1960s, for example. The more rebellious eras in politics are often also high-water marks of transgressive artistic movements, and many of the artists and thinkers in those periods are actively politically radical or sympathetic to the rebels. Later in life, of course, some of them become conservatives, if they become financially successful and/or if their early illusions were too brutally dashed. Fyodor Dostoyevsky offers an archetypal example of someone whose disillusionment with utopian radicalism ultimately led him to a very conservative outlook. And he is far from alone. A cold, hard look at human behavior leads many subtle artists and thinkers to a Hobbesian pessimism more in tune with a rightist ideology or at least individualistic apolitical cynicism than with the often naïve and utopian aspirations of the left.

In the last few centuries in Western art it has almost become a rule that yesterday's rude avant-garde will become today's stodgy establishment, as yet another generation of rebels "sells out." It has become a predictable cyclic ritual: mainstream culture vampirically sucks dry and digests one artistic rebellion after another, its only hope of avoiding terminal cultural sclerosis. But still, during those periods when heightened political ferment is coupled with dynamic new cultural movements one does see an outpouring of politically flavored artistic expression, some of which is powerful and genuinely interesting. But those bursts of Dionysian creativity tend to be short-lived, and the comedown after the party is often harsh. Also the relationship between the artists and the activists is rarely smooth.

In the twentieth century a brief ecstatic period in Russia before and after the 1917 revolution witnessed extraordinary artistic and socio-sexual experimentation in certain creative circles with high hopes for a new era, but it was brutally suppressed by the party apparatchiks. Soon the extraordinary works of artists such as Malevich and Goncharova were hidden in basements, and the dark Soviet era settled in. Not too long after, in France, there was a classic example of the tension between a political organization and radical artists—that between the Surrealists and the Communist Party. Most of the Surrealists had left-wing political views but their revolutionary aspirations extended to the recesses of the unconscious and many were instinctually hostile to all authority. The French Communist Party liked having well-known intellectuals support some of its positions, but these people were, by and large, just too wacky and impossible to control, though, ironically, André Breton often behaved like an authoritarian party boss himself in trying to control the Surrealist movement. And Salvador Dali wound up supporting the fascist Franco regime.

In the 1960s, groups such as the Provos in Amsterdam and the Yippies in the U.S., for example, were able, for a very short time, to strike a chord by creating a sort of funny, anarchically disruptive political performance art. But even in those wildly experimental years, there was an often tense relationship between those musicians, writers and artists who, while against the Vietnam War and for greater social justice, had no resonance with the shrill Marxist rhetoric of the main radical groups. And the artists for their part, in that loopy era, didn't usually have very coherent political ideas or a good grasp of the realities of political organizing. And selective memory should not make us forget that attempts at overtly political art were frequently as painfully didactic in that period as they usually are. Most people who were around that scene most likely remember political artifacts such as, say, the striking activist puppetry of the Bread and Puppet Theater (not its stiff performances), but they have probably erased from their minds the embarassing memories of the Black Panther Party's singing group "The Lumpen" or the Weathermen's rewriting of pop and rock songs with revolutionary lyrics.

To rally widespread support political movements need to have easy-to-communicate, readily understood themes. This is problematic for anyone who understands how complex social phenomena are. For scholars, intellectuals and artists who revel in unearthing subtle distinctions, over-simplification is anathema. Reducing reality to slogans is insulting to anyone attracted to novels or plays or films that are great precisely because they are nuanced and multi-faceted and open to multiple interpretations.

If we are honest with ourselves, we all know we frequently have a whole range of contradictory responses to people and events. Don't we sometimes love and hate someone at the same time, or feel genuine affection for friends but also resent their success? I can both feel compassion for victims of a natural catastrophe but also be secretly excited by a big storm or flood or earthquake and more thrilled the bigger it is (preferably if it is affecting someone else far away). The human psyche is incredibly convoluted and mysterious. Many spiritual traditions and schools of psychology devised elaborate techniques of self-examination precisely because they understood how tangled a labyrinth the mind tends to be. The mischievous spiritual teacher George Gurdjieff said most people have no right to use the pronoun "I" because their mental process resembles a team of out of control horses pulling them hither and yon. An Eastern teacher referred to the flow of thoughts in most people's minds as the chatter of "100 monkeys." And Immanuel Kant hit the nail on the head in writing "from such warped wood as is man made, nothing straight can be fashioned."

This complexity is obviously why thoughtful people tend to find Hollywood films or bad novels with Manichean distinctions between "good guys" and "bad guys" so shallow and uninteresting, but nearly all political discourse stays on that simplistic level. To some extent that is inevitable. A political figure asked to respond to a crisis can't really say: "Well, Bob, I have a wide range of seemingly contradictory feelings about that." Rallying large numbers of people to achieve specific social goals inevitably requires some leveling of reality and an exclusion of subtleties. It can't be as exquisitely nuanced as a refined artistic or philosophic quest. That said, there are on occasion inspiring and aesthetically appealing political gestures, statements and actions. They are rare, but they are the ones that tend to have a major and lasting impact.

Some political art can be both direct and elliptical and subtle and deeply affecting—Billie Holliday's rendition of Abel Meeropol's "Strange Fruit" or the work of the influential German Anthroposophic artist Joseph Beuys, for example. It can also be effective when it is totally straightforward, *elegantly* simple and viscerally powerful. In very different ways, Woody Guthrie or early Bob Dylan songs, the paintings of Leon Golub, Picasso's "Guernica," the caricatures of Honoré Daumier, the film *The Salt of the Earth* or John Sayles' *Matewan*, some of the best political rap music, to cite only a few random examples, all strike me as beautiful and effective without necessarily being subtle or even-handed. Why one piece of overtly partisan political art works while most others are awful is hard to explain. Perhaps power and directness in political art require a special type of unadorned spontaneity, similar in spirit to what Zen-inspired artists seek to achieve, but with more passion and less detachment. But the line between honest emotion and maudlin manipulation or pat political-correctness is easy to cross.

In recent years the direct actions of Earth First! and other tree-sitters such as Julia Butterfly-Hill, or of Greenpeace members climbing high bridges or smokestacks to put anti-pollution banners on them, or Sea Shepherd vessels placing themselves between whaling ships and whales, or even ramming illegal whaling vessels, have captured the imagination of many young people. Political actions that are noble and courageous but non-violent and life-affirming, easy to understand and symbolically resonant have a type of clarity and beauty to them, as the lunch-counter sit-ins of the early Southern civil rights movement, the seizure of Alcatraz by Native Americans, and the extraordinary image of the lone student in front of the tank in Tiananmen Square all did. And of course great political eloquence such as Martin Luther King's "dream" speech can have an impact for generations.

The intelligent use of humor is also a powerful form of communication, as the guerrilla theater antics of Abbie Hoffman's disruption of the New York Stock Exchange by throwing dollar bills off its balcony, and the work of a number of contemporary political pranksters (Andrew Boyd, the political direct-action performance artist "Reverend Billy," the cyber-trickster "Yes Men," Adbusters, and the transvestite "Sisters of Perpetual Indulgence" collective, to name a handful) illustrate. But bad humor is among the worst things a human being can be subjected to (at least aesthetically).

These types of actions, artistic expressions and memorable discourses are remembered precisely because they are rare. Dramatic actions cannot be mindlessly repeated over and over or they lose their effectiveness. The best tactics usually evolve organically, but all too often activists seek to reproduce mechanically something that is no longer resonant, like unimaginative Hollywood executives making endless sequels. In most cases, only a few people participate in the dramatic episodes, and most of the political work that needs to get done to produce lasting results will never be that glamorous. The memorable actions and speeches of a few are only possible because of the work of untold thousands who lay the groundwork and do years of often dreary and depressing work to set the stage and build the support networks. They are the unsung and unseen mycelial mats under the forest without which no trees will grow. Still, the work of creating mycelial mats is much less interesting if it never helps produce a forest with some towering trees.

Of course orators try to prepare the best speeches possible and activists to come up with the most effective tactics, but, overall, there has not been enough conscious examination among progressives of the relationship between aesthetics and politics, of the tensions between psychological, inner honesty and the too often soul-deadening demands of political work. I feel this is a crucial discussion because I am convinced that most people respond instinctively to authenticity. There is something about, say, the Dalai Lama or Nelson Mandela or Jane Goodall or Julia Butterfly-Hill that is truly inspiring. The type of heart-felt authenticity such figures display can also be very threatening as it can make us more aware of our own lack of full-bodied commitment, our failures and imperfections. This is one reason saints of all stripes have been routinely sliced, diced and charcoaled throughout history. Ideally, if we are mature, we should be able to appreciate the inspiration such individuals can provide but accept that each of us has a separate fate, and not feel compelled either neurotically to chastise ourselves for not being perfect or to feel obliged to prostrate ourselves before exemplary figures or project too much onto them, as they are, despite their larger than life personas, just flawed humans like all of us.

During the 1960s a great debate occurred within the counterculture between activists who felt a more just and sustainable society could only come with a drastic overthrow and redesign of the political and economic system and those with a more metaphysical outlook who argued real change could only come with the moral/spiritual development of individuals. Like much in that bizarrely excessive if fascinating time, the argument was a bit silly, a lower octave ("Street Fighting Man" vs. "Revolution Number 9" or "We Won't Be Fooled Again") reprise of a sort of Hegel-Marx idealist versus materialist chicken and egg debate. Obviously there's always some sort of dynamic two-way feedback-loop between the beliefs and attitudes of people and the structure of their dominant social institutions, though, at different times, one can lag behind or stifle the other, sometimes for long periods. But it may be valuable to explore the relationship between activists' self-awareness and aesthetic acuity and the flavor and tone of political movements.

Some of the progressive movements that have generated the most enthusiasm have had appealing aesthetic dimensions, usually a festive and celebratory aspect, from the International Workers of the World's (IWW) singing hobos to the light-hearted anarcho-dada sensibility common in the 1960s. Most of us respond far more readily to colorful costumes, music and self-deprecating humor than to pompous hectoring. On the other hand, bad music and unfunny attempts at humor are far worse than a decent, dry speech. The crucial element is authenticity (though some actual talent is very helpful). People have a very sensitive, often unconscious, radar that detects insincerity, arrogance and neurosis in public figures and speakers and instinctively recoils, even though (or perhaps because) nearly all of us are frequently disingenuous and inauthentic ourselves. This radar is far from perfect; people are also often seduced by maniacally charismatic egotists and hucksters, but it is nonetheless an important human capacity with real political significance. If we too take the path of least resistance and seek to manipulate people's basest instincts or knee-jerk responses for short-term political gain, nothing really differentiates us from our adversaries.

Politics can never be all fun and games and celebratory self-expression even in the best of times. There are historical moments when a festive, playful tone is resonant, and others when deep sobriety is called for. There is always important analytic, dry, cerebral work to accomplish as well as enormous amounts of plain old dull grunt-work that need to get done, as in most other serious endeavors. But, in the same way that a Zen temple is designed (and cared for) to embody ideals of awakened equanimity, mental one-pointedness and spare beauty, or a cathedral is designed to express divine awe and a thirst for transcendence, a political movement's aesthetics and tone may tell us as much or more about its essence than its position papers.

Demonstrations, for example, important mainstays and historic markers of left politics, can range from upbeat, empowering occasions, to excruciatingly depressing affairs. This has a lot to do with the levels of energy and spontaneity and the overall mood of the participants, and most of that depends on the historical context, the depth of feeling and the level of support for the cause of the moment. Activists do often put a lot of effort into the aesthetic dimensions of these events, creating elaborate costumes, satirical puppet-sculptures, colorful banners, political performance art, drumming ensembles, and the like. At its best, this is a vital folk-art tradition. When it all works well, it can be magical. Most often, though, demonstrations feel flat, the chanting mechanical, the speeches from the podium shrill and pandering to the already converted. As with political art, it's not always easy to pinpoint exactly why one event works and others don't.

I've noticed that large marches with a very wide range of people coming together over a common, emotionally-charged concern at important historical junctures do tend to have a mix of both gravitas and ebullience that makes them memorable. The sillier sectarian groups one inevitably finds at such events tend to be subsumed by the sheer numbers. Smaller demonstrations that are done tastefully as a sort of ritual by a disciplined group with a high level of shared purpose can be very effective at times as well. But those occasions in which narrowly sectarian organizations represent a sizeable share of the participants or control the roster of speakers are often jarringly shrill. Demonstrations are an important tactical tool in the activist repertoire, but it is important to think constantly of novel forms and novel approaches to existing models. Might, for example, on occasion, the sight of thousands of demonstrators marching in total silence be more powerful than the usual chanting of slogans? Ultimately, a life-affirming movement that has a profound, lasting emotional/aesthetic as well as intellectual appeal can only be created by people who have achieved a high degree of self (as well as political) awareness, people who can march in a crowd but not be caught up in collective hysteria or lose their critical perspective.

I would like to see at least a significant swath of the progressive/eco-conscious movement attempt to be not only radical in its positions but radically authentic in its political and personal style and behavior. Could we learn to have the courage to be ruthlessly self-examinatory and regularly subject our own positions and knee-jerk reactions to honest and thorough scrutiny? Could we work diligently to stay aware of and mitigate our tendencies toward smugness, self-righteousness, self-importance, arrogance, paranoia, sloganeering, intellectual laziness, ad hominem attacks and suffused rage? (And I speak as someone who suffers from all those traits in very large doses.) I am far from naïve. I know this would make our work even harder. Lying, corruption, distortion, cynical manipulation, character assassination (not to mention real assassination) and intimidation frequently *do* succeed in politics. We're already so weak; it seems unfair to tie our hands behind our backs by asking we hold ourselves to a far higher standard than our opponents. And, without a doubt, there are times political ruthlessness is necessary.

And yet, this may sound utopian, but if we claim we are seeking to build something new, a more equitable, earth-honoring, joyous and less alienated civilization, it behooves us to at least begin, as much as possible, actually to embody the values we tout to others. This entails very hard, painful inner work, more frustrating than lashing out at external foes. It is a continuous process. No one ever achieves perfection. It is not perfection but depth, thoughtfulness and authenticity we should seek. But if I am right, and many people do respond on some level to genuine honesty and a lack of arrogance, even if they disagree with a position intellectually, this path would ultimately pay political as well as personal dividends. This doesn't at all mean one has to be wimpy or abandon one's core passions and guiding ideals or be any less radical in one's positions. But it does mean being open to complexity and uncertainty, and looking with fresh eyes as often as possible. I know this is tricky because movements at times need common positions, cohesion and group discipline, but we must find a way to include a broad range of ideas and approaches and enjoy constructive disagreements, or we become an ideological monoculture, as dead and ugly as a pesticide-laden field of a genetically identical crop.

One crucial area we need to examine is the caliber of our rhetoric. We must strive for linguistic precision. It is truly painful to attend a rally or conference and hear speaker after speaker pander, exaggerate and distort or misinterpret data. Our arguments are strong enough without resorting to blatant attempts at crowd-pleasing. So often I've heard progressive speakers advocate "real democracy" as a cure-all to loud applause, when very often the attitudes of a majority of the people in a situation (Germans in the Nazi era, Hutus in Rwanda, Serbs in the 1990s, white southerners in the 1950s/1960s in the U.S., most Americans in the early/middle stages of the Vietnam and recently during the Iraq War) are a big part of the problem. At a large demonstration the speakers will cite the thousands present as proof that "the people" are with us. No, some people are with us and, usually, more aren't (or don't care either way) and being honest is a better way to begin to tackle a real situation. And, no, the Seattle protests didn't mark the beginning of a real "red/green" (worker/eco) alliance, but a temporary marriage of convenience. "Right Speech," to borrow a Buddhist term, is harder to achieve but less personally deadening and, I believe, more politically productive in the long run. We must hold ourselves to a higher standard of truth telling than our enemies, even if it is not convenient.

Another very frequent domain of hypocrisy within our movements is in our choice of tactics and our response when these are turned against us. If we are amused when cyber-hackers disrupt a mega-corporation's website (and it's hard not to be if you detest most corporate behavior and culture), it is hard to find a rationale to be outraged if right-wing hackers then disrupt our own on-line networks. I am not saying such behavior is necessarily always indefensible, but we pay a price when we wink at our own moral inconsistency. If one decides one is a genuine, avowed revolutionary interested in overthrowing the social order, violently if need be, it seems demeaning to plead that one's civic freedoms are being violated by being incarcerated if one is caught in an act of violence. If one chooses to fight police in the streets, it is hard to be outraged that they respond with brutality (a very different matter than their very frequent excessive reaction to essentially non-violent civil disobedience or than real self-defense).

I myself have a history of involvement (in my youth) with political street fighting and revolutionary movements and still have a soft-spot for some very radical perspectives, but, whatever one's ideology, internal consistency and honesty are paramount. I'm not telling anyone what to believe or do, but I can ask for *integrity within your avowed value-system.* If you're really a revolutionary, denounce the system in your trial and proudly refuse to acknowledge the authority of your judges as you are led off, and I will respect you. If you are a real street samurai, accept your lumps and casualties and fatalities without whining (and don't hide behind a bunch of pacifists and throw stuff at the cops and run away as they get stomped), and I'll respect you. I may think you're misguided in your analysis of what is politically productive or tactically sane or morally justifiable in the current context, but I'll respect your consistency and your commitment, even if I might abhor something you've done.

Very few revolutionaries live up to this standard. And I'm not personally saying revolutionary violence or armed self-defense are never called for. Without them there would have been no American or French revolutions and later no end to colonialism and apartheid. But I'd argue they only make political sense in very rare historical circumstances, and are almost always counter-productive if a genuine revolutionary context is not present. I realize far left militant groups always think they're living in a revolutionary context, and they argue all means including lying, the political manipulation of moderates, and violence are allowable in overthrowing an ultimately evil system. Communist and nationalist movements that used these strategies were often far more successful than other more squeamish leftists at seizing power in the twentieth century. True enough, but they ultimately failed disastrously, and their ruthlessness and hypocrisy tainted them to their core, so that nothing they touched could lead to good. If one is to argue, as the revolutionary cannibals in Jean-Luc Godard's 1968 film *Weekend* do, that "to destroy the horrors of the bourgeoisie requires even more horror," at least be prepared to go into the caldron with your head high without bitching and moaning if the bourgeoisie decides to have you for dinner, and I'll consider you a noble cannibal. But hypocrisy and unconscious inconsistency are ugly and ultimately damaging to oneself and to one's political goals, especially for those on the left.

And the left is once again at a disadvantage in this regard in that it frequently invokes a more exalted view of human ethical possibilities, so its moral inconsistencies are harder to forgive and its failures easier to mock. The Hobbesian pessimism encoded in the right's DNA has fairly low expectations of human behavior, so the right is over and over able to invoke the need for ethically dubious measures or violent repression to maintain order and get away with it, because it's not promising a new Jerusalem, just a flawed absence of chaos. It is not fair, but we need to understand it and accept that we have a greater burden than our enemies, and get on with it.

To be genuinely different from our opponents in our essence, we must do the hard work of awakening some of our higher capacities—the better, more interesting and generous parts of our natures that allow us, on occasion, to be generous even to our enemies. It certainly doesn't mean aspiring to sainthood. That would be even more pompously irritating than mere political fanaticism. In fact, admitting just how far from sainthood we are (and will always be) with honest humor, and even happily consciously reveling in our vices on occasion can be a helpful part of the process. It is not saintliness but a tone of emotional honesty that is key. Acknowledging one's dark side has certainly been a real political taboo in our culture. Jimmy Carter was humiliated for the most banal of self-evident statements about lust, for example. But it is time for a new breed of political leaders who are not afraid to reveal the full range of their humanity, even to admit they are occasionally wrong! They don't have to wallow in sordid Oprah-esque confessionalism, just refuse to present only a polyurethaned, blow-dried surface to the world. The current crop are nearly all afraid to try or are incapable of it, but I suspect one day we will be surprised at how successful a sane, emotionally honest and mature, complex public figure might be, and how much hunger there would be for this type of adult leadership.

In the Bhagavad-Gita section of the ancient Vedic epic, the *Mahabharata*, Arjuna, the hero, agonizing over the necessity to fight and kill his relatives in a crucial battle, is told by divine revelation he must fulfill his historical destiny and do it with total commitment but also without rage or attachment. This is perhaps an impossible standard, especially for Westerners whose culture extols passion more than detachment, but it captures an interesting view of life one finds in some meditative and martial traditions. In these ways one intensely (but ideally joyously as well) develops one's physical, emotional, artistic, intellectual and spiritual capacities to the greatest extent possible while rigorously (but dispassionately, and ideally good naturedly) observing one's psyche and thought flow. One of the ideals of such a path is to emerge with a sense of exquisite appropriateness, a deeply centered capacity to act un-neurotically and effectively for the greater good. This is not necessarily a template most of us can adopt wholesale, but we can draw some lessons from the model.

Unless a good number of progressive activists are willing to "boldly go" outside their knee-jerk comfort zones and really explore their doubts and fears and become more conscious, open-hearted and open-minded, our movements will continue to be weak, divided, stupidly sectarian and unappealing. The people in a movement are the only real advertising for its ideas and ideals. We have to try and create movements thoughtful people with a richly nuanced view of life can support without reticence. If we begin to challenge ourselves as well as our enemies, and think very hard about what makes for good political aesthetics and what doesn't, we might begin to build movements that are far more effective, far more interesting, and, ultimately, far more beautiful.

Notes

There have been several "revisionist" looks at Galileo and Socrates' trials in recent years. These include Rowland, Wade. *Galileo's Mistake: a new look at the epic confrontation between Galileo and the church* (Arcade, 2003); and I. F. Stone's *The Trial of Socrates* (Anchor Books, 1989). For a more balanced view see Brickhouse, Thomas C., and Smith, Nicholas D. *The trial and Execution of Socrates: sources and controversies* (Oxford University, 2002).

Poet Robinson Jeffers' (1885-1962) eco-political wisdom can be found in: *Not Man Apart; lines from Robinson Jeffers/ Photos of the Big Sur Coast, by Ansel Adams*, edited by the legendary eco-activist, David Brower (Sierra Club Books, 1965).

Futurism is a rare example of a mostly right wing avant-garde artistic movement. An Italian group of painters, architects, sculptors and writers that emerged in 1909 with Marinetti's manifesto of futurism, it lasted until the end of World War I. Carrà, Severini and Balla were its most well-known painters and Boccioni its main sculptor. The futurists viewed themselves as anti-establishment rebels. They glorified war and the machine age and were mostly pro-fascist. Their work did influence many painters, including Marcel Duchamp and the Russian constructivists. See Perloff, Marjorie. *The Futurist Moment: avant-garde, avant guerre, and the language of rupture* (University of Chicago Press, 2003); Martin, Marianne W. *Futurist Art and Theory, 1909-1915* (Hacker Art Books, 1978); Lista, Giovanni. *Futurism*, Susan Wise, trans. (Paris: Terrail, 2001); Berghaus, Günter. *International Futurism in Arts and Literature* (Walter de Gruyter, 2000); and: Orban, Clara Elizabeth. *The Culture of Fragments: word and images in futurism and surrealism* (Rodopi, 1997).

Russian art and avant-garde socio-sexual experimentation were remarkably creative in the pre-revolutionary and post-revolutionary era from 1908 to 1928. By 1932, Stalin completely clamped down and only Socialist Realist art was allowed. Some of the most prominent schools of art were the Neo-primitivists, the Constructivists and the Suprematists, led by Malevich. Many of the leading artists of the period were women: Goncharova, Popova, Rozanova, etc. For more on the clampdown on freedom in Russia at the time, see the renowned anarcho-socialist Emma Goldman's *My Disillusionment in Russia* (Dover, 2003).

For more on Surrealism, see Polizzotti, Mark. *Revolution of the Mind: the life of André Breton* (Da Capo Press, 1997); Breton, André. *Conversations: the autobiography of surrealism*, Mark Polizzotti, trans. (Paragon House, 1993); Durozoi, Gérard. *History of the Surrealist Movement* (Alison Anderson, trans. (University of Chicago, 2002); Etherington-Smith, Meredith. The *Persistence of Memory: a biography of Dalí* (Da Capo Press, 1995).

The quote from Immanuel Kant (1724-1804) is in *Immanuel Kant: Perpetual Peace and Other Essays*, Ted Humphrey trans. (Hackett, 1983), p. 34.

George I. Gurdjieff (1872?-1949) was a highly-influential spiritual teacher and colorful character who still has an active following. There are countless books by his followers. The most famous is P.D. Ouspensky's *In Search of the Miraculous*. Gurdjieff's only accessible book is his allegorical *Meetings with Remarkable Men* (Dutton, 1969), made into a film by Peter Brook.

I mention a number of examples of political artists and works. For more on the song "Strange Fruit" see Margolick, David. *Strange Fruit: Billie Holiday, Café Society, and an early cry for civil rights* (Running Press, 2000); for more on the pioneering artist Joseph Beuys see Adriani, Götz, Konnertz, Winfried and Thomas, Karin. *Joseph Beuys: Life and Works* Patricia Lech, trans. (Woodbury, 1979); Stachelhaus, Heiner. *Joseph Beuys* David Britt, trans. (Abbeville Press, 1991); about the painter Leon Golub: Kuspit, Donald B. *The Existential/Activist Painter: the example of Leon Golub* (Rutgers University Press, 1986), and Marzorati, Gerald. A *Painter of Darkness: Leon Golub and our times* (Viking, 1990); about the blacklisted film, *Salt of the Earth* (1954, Director: Herbert J. Biberman), see Lorence, James J. *The Suppression of Salt of the Earth: How Hollywood, Big Labor, and Politicians Blacklisted a Movie in Cold War America* (University of New Mexico, 1999); John Sayles' *Matewan* (1987); about the great nineteenth century political cartoonist Daumier, see *Honoré Daumier, 120 great lithographs* Charles F. Ramus (Dover, 1978), Stasik, Andrew. *Honoré Daumier, a centenary tribute* (Pratt Graphics Center, 1980), and Laughton, Bruce. *Honoré Daumier* (Yale University Press, 1996).

I mention several direct action activist groups: Greenpeace is a well-known international organization; Earth First!, a much smaller, U.S.-based more countercultural group, has been very active in civil disobedience in defense of old-growth forests; the Sea Shepherd Society, led by Paul Watson (see his book: *Ocean Warrior: my battle to end the illegal slaughter on the high seas* (Key Porter Books, 1994) is a sort of small but scrappy high seas civilian eco-police, trying especially to stop the slaughter of marine mammals.

Julia Butterfly Hill became world famous for her two year tree-sit in the battle to save the Headwaters redwood forest in northern California. See her book *The Legacy of Luna: the story of a tree, a woman, and the struggle to save the redwoods* (Harper San Francisco, 2000).

A 19-month occupation of Alcatraz island began when approximately 80-90 American Indians—mostly college students—took over the island on November 20, 1969. That action dramatically brought the emerging movement for Native American rights to national attention.

The contemporary political "trickster" activists who use comedy and/or "post-modern" performance as their prime tactics I mention are: Andrew Boyd, a labor activist and comic writer, organizer of, among many other pranks, the "Billionaires for Bush" campaign; the performance artist Bill Talen, known as his alter-ego, "Reverend Billy," leader of the "Church of Stop Shopping;" the shadowy "Yes Men," who convincingly posed as World Bank representatives at international business conferences offering radically Swiftian, socially-Darwinian free-market proposals, including theoretical defenses of slavery, without raising any eyebrows; *Adbusters*, founded by Kalle Lasn, a very clever magazine of parodies of corporate ads; and the San Francisco based transvestite collective "The Sisters of Perpetual Indulgence," pioneers in gay rights direct action, most famous for their mayoral candidate, Sister Boom Boom, who garnered a surprising share of the vote.

Mycelial mats are fine webby fungal filaments which permeate nearly all land masses on this planet in the first two to four inches of soil. A mushroom is just "the tip of the iceberg," an occasionally emerging fruiting body of a vast hidden network. These fungal structures are crucial parts of forest ecologies, helping the roots of many trees and plants assimilate nutrients.

Rock music reflected the ideological divides in the 1960s between left activist radicals and more spiritually oriented hippies. To cite only a few examples, the Rolling Stones song, "Street Fighting Man" (and much of the *Beggars' Banquet* LP) seemed to side with the revolutionaries (as did some of the Jefferson Airplane's work) while the Beatles's song "Revolution # 9" and the Who's "Baba O'Riley" ("we won't be fooled again") seemed to be in the other camp. I'm tossing out that this is a sort of pop-cultural echo of the debate between idealists (such as Hegel) who see the realm of ideas as the primary generator of change on the physical plane and Marxist materialists who, conversely, see changes in the physical world (in technologies, economies, class structures, and so on) as the generators of ideas.

The IWW (aka "Wobblies"), founded in 1905 in Chicago, was a very radical and militant anarcho-socialist union, especially active in Pacific Northwest logging and mining industries. Involved in legendary bloody clashes with authorities in Everett (1916) and Centralia (1919), Washington, the IWW had a very strong cultural component in which singing, guitar-picking hobo activists featured prominently.

For an example of left "cyberspace activism" that raised a whole series of complex legal, artistic and ethical questions, see: "Cyberspace Artists Paint Themselves Into a Corner" by Matthew Mirapaul in the *New York Times* of December 23, 2002. I personally have less problem with parodies and pranks such as those the brilliant "Yes Men" pulled off by passing themselves off as World Bank affiliates, which I feel can be valid means of political expression, than with out and out cyber "attacks" on sites of opponents.

As far as Jimmy Carter's banal, self-evident honest confession about lust he received so much grief for, I'm referring to an interview published in the November 1976 issue of *Playboy* magazine in which then-Governor Carter talked about the role of religion in his life. At one point he said: "I try not to commit a deliberate sin. I recognize that I'm going to do it anyhow, because I'm human and I'm tempted. And Christ set some almost impossible standards for us. Christ said, 'I tell you that anyone who looks on a woman with lust has in his heart already committed adultery.' I've looked on a lot of women with lust. I've committed adultery in my heart many times. This is something that God recognizes I will do—and I have done it—and God forgives me for it."

Section III:

Know Yourself, Know Your Adversaries, Know the Terrain

Know Yourself/Know Your Opponents

The Socratic injunction to "know yourself" and its companion "The unexamined life is not worth living" have been central tenets in Western ethical life (though a clever wag did point out that "the *unlived* life isn't worth *examining*"). In fact, self-inquiry is at the heart of nearly every serious philosophical and spiritual tradition and also permeates nearly all of modern life in more watered-down secular versions in the various psychotherapies and in pop-psychological self-analysis. Because politics is a highly charged domain in which knee-jerk reactions, obsession, and wishful thinking are the norm, I am proposing that it may be of great benefit for us to extend this introspective approach into the realm of politics and engage in a form of personal and collective political self-examination. It is not an easy process, because, outside of sex, food, money, and religion, politics may be the domain where we are least conscious and most uncontrollably, paradoxically, emotive and robotic in our responses.

The first step in such a process might be to analyze where our political beliefs come from. How much did I simply unconsciously inherit from my family, my milieu and local norms, and how much did I reject simply out of adolescent rebelliousness? What role did influential figures or teachers or ideologies that were in vogue in my formative years play in shaping my ideas? And so on. A subsequent step would be to look at how my ideas have evolved or changed and why. For example: have I drifted to the center or right because I have become more reasonable or less utopian with age, or out of economic self-interest and a narrowing of my concerns? And then we might try to review and critically evaluate our ideological make-up and beliefs, a sort of fresh look and conscious ideological "spring cleaning." Is this position tenable? Are my ideas filled with contradictions I hadn't noticed? Am I unconsciously absorbing widespread social assumptions or those of circles I am embedded in that I haven't scrutinized with rigorous independent analysis?

Do I say I espouse democracy as a universal value? What then of the many atrocities committed with the blessings of large majorities, or of the authoritarian regimes supported by most citizens? How do I reconcile these apparent contradictions? Do I have double standards, bitching and moaning when public figures whose views are closer to mine are attacked for peccadillos, but gleeful when opponents are similarly besmirched? Am I outraged when governments or corporations use dirty tricks to harm their opponents, but amused when those on my side use similar tactics? Do I believe polls if they support my argument or belief but dismiss them as manipulated propaganda if their results displease me? If my beliefs are so right, why are they generally shared by only a small minority? Does my explanation for this sound paranoid? And the goal here is not to iron away all paradox and contradictions in our thinking, which is impossible and undesirable, but simply to become aware of them, and, ideally, wind up on a higher plateau of awareness, with more refined, conscious contradictions.

I realize this process, if engaged in honestly and courageously, can be wrenching and painful, and I suspect that not many have the stomach to tackle it. It will certainly seem absurd to fundamentalists of all stripes, including those types of Marxists (the few still around) for whom the word "revisionism" is, tellingly, a base insult. It is a bit like taking a psychoactive drug that forces you to look at the contents of your mind and the reality of your life. It is not for the squeamish or the rigid. You risk coming out no longer believing as assuredly in what you had assumed to be core tenets of your worldview. Political beliefs are as (or more) based on inheritance, temperament, emotion and instinct as on reason, so this is not just a mental exercise but a challenging, emotional undertaking. And I am not suggesting there is any absolute objective standard of measurement to gauge the worth of political ideologies or views. There is no guarantee your political positions will be "better" or more "correct" when you're done, but the very process of honest reevaluation can be powerful and transformative and lead you to be to a more sophisticated and fluid political actor, capable of understanding other perspectives with more depth.

Another aspect of political self-knowledge is collective: undertaking a careful but ideally constructive examination of the movements and groups we belong to or with which we identify. How honest or opportunistic, accurate or demagogic, centered or manic, thoughtful or half-baked, sophisticated or simple-minded, charming or shrill are our leaders, publications, positions? Do their strategies make sense? How do various parts of these movements cooperate or compete with or hinder each other? And so on. In martial and military traditions self-knowledge means having a very accurate sense of your strengths and your weaknesses so you can attempt to confront your enemy in terrain and with timing and tactics that favor your structural advantages and minimize his ability to exploit your vulnerabilities. Unrealistic assessments of one's weaknesses are often lethal errors. In my view the left/progressive movement in the U.S. has been very unrealistic in its analysis of its own weaknesses and of its opponents' strengths, and this has frequently made its already daunting Herculean challenges Sisyphean ordeals.

Political self-knowledge requires a dispassionate look at the actual facts on the ground: the level and depth of support you enjoy, the social and ideological divisions in your ranks, the weaknesses in your arguments, and so forth. In electoral politics some canny pollsters and local strategists can, for example, tell a candidate where to focus her/his last-minute vote-seeking attention with great precision, e.g. "Don't bother with this suburb up to Avenue X which has overwhelmingly voted for far-right candidates since the dawn of time, or with that apartment bloc which is safely in your column, but rather focus on this series of historically toss up trailer parks." And so on. Gauging more deep-seated cultural attitudes and shifting paradigms is far trickier than elections.

These realms are more fluid and open to interpretation, but, by and large, it is painfully obvious the left (outside of ruthless Stalinist types who are, mercifully, nearly extinct) is very bad at realistic assessments of the genuine *"rapport de forces"* in political struggles. Its view is distorted by an absolute certainty in the moral superiority of its convictions, which makes it very difficult to believe so many others might reject its arguments. Religious fundamentalists suffer from a similar reflex, but they expect strong opposition since they interpret such opposition as somehow influenced by Satan who is, after all, a formidable opponent. (Though, to be fair, quite a few on the left subscribe to conspiracy theories that are secular equivalents of Satan.) And certain strains of progressives want so badly to believe a better, more compassionate, peaceful world is inevitable, they are periodically attracted to a variety of prophecies or predictions which promise "paradigm shifts" or "turning" or "tipping points" of some kind. Naked reality is usually too painful to stare down without ideological crutches of some kind.

I discuss elsewhere the particular form of intellectual arrogance and the over-certainty in the absolute truth of its positions the left inherited from its origins in Enlightenment thought that I think are among its major problems, but a related and even more serious tendency which distorts many left-progressives' views of the world is what I call the "paranoia/naïveté dyad." A great many people on the left are convinced the majority of people would support their anti-war or pro-environment positions if they weren't deceived, distracted and manipulated by the powers that be. And the corollary to that is that a very powerful cabal of government, corporate interests and media conglomerates conspire to dupe and exploit the populace.

There is no question that there is some truth to that analysis. Governing elites always attempt to control and manipulate the masses of people, and these elites usually share core values and worldviews that are accepted as the mainstream norm and permeate much of a society's communications media. And there are periods during which the level of propaganda intensifies to a fever pitch and dissent becomes far more difficult and even dangerous. That said, it is condescending and arrogant to assume people are all so easily brainwashed, and that they would automatically rally to your cause if the media suddenly became objective. That is an absurdly simple-minded assumption. Propaganda is a two-way street. It works best when it reflects and reenforces pre-existing chreodes. And often people in positions of power and influence act in lockstep on major issues not because they were ordered to do so but because they too share the dominant values of their class and peer group.

Furthermore, while politics of all types (office, local, international) are by their very nature conspiratorial in that they involve plotting and planning to maintain or accede to power, that does not mean conspiracies are invariably omnipotent or even successful. Yes, of course there have been important conspiracies and secret meetings that have had important historical consequences. The early twentieth century cooperation of the automobile, rubber, steel and oil sectors to undermine public transport and assure a suburban, auto-centered America comes to mind; or the secret deals at Yalta to divide post-WWII Europe; or the FBI's "Cointelpro" operations against 1960s radicals; or the Iran/Contra affair, and so forth. But the difference between astute historical analysis and psychotic paranoia is that the paranoid assumes his enemies' conspiracy is by definition omnipotent, that they can control nearly every aspect of life or politics.

This flies in the face of reality. First, the powerful are always, first and foremost, competing and plotting against each other, and some win and some lose. And they are just people, with migraines and bad hearts and backs and problem children and unrealized dreams and sexual fetishes and secret fears, just like the rest of us. Their beliefs and values may be anathema to us, but they are not members of some other species, even if the institutions they run certainly do most often seem to act in ways that are detrimental to the best interests of most of the world's people and species.

If you think that government intelligence organizations are trying to monitor the communications and discussions of dissident groups and infiltrate them, and are incessantly engaged in questionable plots to undermine "our enemies" at home and abroad; corporations are frequently colluding on prices and dividing markets and getting away with as much as possible; the revolving door of military contractors and Pentagon officials makes defense spending an extraordinarily corrupt and sleazy affair; politicians and judges are usually swayed by the most powerful, most moneyed players; electoral politics is as much about plutocracy as democracy; oil is a major factor in U.S. military interventions, and so forth, then you are simply a reasonable observer of reality.

But if you think the world is being completely run by the Trilateral Commission, or the Carlyle Group, or the Bohemian Grove, or the Illuminati, or lizards from another planet, you need some serious paradigmatic therapy. Conspiracy thinking is obviously not limited to the left. It is even stronger on the extreme right and permeates many nooks and crannies of the modern cultural landscape, sustaining many a subculture from UFO abductees to sci-fi geeks. It also pops up in more mainstream guises, in, for example the solipsistic *"déformation professionelle"* revealed in books by former intelligence specialists arguing this or that broken code or intelligence coup won this or that war. Obviously, if intelligence were so paramount the Russians would have easily won the Cold War as the KGB repeatedly outwitted the CIA. In any case, conspiracy thinking is a far more widespread syndrome than acknowledged by mainstream analysts, and is a fascinating phenomenon, but it is a political black hole.

The flip side of paranoid conspiracy thinking is millenarianism, and that too sucks in many in the counter-culturally tinged sectors of the left and eco-movements. In its eco-lefty form it usually involves a quasi-religious faith in the inevitability of the coming of a new dawn, a new paradigm that will, of course, ultimately usher in a kinder, gentler utopian era of social justice, sustainable economics, restored ecosystems, full equality in every sphere for women and minorities, and the like, though usually after a series of disasters. In fact, most totalizing prophetic ideologies of all stripes incorporate dark and light elements and somehow balance paranoid and manic worldviews, the catastrophe first then the utopia.

The millenarian impulse has obviously been very widespread throughout nearly all of human history and has taken and continues to take an extraordinary range of forms. It is clearly a potent, fundamental archetype of human thought. And it is potent because local and regional apocalypses have occurred and continue to occur fairly frequently: floods, fires, plagues, volcanic eruptions, invasions, droughts, genocides, and massacres. But millenarian ideas tend to globalize and mythologize such scenarios so they will affect everyone on the planet at the same time and be pregnant with universal psycho-spiritual significance, ignoring the fact that usually, disaster in one locale co-exists with prosperity somewhere else.

Clearly the strongest and most widespread current form of millenarianism in the U.S. resides among Christian fundamentalists who are obsessed with Armageddon and the rapture and so on, and, incredibly, their reach extends deeply into the Republican conservative clique in power as I write this—to an extent unseen in American history. Among those with eco-left leanings millenarian/apocalyptic tendencies tend to be less extreme and less rigidly adhered to than the variants on the "black helicopter" or *Left Behind* right, but they are influential nonetheless. They take a few forms. One is a fascination with apocalyptic eco (or nuclear or telluric or climatic) catastrophes, especially as warned about in a range of indigenous prophecies (Mayan, Iroquois, etc.); or among certain sects in Eastern traditions; or in the predictions of psychics such as Edgar Cayce or various more contemporary "channelers;" or in highly original cyber-psychedelic versions such as the late Terence McKenna's "Time Wave" software, which combines algorithms and psilocybin-induced revelation to predict a radical global change in 2012, coincidentally resonant with the end of the Mayan calendar for this era.

Now obviously only idiots aren't legitimately horrified about the very real environmental devastation and biodiversity crises we are facing or the very real risks of nukes (or other Weapons of Mass Destruction). Prophecies add the *frisson* of a mystical/visionary element to the well-founded fears. It is hard to say whether this might make fears psychically easier to deal with, or be a form of escapism, or if, in fact, some of these types of prophetic warnings may actually be helpful mythic galvanizers, encouraging people to act to avoid the worst. Many of these prophecies are fascinating, but their uncritical embrace exacerbates the already rampant romanticizing of indigenous and exotic "others" and the tendency to make all incoming data fit into one's preconceived scenarios.

One might wonder why I am lingering on this type of conspiratorial and millenarian mindset in looking at the eco/progressive political landscape when none of the literature or positions of its major groups or any of its leaders seem to espouse such beliefs, and, in fact, the dominant tone of these movements is profoundly rooted in secular rationalism. The reason is that I know from my decades of exposure to the eco- and left universes that there is a big discrepancy between the official positions of groups and the mindset of their leaderships (and funders), and the ideological currents that roil grassroots activists, supporters, and sympathizers. These currents, unacknowledged and unaddressed within our movements and unseen by the mainstream, are, in my opinion, very significant. They are akin to repressed psychological material in an individual which can bubble up in myriad disruptive and self-defeating behaviors, so it behooves us to study ourselves, our movements and our beliefs, no matter how seemingly strange, with curiosity and honesty, or we will continue to flounder.

A more secular sort of millenarianism-lite that is very widespread in eco-circles is rooted in "whole systems" thought, which argues that the old nineteenth century positivistic, mechanistic paradigms are gradually being supplanted in nearly all disciplines by more holistic approaches, and that as our old industrial, fossil fuel-based economy experiences its last convulsive death-rattles, a new "greener," sustainable era will emerge. This is obviously a more sober and somewhat science-based analysis than those above, and has some merit. Some of its leading proponents, such as Fritjof Capra, are highly intelligent, reasonable thinkers, but many take these types of speculations and make a leap of faith to assume these scenarios are inevitable. The alternatives are so bleak, it is certainly understandable some activists feel a need to believe a green utopia is inevitable, or they wouldn't be able to sustain any hope for the future and would have no motivation to keep working on their projects.

The problem with this, as I argue elsewhere, is that social change is fundamentally unpredictable, and the forms that will emerge as new ideas, movements, and technologies mutate and collide with vested interests and inertia (and each other) are unknowable. To assume the outcome of the mix will be exactly what we want—an eco-friendly, harmonious, tolerant paradise—is wishful thinking of the highest order, and so very American in its insistence on happy endings and on a refusal of nuance and imperfection. Why would, say, a more egalitarian society or women's emancipation or eco-sensitivity automatically go hand in hand with democracy? One could, for example, envision, as several science fiction writers have done, an eco-totalitarian future in which environmental degradation was so severe governments would have no choice but to mercilessly protect what was left of ecosystems from the predations of the desperately poor majority. If we don't make serious environmental progress soon, this scenario might, in many parts of the world, actually be the most likely.

The remarkable women of Sparta (assuming historians have correctly interpreted the few clues they left behind), were by far the most emancipated women of all Antiquity, but were seemingly among the staunchest defenders and boosters of that city-state's brutal and authoritarian warrior culture and its use of slaves. Figures such as Margaret Thatcher and Condoleeza Rice reveal how silly it is to assume the leadership of women is automatically enlightened and humane, and the Dutch political figure Pim Fortuyn highlighted that gay leadership does not automatically imply tolerance. Societies take many strange forms and turns. We have to be ready for unpredictable change and surreal juxtapositions, not locked into pious certainties about the future.

Other forms of wishful thinking and self-deception also plague the left. Speakers at rallies often cite the amount of people present (when it is a large crowd) as proof the majority is with us and that we will prevail. Obviously, if half a million people turn out to protest a war, it is exhilarating and empowering at the moment, and it indicates at least that an important subset of the population opposes the conflict; but, in a nation of nearly 300 million, the vast majority might still support it. Furthermore, those 500,000 people won't all sustain their opposition for a protracted period. Few of them are hard-core activists. Most have lives they must return to and are easily discouraged when their protest fails to influence policy and seems merely symbolic. But on the left making extravagant claims about the effectiveness of protests is the norm. It's demagogic hype and counter-productive in the long run.

Environmentalists often cite polls that indicate 70% of Americans are sympathetic to environmentalism as a sort of mandate, but that support is very shallow in that few of those people are prepared to take much action or to alter their lifestyles in any significant fashion or think much about environmental issues when voting. Citing that figure is perhaps understandable in campaigns to attempt to pressure reluctant politicians with a lot of suburban women in their districts into supporting environmental legislation, say, but it's very dangerous if you start believing it really means something yourself. Overestimating your real level of support and its depth is among the worst of all strategic miscalculations, as is believing your own hype in general.

The Seattle anti-IMF demonstrations did bring together an interesting coalition of eco-, labor and "developing world" groups, but the longevity and solidity of that coalition was oversold as the beginning of a formidable "red/green" or "turtle/teamster" alliance. Not long after, some of the same American labor unions which oppose globalization's threats to American industrial jobs and marched in Seattle were instrumental in torpedoing higher gas mileage requirements for trucks and automobiles in the U.S. Congress, which would have been a critical step in reducing our oil-dependence. Labor and environmentalists and developing nations' non-governmental organizations (NGOs) may on some occasions find common ground but also often have divergent interests. Unions and corporations frequently work together on blocking or advancing legislation when they see mutual benefit, often to the detriment of consumers and the environment. This has been very pronounced recently in the automotive and communications sectors but has a long history in the U.S. Pretending over and over that a new dawn of green/red, concerted action has permanently arrived is again hype. If we are to fashion even short-term coalitions that are effective in achieving specific goals, we have to remain completely unsentimental and brutally lucid about the real divisions amongst us.

We need to stop exaggerating, sloganeering and over-selling. We would do better to cultivate honest and centered discourse, so that even those who disagree with us could respect our integrity. The payoff in the long term would exceed any of the short-lived boosts we might reap from shrill hype. We need to challenge some of our reflexive responses and ideas, take a hard look at our unexamined assumptions and be willing to face the pain and uncertainty that define reality. This doesn't mean we can't study interesting prophecies from cultures we might have much to learn from, or have some fun and dabble in speculating about conspiracies, or be a little utopian at times, or occasionally use a little clever spin or take some poetic license in a campaign. But we do have to resist the urge to completely embrace all-explaining ideologies and pious certainties that paralyze real thought and impede our capacity to be lucid and nimble in interpreting new information. We need to have aspirations for a better future, but if we shield our eyes from the facts on the ground with pie-in-the-sky fantasies, and wish away the messy contradictions and painful ironies that characterize the human condition, we will never achieve even the minimal level of personal and political self-knowledge that is a pre-requisite to successfully engaging our opponents.

Knowing the Adversary

The corollary to knowing yourself is to know your opponents. This requires, first, careful and thorough study of their organizations, their positions and the socio-historical and philosophical roots of the impulses that propel them, not unlike what takes place at the highest levels of sport, a realm in which coaches and their staffs painstakingly dissect opposing teams' and players' strengths and weaknesses to prepare for encounters. There are a few individual researchers and academics and some small organizations on the left specializing in tracking and analyzing right-wing movements. Some of them do very good work, and we need to support them and, ideally, build more state-of-the-art institutes to study the right (and the center) and pay close attention to their findings. But, for now, there are too few of them, and their efforts are, of course, dwarfed by the scale of the intelligence gathering done by government agencies that monitor all potential threats to the established order (and seek to penetrate and disrupt them). And a plethora of deeply-funded think tanks, research institutes, private security firms, and corporate advertising and consulting groups on the right which study and track and attack and undermine progressive groups at every opportunity are vastly more powerful than anything the left can muster for the foreseeable future.

Rigorously studying your opponents is an essential first step, but, in my view, it can't be limited to dry, cerebral observation. If, as we study our adversaries, we distance ourselves by maintaining a smug sense of our own superiority throughout, we will fail to penetrate deeply into the essence of what makes them tick. We need to make real attempts to engage in visceral mental and emotional experiments in which we try, as much as possible, to see things as our opponents do, to live for a short time with their worldviews. This is similar to the preparatory work some actors do as they rehearse a role: they seek to become the person they are playing, to perceive the world and respond to it as that person would. Many spiritual disciplines also offer a variety of techniques to change habitual response patterns, including exercises that involve listening intently but without assent or dissent to views or people one may detest. An even more radical example of this attempt to inhabit the consciousness of an alien "other" is the mindset of indigenous hunters whose entire culture loves and celebrates the species it hunts to survive. Those hunters have for countless generations studied that animal in such extraordinary detail that they feel that they share in its essence. That might be a bit extreme, but we must at least borrow a little of the impulse to more than intellectually "understand" our opponents, but actually to "grok" them.

We have to constantly remind ourselves that our adversaries feel the same types of political emotions we do—the rage, frustration and sense of impotence in the face of injustice. They just have different triggers. A bomb that kills Vietnamese or Iraqi children infuriates us; cutting short the potential for new life in an abortion horrifies them. We get upset when governments jail free speech or labor or human rights advocates; our opponents focus on the jailing of proselytizing Christians exercising their freedom of religious expression in hostile lands. We certainly can't just roll over and accept their worldview and allow them to impose their vision of socio-political life on the rest of us, but we must understand that they feel we are doing that to them. There is no ultimate way to resolve this in that, to a large extent, we are dealing with fundamentally incompatible sets of values in which one's group's concept of civilized norms of freedom and justice automatically impinge on the other group's. But that makes understanding our adversaries even more critical, and that's where these types of exercises can be helpful.

Let's say I am watching the news and a government official I loathe is touting a position I abhor. Instead, for once, of screaming at my television, or engaging in a torrent of snide comments, I might decide to attempt a thought experiment. I will put myself in an altered state and try hard, for a few moments or as long as I can maintain it, to become that official or perhaps someone who agrees with what is being said and who has well thought-out reasons for it. What does the world look and feel like? Who seems threatening and dangerous and who seems worthy of respect and affection? Where do my ideas come from? And, when I come out of this state, have I learned anything? Have I discovered a way of looking at an issue I hadn't thought of before? And, most importantly, have I learned something about my opponent's worldview at the gut level I hadn't realized?

Once again, as in the case of rigorous personal political self-analysis, if done whole-heartedly, this is a very demanding and frightening exercise, a "trip" whose outcome is unpredictable. What if I suddenly see some merit in my opponent's argument? What if, say, I am a hardcore anti-capitalist, but I suddenly see that, under current conditions (at least until the revolution or workers' utopia I long for arrives) markets might indeed work better in some sectors of an economy, that an argument for privatization may in some cases make sense? Or I am a pacifist who invariably opposes military intervention but realize a genocide will result without armed intervention in a specific situation? Or I am pro-union but realize a change in my country's pension structure that somewhat reduces benefits is inevitable in order to save the entire system given the aging of the population? Obviously this type of exercise can be attempted by people of any political persuasion. A gung-ho free marketer might have a *satori* riding a French high-speed train and realize some state-run enterprises might indeed be a good idea; a militarist finally exhausted by one more bloody war might suddenly "get" what pacifism is really about; and so on. I am not advocating any particular positions, just describing a thought exercise and some of its possible repercussions.

I realize some will say what I am recommending sounds like a prescription for psychosis and wishy-washy new age nonsense and will only confuse us politically, but I would argue that the weaker you are (and we are very weak) the more you need to elevate your capacities of awareness and observation, and the more you need to be able to know as much about your opponents as possible. If we are so afraid we might weaken our convictions if we let down our guard, they must not be solid enough to begin with. Somehow we must, in the words of the fascinating, complex early twentieth century revolutionary figure, Victor Serge, find a way to balance "the intransigence resulting from firm convictions, the maintenance of a critical spirit with regard to those convictions, and …respect for any differing convictions."

While the best caricature can certainly be an exalted form of art (Daumier, Doctor Strangelove, etc.), in general the most powerful and lasting literary, theatrical and cinematic works are those that empathize with their characters, that make us feel the motivations of even the most unsympathetic and obsessed. Human beings are complex creatures. The best art avoids condescension to any of its protagonists and doesn't offer us one-dimensional bogey-men but nuanced, multifaceted, conflicted people struggling to come to terms with existence, meaning, history and social reality. Why then do otherwise sophisticated people accept styles of politics on the level of the dumbest and most simple-minded caricature?

Far too often we progressives paint all our adversaries with the same brush, carelessly bandying about words such as "fascist" or "right-wing" or "fundamentalist," but this is self-defeating. Our lack of linguistic precision makes it hard for thoughtful people to take us seriously. Our government may fight unjust wars for the commercial gain of business elites and abuse civil liberties and human rights, and our system may be as much a plutocracy as a democracy, but it is absurd to call it "fascist" or "totalitarian." Instead of hurling insults, it would be far more useful for us to look very precisely at the political landscape of the right, the whole ecosystem of often competing ideologies and groups that comprise it, and to see where there are fault-lines and divisions we could deepen, as well as where we might find common ground with potential allies on very specific initiatives in "strange bedfellow" coalitions. We have seen recently that on matters of civil liberties and invasions of privacy as well as on the concentration of communications media, alliances of far right and left civil libertarian groups were able to partially contain power grabs embraced by the vast bulk of the center of the political spectrum. In these instances the libertarian and small community autonomy impulses transcended habitual right/left divides and were able to at least slow down the society's most powerful players in their quest for yet more power.

We have no choice but to fight tooth and nail to retain what are, to us, essential, sine qua non rights—a woman's right to choose an abortion, the separation of religion and the state, and so forth, but there may be ways we can be more clever, more respectful and, when core rights are not at stake, more accommodating to people whose values we may not share. These people do have values, and powerful groups we will have to deal with for the foreseeable future, and with whom, on certain issues, we may be able to find common ground. If we can avoid ramming our values down their throats when it isn't necessary and finding ways to create social space for them to operate in the commons so they feel less put-upon, or at least ways to deflect and temper their rage, we might waste less political energy in exhausting stand-offs. After all, if we really believe in multi-cultural tolerance, and we try to accommodate groups as diverse as the Amish and Hasidim, shouldn't we find ways to, within reason, accommodate fundamentalist Christians as well?

This certainly won't be easy in that it takes two to tango, and the most rabid activists among these folks are very well organized, relentless, often covert, well-funded and tactically sophisticated, and they are enjoying their greatest access to power at the highest levels in our history. They are in no mood to accommodate us, for the moment, as the wind is in their sails. That said, history is probably against them. The march of secular rationality has (for better or worse) been fairly inexorable. Though religion is still a dynamic force and new spiritual movements arise constantly and undoubtedly will for a long time to come, and the mytho-poetic component of human life will never vanish, it seems highly probable secular-scientific norms in the European/UN mode will dominate the lingua franca of state-craft and the political commons of nations, even eventually in Islamic nations, and ultimately even in that most religious of all industrial nations, the U.S. And when we achieve victories in this sphere we must take care not to gloat and engage in triumphalism, lest we wind up creating equivalents of the Versailles treaty, humiliating our opponents so they rise up more rabid than ever decades later.

The corporate "low tax" business right is a different universe than the moral, Christian right. And fundamentalists are by no means some monolithic entity. There are many centrist and even some left-leaning evangelical Christians, and they were key groups in electing (for better or worse) the Democrats Jimmy Carter and Bill Clinton in U.S. presidential elections. These southern candidates spoke their language, frequently quoting scripture and employing the cadences of southern church oratory. Many people in the "bible belt" are immersed in scripture from a tender age, but that doesn't mean they all think alike. It is one of the main lenses through which they interpret the world, but they can interpret it very differently. Recently, conservative Christian Republican Alabama governor Bob Riley invoked biblical ideals in attempting to reform his state's tax code to make it fairer to the poor and thereby increase taxes on the rich and businesses. This is obviously an exceptional case, and his initiatives were not warmly embraced by other conservatives in his state, and he failed, but it challenges us to take a broader view of the variety of views that exist among self-described conservative Christians.

There are major divisions in theology and approach between Baptists and Pentecostals as well as wide ranges of views within denominations. The most powerful radical and populist movements in American history have been left/right hybrids, and religion has often played a major role in those movements. We need to understand the socio-cultural matrix from which the right has been drawing so much support and strength. Denouncing and bemoaning is not a strategy. These people are not just archaic relics who will soon fade away. We will have to share this continent and many communities with them for a long time to come. We had best sincerely try to understand them, for we will have no chance of succeeding in even the most modest of political goals if we don't have an exquisitely sophisticated understanding of the forces arrayed against us.

In a recent book, *Made in Texas*, the once neo-conservative and now center-left, often highly astute political analyst, Michael Lind describes the complexities of that state's political landscape, explaining that the part of the state that produced Lyndon B. Johnson is largely populated by folks of German, Czech and Scandinavian stock who were historically pro-Union and anti-slavery. On the other hand the region that produced George Bush the younger is inhabited mostly by Anglo-Celts originally from Ulster and Scotland, among whom an ideology combining devout Protestantism, militarism and anti-intellectualism has become dominant, and has now allied with rabidly pro-Likud Northeastern neo-conservatism with imperial designs for America. For the moment these two ideological currents are, horrifyingly, jointly in power. This is the type of detailed analysis we need, and it is interesting that some of the most thoughtful and sophisticated critiques of American socio-political trends have come from thinkers who were formerly or are still on the right. Center-right historian Kevin Phillips' *Wealth and Democracy* is by far the most detailed analysis of long-term wealth trends in the country and its drift to plutocracy. We need to be open to intelligent input whatever its source.

Besides the Christian right, another critically important social milieu we on the left tend to view one-dimensionally is the military. Yes, we have good reason to be historically anti-militaristic and anti-imperialist, and the extraordinary excess of the U.S. military budget is a massive, epic, tragic misallocation of precious resources in an era of global environmental degradation, the HIV plague, and so forth. Yes, the officer corps is probably 90% Republican, but the military has also been a driver of social change. The black soldiers who fought in WWII and returned to the South brought a new militancy which became the key to the early Civil Rights movement. And, starting with Harry Truman's integration of the armed forces, the military, though far from free of racism, has actually frequently been ahead of the curve on racial integration and provided an important source of leaders in the African-American community and one of the main avenues to upward mobility for many poor and working class youth of all ethnicities (and now both genders.)

Furthermore, the military is not some abstract idea; it's an immense social apparatus that employs millions upon millions of civilians as well as uniformed personnel. Enormous regions of the country depend on it to sustain their economies, and while these military provinces are often among the strongest supporters of the Republican Party, we need to realize we are dealing with a complex social structure with its own divisions, rivalries and competing ideological currents. The military brass are not invariably the most gung-ho of imperialists. They are often more reticent about sending troops into conflict than some saber-rattling civilians.

A major factor in the American defeat in Vietnam was the large-scale quasi mutiny of so many front-line soldiers, who were black or Hispanic in numbers vastly disproportionate to their representation in the U.S. population. In fact, the racial polarization of the troops so hindered the war effort that many generals today, eager not to see such a situation again, are strong supporters of affirmative action programs. The increasingly militant civil rights movement and the dynamic counterculture of the day had a profound effect on the troops. Many more "fragging" incidents, in which pissed-off soldiers tossed grenades under officers' (usually second lieutenants') beds, occurred than was reported at the time. To a large extent, by the last few years of the war the military had lost control over its front line troops. The Vietnam era anti-war movement understood this and understood the powerful appeal of the counterculture, and made substantive efforts to reach soldiers with its message, including the opening of a number of coffee-houses near military bases. And the groups of Vietnam veterans who organized against the war upon their return, while small in number, had an enormous impact and were a crucial factor in turning opinion against the war, as Oliver Stone's film *Born on the Fourth of July* documents quite effectively.

In a similar vein many of us on the left fail to appreciate the ways in which most of the police forces around the nation (and the world) form distinct cultures with unique ideologies and family traditions centered in specific geographic locales, a theme well captured in one of Sylvester Stallone's few interesting films, *Cop Land* (1990). That tribal aspect of police culture has waned a bit with the beginning of racial and gender integration in these institutions, as some organizations of minority police officers have formed, but it is still a potent force. In

France, the dreaded CRS, the special riot police, are often housed in their own communities so they feel no sympathy for the populace they might be called upon to suppress. The Chinese government is reported to have brought in Mongolian and other non-Han, non Beijing-dialect-speaking troops to quell the Tiananmen protests.

Nearly every successful revolution or insurrection in history has involved the defection of some parts of the military/police apparatus. Occasional urban riots are a virtual certainty but an actual revolution from the left is a totally unlikely scenario in the U.S. (where a rightist putsch or right-populist regional insurrections are far more plausible). But at some point in the future unstable periods and breakdowns in social cohesion are certainly possible. The more outreach the left of the political spectrum might have done to segments of the military and police communities, the more chance progressives leaders of the day will have of having some positive input in a crisis, rather than automatically winding up as victims or interned political prisoners. In any case, the military/police sector is just too big and important a social force to be completely ceded to the right.

Evangelical Christians, the military and police are examples of important groups we progressives don't sufficiently study and figure out how to engage in dialogue with, but there are others. The intelligence community is also a far more nuanced world than our often (unfortunately frequently justified) paranoid view of them lets us see. Many of these folks see themselves as public servants and are horrified when their work is distorted and politicized to further dubious agendas, as we saw in the recent brouhaha in the U.K. and U.S. over the "sexing up" of data about WMDs in Iraq. Some in the CIA are intellectuals with a deep appreciation for a part of the world they study, and are annoyed by simplistic and shortsighted foreign policy. Others have studied global environmental trends and are deeply concerned.

This doesn't mean we have to embrace the military and intelligence complex and its values, but at crucial times someone inside that apparatus who rebels against its excesses can have an enormous impact (Daniel Ellsberg, the leaker of "The Pentagon Papers," is a classic example). Again we can't just be broadly dismissive of whole groups; we must find ways to cultivate dialogue with as many key segments of the political landscape as possible. We have to do this without selling out our values, of course, but what is required is often a change of tone, not one of content. We should be honest and clear about our beliefs and not become opportunistic to curry favor and influence, but we can, at least on occasion, be more respectful and clever in our modes of communication.

The small business community is another very important constituency that has been crucial to the success of the right, a pillar of the Republican Party. It has been a major failure on the part of progressives that a credible attempt to carefully study and dialogue with this community has not taken place, especially since, on many issues, its interests run counter to those of mega-corporations. This potential faultline has barely been explored, but could be critical in undermining the right's electoral base.

In general, we have to generate far better analyses of those social groups, communities, institutions and social sectors from which our opponents draw their strength, with which we so often enter into conflict or which we want to reform, and really try to understand what makes them tick, to probe for areas where common ground can be found or at least ways in which we can divide the adversary. We need to find points of entry and leverage and ways to make our very powerful opponents less cohesive, not insult them across the board so they instinctually band together.

Notes

"Know thyself" was, reputedly, an inscription on the temple of the Oracle of Apollo at Delphi in Ancient Greece. And "The unexamined life is not worth living for man" is in Plato's (469–399 BC) *Apology of Socrates*.

"*Le rapport de forces*" is the objective strength of the respective forces arrayed against each other in a conflict.

For info about the FBI's "Cointelpro" operation and other episodes of covert repression of dissent see Churchill, Ward and Vander Wall, Jim. *Agents of Repression: The FBI's Secret Wars Against the Black Panther Party and the American Indian Movement* (Boston: South End Press, 1988); Blackstock, Nelson, *COINTELPRO: The FBI's Secret War on Political Freedom* (Pathfinder, 1975); Donner, Frank J., *Protectors of Privilege: Red Squads and Police Repression in Urban America* (University of California, 1990);

Gelbspan, Ross, *Break-ins, Death Threats and the FBI: The Covert War Against the Central America Movement* (South End Press, 1991); Matthiessen, Peter, *In the Spirit of Crazy Horse* (Viking Press, 1991); Theoharis, Athan, *Spying on Americans: Political Surveillance from Hoover to the Huston Plan* (Temple University Press, 1978); Ungar, Sanford J., *FBI: An Uncensored Look Behind the Walls* (Little, Brown and Company, 1975).

Some of the groups I list that come up often as the *bêtes noires* of conspiracy theorists are: "The Trilateral Commission," a policy-oriented discussion group of some 350 high-powered business and government leaders from Europe, North America and Pacific Asia, launched in mid-1973; "The Bohemian Grove" in a redwood forest near Monte Rio, CA, a private, all male club, formed in 1872, now an association of rich and powerful men whose membership list has included every Republican U.S. president (as well as some Democrats) since 1923, many cabinet officials and CEO's of large corporations (the grove is the site of a two week retreat every July); "The Carlyle Group," a private equity firm established in 1987 with over $17.5 billion under management, whose management and investors include many former high-ranking government officials including former president George Bush (senior) and James Baker.

"Déformation professionelle" is a French expression which describes some people's tendency to see or approach the world with a perspective strongly shaped by their occupation.

For an account of the KGB's war with the CIA, see former KGB general Oleg Kalugin's *The First Directorate: my 32 years in intelligence and espionage against the west* (St. Martin's Press, 1994).

I mentioned "black helicopters" earlier, but because they're such a fascinating example of conspiratorial mythologizing, here's a bit more backround: paranoia about mysterious "black helicopters" seems to have its origins with UFO sightings and cattle mutilations in the 1970's. A strange character named Jim Keith popularized these icons in the 1990's, linking black helicopters with "Men in Black" and the "New World Order." (See: Keith, Jim. *Black helicopters over America: strikeforce for the New World order* (IllumiNet Press, 1994). Keith, also the author of *Mind Control/World Control, Casebook on the Men In Black*, and many other works about conspiracies, died from surgical complications after falling from a stage at the Burning Man arts event. For a good, sober look at contemporary conspiratorial thinking, see Michael Barkun's *A Culture of Conspiracy: apocalyptic visions in contemporary America* (University of California, 2003). Barkun analyzes how, in the age of the Internet, various conspiracy theory subcultures mutate and recombine, creating wildly baroque "superconspiracies." The dread of the antichrist among fundamentalists and the long standing, far-right-wing paranoia regarding Masons, Jesuits, Jews, "the Illuminati," etc., started combining with fears of extraterrestrials in the 1980s, yielding new bizarre belief structures.

The *Left Behind* series of action novels with apocalyptic themes based on the Book of Revelation by the fundamentalist preacher Tim LaHaye and co-author Jerry Jenkins have sold 58 million (!!) books since 1995.

I mention a number of millenarian prophecies popular in countercultural circles. For more on the most famous psychic in U.S. history and his predictions, see Stearn, Jess. *Edgar Cayce, the sleeping prophet* (A.R.E. Press, 1997). The late Terence McKenna, the most eloquent and interesting advocate of hallucinogenic plant usage of the last few decades, author of, among others, *Food of the Gods* (Bantam, 1992), and *True Hallucinations* (Harper San Francisco, 1993); and Jose Arguelles, originator of the "Harmonic Convergence" (author of several books, including, *The Mayan factor: path beyond technology* (Bear, 1987), both made somewhat hazy but dramatic predictions about massive global transformations that would occur at dates that correspond to ends of a major Mayan calendric cycle, with 2012 a frequently cited year.

There are countless sci-fi books about a bleak environmental future. A great classic with that theme is John Brunner's 1972 *The Sheep Look Up* (Ballantine).

For a discussion of Sparta's women, see: Pomeroy, Sarah B. *Spartan Women* (Oxford University Press, 2002).

I'm referring to the emergence of the anti-immigrant political party in Holland led by the gay academic Wilhelmus Simon Petrus Fortuijn, known as Pim Fortuyn, who was murdered in May 2002. His movement was a strange permutation in that it was certainly, by Dutch standards, a right-wing populist one, but one of Fortuyn's main gripes was that many (often Muslim) immigrants were culturally reactionary and not sufficiently feminist or tolerant of differences in sexual orientation and therefore did not fit in with permissive Dutch norms!

For more on cooperation and differences between unions and environmentalists, see "Green Collar Workers" by Jim Young (in *Sierra* magazine, July/August 2003).

For an example of the types of techniques used in spiritual traditions to enhance perception skills, a fascinating book that details specific methods of expanding one's spiritual abilities, including the ability to understand other people's deep intent and innermost states, is the Austrian mystic Rudolf Steiner's *Knowledge of the Higher Worlds and its Attainment* (Anthroposophic Press).

The term "to grok" comes from sci-fi author Robert A. Heinlein's *Stranger in a Strange Land* (Putnam, 1961). In Heinlein's invented Martian language, "grok" literally meant "to drink" and figuratively "to understand," "to love," or "to be one with," all at the same time. It became a widely used expression among sci-fi fans and hippies and is now found in computer parlance and even in some dictionaries.

For more on the early twentieth century revolutionary figure, Victor Serge, see Susan Weissman's *Victor Serge: The Course Is Set on Hope* (Verso, 2001).

Lind, Michael. *Made in Texas: George W. Bush and the Southern Takeover of American politics* (Basic Books, 2003).

Daniel Ellsberg is probably the most famous insider turned "whistle blower" of all time, certainly in US intelligence and foreign policy circles. A Rand Corporation consultant at the Pentagon in 1967 working on a top secret Robert McNamara study called "U.S. Decision-Making in Vietnam, 1945-68," which later came to be known as the

Pentagon Papers, he photocopied the 7,000 page study in 1969 and gave it to the Senate Foreign Relations Committee; in 1971 he gave it to the New York Times, Washington Post and seventeen other newspapers. See *The Pentagon Papers: the Defense Department History of United States Decision Making on Vietnam* (Beacon Press, 1971-72); Herring, George C., ed. *The Secret Diplomacy of the Vietnam War: the Negotiating Volumes of the Pentagon Papers* (University of Texas, 1983); or *The Pentagon Papers: as published by the New York Times, based on investigative reporting by Neil Sheehan* (Bantam Books, 1971).

The Utopian/Realpolitik Axis

Virtually all political beliefs combine practical and utopian elements. A political ideology is nearly always based on some model of the best possible society, even if that model is relatively pessimistic. And practical concerns arise immediately, as soon as one actually tries to influence society to organize itself according to that optimal model, or to tend in that direction, as resistance and obstacles flare up and must be negotiated.

Even a perfunctory look at any political/ideological landscape reveals a range of tendencies from the most utopian to the most pragmatic. Within movements the pragmatists invariably ridicule more extreme tendencies as hopelessly idealistic and/or frankly dangerous while the more radical denounce the more moderate as sell-outs with little courage or imagination. It's a tiresomely familiar ritual, and a delicate dance, because in certain situations a dynamic radical wing can be very useful to more moderate leaders in a movement, helping pressure opponents to concede more in negotiations with the "reasonable" elements, the classic "good cop/bad cop" routine. Most large-scale social movements such as the civil rights or women's movements have involved the political and cultural activities of a very broad range of groups and individuals with a wide spectrum of ideologies. To achieve some success, movements of that magnitude require both very dynamic, radical forces "in the streets" and more mainstream sympathizers inside a broad swath of society's institutions. But at other historical moments, especially when actual power is within reach, the tacit or unconscious symbiosis between radicals and moderates in a movement can break down into intense, even bloody, conflict.

Tensions between innovators and conservers, egalitarians and elitists, and a broad spectrum of extremists, radicals, and moderates within all movements will always exist in a wide range of forms, as long as there are human societies. People who are passionate about their politics have their beliefs shaped by their milieu in one way or another of course, and we can often readily see, in hindsight, how individuals' ideas were shaped by rebelling against their family or cultural background or, conversely, by embracing it. But ultimately the particular form political passion takes is largely unpredictable. In most cases, why one individual becomes an animal rights advocate, another a religious missionary, another a pacifist-anarchist, another a mainstream party apparatchik, another a radical libertarian, another a military enthusiast, will remain as mysterious as people's aesthetic preferences. Different "ideological attractors" resonate with some people and not others, and there is very little chance to convince folks that their passion is not as objectively relevant as yours. So no one is going to have much luck, most of the time, trying to talk someone out of a core ideological stance, because it usually reflects her/his fundamental temperament.

People do tend to get more moderate with age, but that's undoubtedly as much a result of hormonal decline as of ideological reflection. And life experiences, events, political failures, successes, and so forth, do alter beliefs, so there are "window" moments when someone (or a society) is ready to make an ideological shift, especially in periods when a paradigm is suddenly discredited. A society's ideas of what is acceptable and desirable also obviously change, sometimes gradually and sometimes suddenly in response to dramatic events, but these things happen in their own unpredictable ways. In general, changing very many people's core ideas at any particular moment is unlikely to happen, but a deeper understanding of the utopian/pragmatic tension within political movements and within one's own personal political stances can still be very productive.

A classic case of a utopian/pragmatist divide occurred among U.S. progressives during the 2000 presidential election. The Democrats were livid when they lost such a close election under dubious circumstances and laid some of the blame at the door of the somewhat populist third-party run of Ralph Nader. To Nader's supporters, Al Gore, though he might have differed from George Bush in some domains, was as fully committed to a model of global mega-capitalism that they view as the core problem facing the planet. To keep supporting such candidates (who invariably move to the right upon taking office in any case) is nauseating and disempowering, they argued—it is better to begin building authentic alternatives. To pragmatic progressives who supported Gore, a quixotic third party tilt at windmills that risked bringing overtly ecocidal oil executives and their Armageddon-obsessed fundamentalist allies to power, with a lot of tangible environmental and social damage surely to follow, was foolish, no matter what one's reservations about Gore and his ilk might be.

Obviously, one's view depends on one's analysis of questions such as: Was Nader's run a symbolic protest or a serious attempt to build a viable party or movement? Is a third party doomed to irrelevance in a non-parliamentary two-party system so corrupted by big money? Is an electoral emphasis a black hole for a movement as weak and divided as the progressive left in the U.S. in any event? And so on. But, at its core, the divide highlights the difference between a view of politics as an attempt to achieve modest incremental change or at least a minimization of damage, and a politics that seeks to inspire by aiming for loftier goals and insists on leaders and platforms that speak to one's highest aspirations. Nader and Gore supporters seemed to be speaking different symbolic languages, but this type of division is a feature of all politics in one way or another, because both these impulses are profoundly rooted in human culture, and neither will disappear. Utopianism can, of course, be dangerous, but it is also a vital contributor of creativity and novelty to the body politic.

I'm not trying to convince anyone to adopt any particular position or to change beliefs, especially since I believe it is unlikely, but I do advocate we make efforts at political self-knowledge, in the same way self-reflective people examine themselves psychologically or ethically. Almost no one is completely utopian or totally pragmatic. As I said at the onset, all politics combine both those elements in some fashion. Let me suggest, merely as an example of one possible tool of political self-study, a thought exercise. Let's take the over-all political scene or a specific ideological strain we have interest in and map out a "utopian/pragmatic axis" and place various groups and individual thinkers along it, and also attempt to place ourselves on it. In other words, let's attempt to measure how utopian or pragmatic we are on different issues. As I've mentioned, this is obviously only one of many possible lenses through which to examine one's own political profile.

How would this analysis work in practice? First of all, this exercise is obviously arbitrary in that a wide range of models is possible, and not everyone would agree on where someone else places a particular group or thinker. But, let's go ahead and consider a utopian/pragmatic axis delineating, say, the environmental movement in the U.S. And I'm not at all attempting to be exhaustive in this example; I'm just picking a few groups to illustrate the model. At the utopian end of the spectrum we could place a variety of very different organizations and tendencies, from small direct-action militant (but still basically non-violent) groups such as Earth First! and Sea Shepherd, the conservation biology organization; the Wildlands Project, which envisages a radical expansion of linked, protected wildlands from Mexico to the Yukon; to groups of people who believe a "new paradigm" of heightened spiritual awareness and "voluntary simplicity" will spread and a new eco-friendly era will emerge; and even some techno-utopians who believe scientific progress will lead to wondrous "end run" technological solutions to the environmental crisis.

Now some of these groups/tendencies have far more gravitas and real track records of accomplishment than others, and they would vehemently disagree with each other in many instances. I am not at all equating them, only placing them at the utopian end of the spectrum, because what they advocate currently seems unrealistic to mainstream opinion. And of course they all might argue, as most utopians do, quite rightly, that many things we now accept as the norm, from woman's suffrage to universal education to social security, were once viewed as utopian ideas. Also, a utopian/pragmatic axis is not necessarily the same thing as a moderate/militant axis. One can be tactically moderate and ideologically utopian or tactically militant but pragmatic in one's expectations. Still, often utopians tend to be more willing to entertain radical tactics. In any event, several of the groups I mentioned are very centered and sane and effective. I'm just calling them utopian because their ideas of what the world should look like are so at odds with current realities.

A little less utopian, perhaps, but still far to the "left" of the axis, would be a group such as Greenpeace, which does both very effective nonviolent civil disobedience on a global scale and also negotiates with governments and corporations. I might place the Rainforest Action Network here too. Toward the center-left of this spectrum I would place some of the somewhat mainstream environmental groups such as the Sierra Club, Wilderness Society and a slew of other organizations. Toward the more "pragmatic" center one finds organizations such as the National Resources Defense Council (NRDC), big moderate environmental organizations and their litigating attorneys, and lobbyists who are jousting with and negotiating with polluting industries and developers, trying to work within the confines of the political and judicial systems and frequently having to make major trade-offs and compromises. A little further to the right one finds organizations that cooperate more readily with corporations but still pressure them, such as Environmental Defense. Yet further to the right of the axis we could place environmentally aware people working in branches of government or major social institutions. And at the furthest right of the axis would be people working with and within polluting corporations to improve their environmental performance (again, this is a subjective, arbitrary model).

Obviously there are broad ideological gradations even within individual organizations, and most individuals live with a range of fluctuating contradictory ideas and beliefs, so many of us undoubtedly will skate all over the scale at different points and in relationship to different issues. Remember, this is just a thought exercise. Still, if you are environmentally concerned and/or involved, you can look at this panorama, and try as best you can to determine where you might fit. If you're an Earth-Firster doing a tree-sit, or on Captain Paul Watson's crew ramming an illegal Japanese or Norwegian whaling ship on the high seas, you might feel some disdain for suited NRDC attorneys and Sierra Club lobbyists safe in their beds at night, let alone some state Environmental Protection Agency official. On the other hand, a well groomed congressional aide to a somewhat environmentally-friendly politician trying to get a bill passed might bemoan that spliff-smoking, dreadlocked tree-sitters are giving environmentalism a bad name.

But, if we are willing to step back and realize any political movement is an ecosystem of sorts, we might entertain the possibility that different types of people with different temperaments who resonate to different ideological tonalities can all serve in their respective niches. The sincere, well-scrubbed aide or lobbyist might see that the direct action folks are culturally distant but nevertheless crucial allies in a broad wave attempting to save as much of the natural world and its vital functions as possible. Some of the radicals might see that, as much as every compromise feels like a small death, the battle for the soul of a civilization requires a broad range of actors both outside and inside the corridors of power. They may still disagree furiously over settlements and outcomes of specific struggles, but a greater degree of conscious symbiotic action and coordination could go a long way to raising the effectiveness and success ratio of the whole movement.

Very few of us are likely to suddenly abandon our utopian or pragmatic orientation or whatever our guiding principles might be, but a dispassionate look at your own worldview and the larger context can change how you look at your role. I believe one can be a utopian with realistic assessments of socio-political facts on the ground as well as a deluded dreamer. One can also be either a narrow-minded cynical or a sophisticated pragmatist. What I am saying is that one's core ideological tendency is likely a matter of temperament and destiny more than choice, but that one's understanding and behavior within that tendency can be more or less intelligent or delusional.

For example, let's say you're a Gandhian vegan pacifist, a perfectly honorable tradition, if one far outside the mainstream. (And I'm picking this tendency at random; the point I am seeking to make regarding political introspection could apply to nearly any political worldview.) If your view of your function in the political ecosystem is that your role is to hold to a very pristine moral and ethical stance so that humanity has exalted models to aim toward, that seems to me to be a very valuable function. And you would be right to argue that human morality has become less tribal and more universal over the centuries, so the eventual extension of moral concern and some rights to animals, say, might very well be a logical continuation of that trend. But if you're a sophisticated observer of political reality, you will also realize that your worldview excludes you from participating in positions of actual power in any government in the world or of being taken seriously by those who hold those positions, since all governments depend, nearly by definition, on the potential and actual use of violence to enforce their laws and interests, and none are about to promote veganism.

This doesn't mean you can't achieve influence on your culture and some political victories: some better laws to reduce cruelty to animals here, less meat and fat-friendly nutritional guidelines or less public support for a particular war there, and so on. Nor does it mean that in the very long term you may not see society edge closer to some of your values. But you and your ilk will not be major players wielding political power for the foreseeable future, which is obviously true for nearly all far-from-mainstream positions.

There are, as always, exceptions to this: one could argue Gandhi himself exerted enormous power, and the Gandhian pacifist civil rights leader Bayard Rustin played a significant role in pushing through important civil rights legislation in the 1960s. But Gandhi was the inspiring leader of a nationalist movement and the values he espoused had deep and wide roots in his culture, and it is hard to see how he could have made the transition to heading a government had he not been assassinated. He would very soon have butted heads with more pragmatic bureaucrats. And Rustin, who had refused to serve in WWII and did prison time for it, withheld any criticism of Lyndon Johnson's Vietnam policy as a political trade-off, to the consternation of his pacifist comrades, in the kind of realpolitikal tactical maneuver very few pacifists would consider. And these figures, as influential as they were, exerted their influence as leaders in movements pressuring governments from the outside, not as insiders, and they were exceptional.

So, in my view, if you hold a utopian position in the ideological ecosystem, but you are clear-headed about it and understand and accept the constraints of that stance and have a realistic perception of your society, you can serve a very helpful function in the political landscape. It is just as important in politics as in art or music or religion to have traditionalists who seek to maintain lineages in their pristine authenticity; experimenters, iconoclasts and creative opportunists who mix and match and break new ground; and popularizers who digest and soften new ideas for mass consumption. Looking at the political landscape as an ecosystem means understanding that others who are more utopian or more pragmatic than we have a real function that might not suit us. But if you have a false sense of what is achievable in a specific time-frame, or how powerful the real forces arrayed against you are, or an inflated messianic, megalomaniacal sense of moral superiority, you are, in general, likely to be far less effective (and far more unproductively annoying to everyone else).

I do have to concede that leaders and movements with extreme, unyielding positions and maniacal one-pointedness have often succeeded or at least had major historical influence, sometimes with good, sometimes with horrific results. And their causes have sometimes seemed totally unrealistic and then suddenly gained traction. Almost by definition, those who are considered great leaders in our culture are driven and relentless. (I'd go so far as to say nearly every successful political or business leader of note in our culture has to be a functional manic.) But for every such leader or movement that has succeeded many more have failed miserably.

I would also argue that in an age of extremely potent lethal weaponry and highly complex technological societies, a politics of maniacal certitude can be far more dangerous than in epochs past. Certainly the very nature of utopian impulses makes nuanced perspective unlikely. Perhaps I am being naïve (or utopian!) by thinking there could be at least some sophisticated, realistic utopians with a keen sense of social complexity, and equally intelligent un-cynical pragmatists, and that they could somehow learn to behave more symbiotically. Given the rise of holistic thought in key areas of science, it doesn't seem like too much to hope for a new breed of less linear political thinkers and doers, and I fear what will transpire if it is not in the cards.

I also have to readily admit it is not always easy to decide who is being utopian on specific issues. For instance when the U.S. is contemplating a war or military intervention, the pacifist wing of the left will of course invariably oppose it while other progressives who are not pure pacifists will on some rare occasions support a war they feel is legitimate. Here the pacifists would, according to my scale, have to be considered utopian and the others pragmatists. But what about some on the left who would like to see the rule of the American corporate elites weakened and who therefore wouldn't mind seeing the U.S. over-reach militarily and get bogged down in imperial wars on too many fronts, as the Romans did?

This is not an uncommon perspective among some intellectuals abroad, but it would likely be viewed as a close to treasonous world-view for an American to hold by current mainstream standards, so those few who subscribe to such views usually don't talk too openly about them (and can't do much of anything to bring their hopes to fruition in any case). It is a very risky thing to wish for, in that a war can sometimes strengthen a regime rather than weaken it, and competing elites may turn out to be as bad or worse than the one you are eager to displace. But if one despises a social order with enough vehemence and nothing else seems likely to depose it, why not hope it will gamble, overreach and lose, one might argue. This type of position is on the surface pure Machiavellian realpolitik hard-ball, but in another way it has a sort of romantic revolutionary, dystopian, apocalyptic, millenarian flavor that is as utopian in its own dark way as pacifism, even though it may have a firmer basis in a sound reading of geopolitics and history. And the currently highly influential clique of thinkers in the U.S elites that overtly embraces absolute global U.S. military and economic hegemony and is confident in the nation's ability to achieve and hold such dominance may be the most naïve and utopian of all.

The exercise in political self-analysis I propose is far from any sort of facile ideological wonder drug that will resolve all differences within a movement. There are inevitably real substantive differences that can't be papered over. Beyond the pacifist vs. pragmatist divide I mentioned above, there are always, even if one is attempting to take a very broad, tolerant, "ecosystemic" view of a movement, certain groups or ideologies that one may consider beyond the pale: either so extreme or so tepid they seem counter-productive or actually part of the enemy camp. The problem is, there are usually very different takes on who is or isn't beyond the pale at which particular historical juncture. We are, after all, dealing with a subjective realm of opinion and belief, and one that is constantly in flux. I may consider the "Unabomber" on one end of the spectrum and those employees of polluting mega-corporations who run what I may view as token, "greenwashing" eco-programs on the other to be outside the range of legitimate environmentalism, but, at least in the second case, quite a few would undoubtedly object to my delineation. People tend to disagree about where to draw lines in the sand.

Also, while nearly all progressives in the U.S. (as I write this) are currently committed to working in a reformist or evolutionary, not a revolutionary, context, there have been other historical moments when that was less true. And a divide between reformers and revolutionaries whose ultimate goal is the destruction of a system of government is a profound one that is one of the hardest to bridge. Committed radicals are often willing to manipulate and betray moderates for whom they hold little respect, and moderates are at times willing to let radicals get dragged off in the middle of the night without making too much of a fuss.

So analyzing where you stand in a utopian-realpolitik continuum is far from easy and may vary from issue to issue and year to year and won't magically solve any political conundrums. But I think it can be very productive because most of us hold a variety of complex, often reflexive and reactive, not fully examined views. To begin being more effective politically, it can't hurt to first examine, clarify and contextualize our own positions and ideological profiles, and a little exercise in seeking to measure one's own utopian and pragmatic ratios on different topics can be an entertaining first baby step in a quest for political Socratic self-examination. We could then use a variety of other axes and lenses to study our political make-up: how libertarian or communitarian, Luddite or techno-utopian, militant or moderate, rational or emotional, Romantic or utilitarian, and so forth, are we on different issues?

One tack that is worth considering is the idea of a two-tiered approach to politics. Those of us whose socio-political aspirations seem utopian to the mainstream can attempt to spread our ideals in a variety of ways, from writing or artistic expression, to educational initiatives, to building working models of alternative economic organization, "green" technologies and cooperative communities, while also understanding that more pragmatic compromises and trade-offs need to occur in short and medium term political life. We might, say, volunteer on a communal farm or visionary neighborhood organization or teach the history of Anarchism, attend anti-globalization protests or participate in tree-sits, but still support a "sell-out" liberal politician in an election because of the greater tangible damage the alternative candidate would cause. But the ability to adopt such a flexible stance depends on one's analysis of the facts on the ground, and many radicals are unwilling to consider that their ideal society lies, at best, far off in the future, and that sometimes ugly trade-offs need to occur in the meantime. Some of us are better suited to spreading utopian ideals and models, and some are better suited to the horse-trading of realpolitik. My hope is that we can become far more self-examinatory and sophisticated in understanding where and how we can each best serve. And if we can begin to see that our role is one of many in the larger political ecosystem, not the only true path, we will already have come a long way.

Notes

I list a number of environmental groups. I've already mentioned Earth First! and Sea Shepherd. The Wildlands Project founded by leading figures in the emerging field of conservation biology and experienced conservation activists, including Dave Foreman, has a fine journal, *Wild Earth* (www.wild-earth.org). The Rainforest Action Network, started by Randy Hayes, has had a lot of success in the last few years using a range of tactics to pressure some of the world's biggest corporations to stop buying old growth lumber and to improve some of their eco-behavior. The Sierra Club, with some 700 000 members, has long been the most significant national environmental grassroots organization. The Wilderness Society, founded in 1935 by the renowned Aldo Leopold and the father of the Appalachian Trail, Benton MacKaye, is smaller and focused completely on wildland issues (www.wilderness.org). NRDC stands for the Natural Resources Defense Council (www.nrdc.org, and see also their fine journal *On Earth*), a crucially important organization that does some of the most important work in pro-environment litigation, education and lobbying. The main purely legal group that specializes in activist eco-litigation is one I didn't list, the admirable EarthJustice (formerly Sierra Club Legal Defense). Environmental Defense is a group more willing than most to cooperate with large businesses to improve their environmental behavior. A group I don't list but that does great work from within a government bureaucracy is FSEEE, Forest Service Employees for Environmental Ethics (www.fsee.org).

There's been a renewal of interest in the life and times of the complex civil rights leader Bayard Rustin with several new books in the last few years. See D'Emilio, John. *Lost Prophet: the life and times of Bayard Rustin* (Free Press, 2003); Levine, Daniel. *Bayard Rustin and the Civil Rights Movement* (Rutgers University, 2000); and: Anderson, Jervis. *Bayard Rustin: troubles I've seen: a biography* (University of California, 1998). Rustin's homosexuality, socialism and pacifism forced him to maintain a low public profile at many crucial historical moments despite his key role in the movement. In the late sixties he infuriated many antiwar activists by his decision to focus on civil rights issues and to work with the Johnson administration despite its Vietnam policies.

Know the Terrain

Besides "knowing yourself" politically (having a clear sense of your beliefs, goals, capacities, strengths and weaknesses) and having a profound sense of your adversaries, nothing is more important than understanding the "terrain," i.e. the socio-political geography of the area, nation, or global region in which you are vying for influence or power, and, of course, the historical roots of the current "topography" and the dynamic forces transforming that terrain. Since my main focus in this text is the U.S., that is the terrain I will look at here. I am not purporting to offer a full analysis of such a complex society. I am only focusing on a few examples of ways in which I think left/progressive/eco-movements have largely failed to accurately analyze the harsh realities of the American political landscape. The reasons for these misreadings are often the same as those that cause our movements to overestimate their levels of support in the population and to fail to study our adversaries with sufficient precision: arrogance, naïveté, and wishful thinking (or, conversely, paranoid conspiratorial ideological sink-holes), but there are also other factors.

My main contention is that progressives consistently fail to appreciate just how conservative a nation the U.S. really is. There are several reasons for this. One of the most important is that they tend to live in communities in which somewhat left (by U.S. standards) perspectives are widespread, such as inner cities, cosmopolitan urban neighborhoods, liberal suburbs, college towns, and the like. They don't encounter in any large numbers many of the social groups that tend to support the right: rural folks, the small town and suburban conservative elderly, military and police families, small business owners, evangelical Christians, permanently pissed-off working class white males, and so forth. So when they go to a large anti-war demonstration and see hundreds of thousands of like-minded people, they have a hard time believing polls that tell them they are a minority, and are shocked again and again that so many Americans can vote for candidates who seem so profoundly unsophisticated and archaic. It is hard for them to accept it is they who may be living in isolated pockets of cosmopolitan modernity.

Another reason the country's core religiosity and puritanical morality are easy to underestimate is that there have also been, from the very beginning of the nation's existence, powerful countercurrents: a strong libertarian streak, a love of technical novelty and strange new cults and fads, wide sympathy for iconoclastic rebels, a deep love of the land and wildness, occasional outbreaks of mass ecstatic hedonism, and a crass commercialism unparalleled in human experience. These are more immediately evident than the deep conservatism. On its surface the culture gives an impression of being a tireless novelty factory, and it does have a remarkable capacity for generating and then re-absorbing and commodifying sub and counter-cultures to replenish itself. And it is often astonishingly adaptable and (admittedly, usually after bitter resistance, and to a point) willing to accommodate many demands for change or inclusion. For example, while racial minority and women's and gay rights activists may have good reason to bemoan the current reactionary period, the gains those movements have made in a few decades and the changes in public attitudes and norms have been extraordinary. That has been true in Europe and some other places as well, so these are international trends, but the U.S has often initially led the way. Other nations, especially in Europe, have been taking culturally liberalizing trends further subsequently, but tolerance and equal rights are virtues that do have deep resonance here; and the Bill of Rights is a real achievement, an important marker in the history of struggles for human rights.

So how could I be arguing that this land—built by oppressed immigrants, a place of youth and optimism, which worships the new and shiny, is abuzz with rock n' roll, Hollywood glitz and rap, awash in (more and more socially acceptable) pornography, gambling, hyper-sexualized advertising and drugs and booze, with its dazzlingly high levels of personal violence and astonishingly gluttonous patterns of consumption—is, at its core, a very conservative place? Well, first, these trends of tolerance and pop culture zaniness are fairly globalized at this point, and all complex systems are multi-faceted with competing dynamic forces reacting to each other. The U.S. clearly does have a very pronounced dual nature, a dancing dyad of wildness and rigidity that can be traced to its earliest colonial settlers who included a bizarre mix of religious fanatics, adventurers, criminals and hustlers. So I'm not saying it is only a conservative country, but that the more tolerant and effusive aspects of its persona I've enumerated are so obviously visible that they mask a far more covert but very deep rigidity, something that would make perfect sense to Jungians who would see this apparent dichotomy as perfectly logical: the more rigid and repressed a psychological system is, the more wild they would expect its "shadow" to be. And the juxtaposition of deeply conservative, apocalyptic/millenarian religiosity and morality with, say, Las Vegas, is nothing if not surreal. I am not denying other aspects of the American mindset and experience, but I am emphasizing the conservative essence of the country because it is an aspect of reality the left has been reluctant to look at unflinchingly, and one it needs to confront.

There is no doubt that it seems paradoxical that a nation as dynamic and fluid as the U.S., whose population has grown so much and received successive waves of immigrants from such varied parts of the world; in which people move to new locations far more frequently than nearly anywhere else; which seems far less interested in its own history than nearly any other nation; and which has witnessed so much social and technological change, nonetheless continues to exhibit many of the same political reflexes Alexis de Tocqueville (still the most astute and prophetic of all those who have studied the U.S.) identified over 165 years ago: a mix of individualism and extreme conformism (especially religious and moral conformism), a deep-rooted, almost fetishistic type of patriotism, and a sense of nearly messianic national exceptionalism unique in the world.

I recall reading somewhere that Lawrence Durrell once said you could take all the French out of France and replace them with Tartars and you would still wind up, after a generation or two, with people who loved wine, cheese, sex, fine food, fashion, baguettes, literature, and philosophy, that somehow the soul of the land expresses itself in its people. I have no idea if that has any truth to it or if some other cultural method of propagation accounts for the mysterious continuity and resilience of national traits over long periods despite major demographic and other radical structural changes, but it is a very real phenomenon, and political actors forget it at their peril.

The U.S. presents a very strange case, ripe with weird contradictions. Its revolution and many of its main founding fathers emerged from the same largely secular-rationalist values as the French Revolution did, yet the new nation stayed steeped in extraordinarily conservative forms of religious fundamentalism. The country has been at the global forefront of technological innovation for two centuries and novel artistic movements for one, yet may at its root be the most solipsistic, anti-intellectual and provincial great power the world has ever seen. Some of this can be explained by the sheer size of the country and the isolation of many communities that permit the survival of very traditional patterns of thought in many pockets. The country's physical enormity, the ebullient, utopian aspirations aroused by its very novelty, and the heroic efforts needed to adjust and succeed in a hyper-competitive culture also force even recent immigrants to get so immersed in this new world they lose interest in the rest of the world—other than, for a while, their place of origin. Then there are the enormous, lasting impacts of slavery and the Civil War, the brutal conquest of the continent's indigenous peoples, the nation's imperial expansion at the expense of Mexico and Spain, and the evolution of very distinct ethnic and regional subcultures in the new country. These all combine to create very deep racial/ethnic divides that stymie attempts at building national class-based grassroots movements.

Also, most immigrants come here to achieve economic success and don't want to rock the boat politically. This thirst for material success and possessions, strongly encouraged (as Max Weber analyzed so brilliantly in *The Protestant Ethic and the Spirit of Capitalism*) by the variants of Protestantism that took root here, winds up being the greatest unifying factor of a heterogeneous population. Another crucial factor is the uniquely dominant role of a very dynamic and ruthless capitalist/entrepreneurial class and a very unfortunate legacy of robber-baron era jurisprudence, which comes close to equating commercial speech with political speech and offers corporations many of the rights accorded individuals without sufficient corresponding legal liabilities. Nowhere on earth have commercial corporations enjoyed as fundamental a role in politics and culture and developed such strange, nearly cultish, fetishistic allegiances. Finally, add to that the protection from invasion and the cultural distance from the outside two enormous oceans confer (though Mexico may ultimately demographically reconquer what it lost militarily), and you have a recipe for a largely a-politicized, paradoxically fragmented yet deeply conformist population. This population is uniquely (for a fully "developed" nation) disconnected from the rest of the planet, wants a government that will provide some order amidst the noise and chaos, and tends to lean to the right, though it is also prone to occasional eruptions of usually localized populist rage.

Well-educated, sophisticated progressives understandably have a hard time accepting the depth and resilience of the archaic values that permeate so much of the nation and the strange political consensus that results. But, as I keep repeating, simply offering arguments that seem self-evidently rational to us and then being shocked/shocked over and over again that they get no traction is a futile exercise. We have to stop pretending the country would really embrace our views if only it were exposed to them, and actually analyze why it is so often immune to a progressive worldview. We have to first take a cold, honest look at the terrain. We need to come to grips with why the left and eco-movements so often seem alien and out of step with the American mainstream consensus.

First, we are living in the world's most powerful empire, a hyper-aggressive mercantile naval power with some military presence in well over a hundred countries, and major garrisons ensconced for over half a century now on many far-flung fronts around the globe. Its military expenditures may now exceed that of the rest of the world. And yet most Americans think of their country as a benign, although powerful and aggressive in business, always well-intentioned entity, reluctant to intervene in other people's conflicts, uniquely innocent and virtuous. This is a long-standing, deep-seated and very widespread belief, a national identity myth, which, as extraordinarily naïve as it may be, is so entrenched in the average citizen, it seems immune, so far, to counter-argument. And, astonishingly, much of the political-intellectual elite buys into it on some level. A very specialized class of global business people, State Department officials, military and intelligence foreign policy operatives, experts and academics (and proselytizing Mormons and evangelicals and peace corps idealists) handle the U.S.' relationships with the outer world, but the average American is more ignorant about other countries than citizens of every other literate society. Less than half the members of the U.S. congress have passports!

Those of us who challenge this view of American exceptionalism, and actually try to argue for universal "Enlightenment" norms (the equality of rights for all humans, the fact that one human life is worth as much as another regardless of national origin, etc.) are treated as, at best naïve and irrelevant, at worst traitorous, especially when conflict looms. To some extent, this is true in every country. People tend to care more deeply about their own folks than others, and this is normal, but it is more pronounced here because we have (other than briefly in 1812) been shielded from military invasions and the forcible need to adjust to other cultures. That anyone would challenge the U.S.' fundamental goodness and righteousness seems unthinkable to the vast majority, and in no other country does fetishism of the national flag elicit the astonishing fervor it does here.

The U.S., as I have discussed at length, is the world's most religious fully industrialized country. References to God are ubiquitous: on our money, in our oaths, on our buildings. Only a tiny minority of Americans professes to being agnostic or atheist. This is a profoundly relevant political factor, and is deeply problematic for much of the left, which is steeped in a tradition of anti-clericalism and is disdainful of religious impulses. As I have discussed in other chapters, there is also a very dynamic progressive religious sector, but the left's overall tone is nonetheless largely steeped in secular rationalism, and this is another factor which makes it seem culturally alien (perhaps too "European") to most Americans.

The American quest for material prosperity, with its particular cult of consumption and its view of the country as a uniquely sanctified engine of wealth-creation unequaled in human history, is an awesomely powerful force, a social glue to those here and a beacon to so many struggling around the world in lands of far less opportunity. And, while we know the Horatio Alger myth is a myth and that the U.S. is very much a class society with increasingly obscene wealth disparities and fewer safety nets than other industrialized nations, we have to acknowledge it still is a place where there is enough possibility of upward social mobility, especially for tight-knit immigrant groups willing to make intense familial sacrifices, and for astute, driven entrepreneurs (including criminals), that the myth does also have some elements of truth.

Many of us on the left and in the environmental movement understand the real global damage American levels of wasteful consumption cause, and also recoil at what we see as gluttony (our own form of ascetic moralism). Many of us, especially white activists, come from middle-class backgrounds (though by no means all; that's also a myth) and, since physical survival and poverty were not our immediate concerns growing up, those of us who had altruistic predispositions had the luxury of extending the range of our concerns to those less fortunate and to the larger world. This certainly doesn't invalidate our analyses and beliefs, but we have to understand why most people don't share them: they are so busy struggling hard to get a piece of the American dream, or to stay afloat and make those car, house and credit card payments once they're in the game, they have no time or patience for our entreaties to look at environmental degradation or systemic inequities domestic and global.

Americans work harder and longer than people in nearly every other "fully developed" economy (and than they themselves did twenty years ago), get less sleep, far less vacation time, are more violent and more frequently go bonkers, take more drugs (prescribed and self-medicated), have higher rates of teen pregnancy and divorce, less health insurance (if any), are less well-educated, spend more time stuck in traffic, are far more obese, and so forth, but they are also far more politically docile and a-political than far more coddled European populations. We are far from the constantly disputatious and argumentative French who have a *bon mot* about education: "The goal of a good educational system is to create a population that is very difficult to govern." Here, making money is the name of the game, and nothing else really has any gravitas. People who distract you from that goal are wasting your time (which, after all, is money). Unless things seem very tangibly, visibly really bad, the President must be doing a good job.

The U.S. also has a bizarre duality vis-à-vis history. On the one hand historical novels sell well, and a subset of the educated public is fascinated by historical narratives. There is nearly an industry of books about the founding fathers. Civil and Revolutionary war battle re-enactments abound. But that's entertainment. Government policy and social issues are discussed in an a-historical vacuum. The historical roots of contemporary policy issues are simply not considered relevant or appropriate to discuss. The conquest of the indigenous Americans and slavery are "ancient history," so "get over it," says the mainstream. For Serbs the battle of Kosovo in 1389, for the French and British the Hundred Years War, for the Chinese the Warring States Period, for Jews the destruction of the temple, for Shiites the martyrdom of Ali in 661, for Christians the life of Christ, for the Japanese Commodore Perry's gunboats' arrival in 1853, to cite only a few random examples, are readily acknowledged to still have resonance and ongoing repercussions centuries or millennia later. But even the fact that the U.S. overthrew Mossadegh in Iran in 1953 or Arbenz in Guatemala, or acquiesced and abetted in Allende's murder in Chile, or was recently allied with Saddam Hussein and Osama bin Laden, are not admissible as worthy of serious concern as causal factors in current crises or as cautionary tales in contemporary policy debates. It's all "old history," blowback be damned. It is always onward to the New Jerusalem. Only can-do, feel good optimism and certainty about the U.S.' pure intentions are allowed.

If history is invoked, it is very selectively, as it was recently in the Iraq conflict to point out how brutal Saddam had been (never mind that we supported him at the time of his worst crimes). Or it is invoked to remind ungrateful Europeans that the U.S. saved them in two world wars, conveniently neglecting to mention why there are so many "Lafayette Avenues" all over U.S. cities, or how the U.S. intervened late in both those twentieth century conflicts after the initial protagonists had exhausted themselves, and used both those wars to establish itself as the world's dominant power, and how few casualties it sustained compared to the other players, especially the Russians who lost fifty times (!!) more casualties than the U.S. in WWII. One could persuasively argue that, at least on the European front, the Russians defeated Hitler with some British help, with a big late boost from the tardy Americans with all their high-tech. But that, of course, would be close to treasonous heresy.

Despite all the factors I've enumerated that can make us feel profoundly alienated from the mainstream consensus, the American left/progressive and eco-movements are also genuinely embedded in American history. They are not subversive alien viruses but legitimate, homegrown ideological strains and a real part of the terrain. The environmental movement can legitimately point back to Native American cultures' land ethics as sources of guidance and inspiration. We should avoid a racist over-romanticizing of indigenous peoples as infallibly noble environmental saints, but, as scholars such as Malcolm Margolin and hands-on practitioners such as Dennis Martinez have shown, many tribes had (and in places continue to have) highly sophisticated, sustainable land management practices and elaborate social mechanisms to regulate the commons from which we could learn a great deal. And John Muir, Ralph Waldo Emerson, Henry David Thoreau, the Hudson River Valley painters, Theodore Roosevelt, Aldo Leopold, Rachel Carson, the fishermen, patricians and other folks who fought to save Storm King Mountain, Karen Silkwood, and contemporary tree-sitters, are all quintessentially American figures.

All those slave revolts, Nat Turner, David Walker's appeal, Sojourner Truth, the Abolitionists and Underground Railroad, Joaquin Murieta, W.E.B. Dubois, Malcolm X, SNCC and the Black Panthers, Chaney, Goodman and Schwerner, Cesar Chavez, and the like, are all part of a profound, vital, component of the American experience. The mix of indigenous people and run-away "maroon" slaves known as the Seminole who fought the U.S. army to a stand-off under the great chief Osceola offers an early example of multi-cultural resistance to oppression. And Tom Paine, the suffragettes, the great populist movements, the brutal labor battles, the "wobblies" of the IWW, the miners of bloody Harlan county, are all important in American history. And no poet is as American as the deeply populist Walt Whitman, an early icon of gay liberation to boot. So let no one deny that we represent an authentic and legitimate part of the ideological landscape from the get-go. The movements that are our ancestors did much to shape this country and to challenge and begin to correct its injustices and represent, in many instances, its most noble strains.

That said, many of these antecedents, while inspiring, contained contradictions that can still haunt us. The strict moralism of the Abolitionist and suffragette milieus later led to Prohibition with all its unintended consequences (the Mafia, for example), and some eugenics movements, and one sees echoes of this moralism in the tragically wasteful "war on drugs" and some puritanical reflexes in parts of the left. The great populist movements also included very conservative rural components and a great deal of racism. Due to immigration patterns, much of the most militant labor unrest was very ethnically specific (Bohemians in Chicago, Irish in New York, Italian anarchists of Sacco and Vanzetti fame in Patterson) and occasionally targeted other minorities as well as the bosses—massacring African-Americans in the New York draft riots, Chinese laborers in California railroad strife, and so forth. And the train robbers who became lasting American folk heroes (Jesse James et al.) were mostly embittered former Confederate soldiers as brutally racist as they were anti-railroad magnate.

Teddy Roosevelt, undoubtedly a major figure in environmentalism and anti robber-baron reform, also had the indigenous inhabitants of Yellowstone thrown out to make it the first national park, and was, of course, a rabid "manifest destiny" imperialist. And the scions of wealthy families who did so much to save large tracts of wooded lands in the Hudson River Valley (and many other places) for posterity, notably the Rockefellers, had usually amassed their fortunes from vicious predatory capitalism and ruthless manipulations on Wall Street. And much of the eco- and progressive movements are to this day funded by foundations set up by altruistic ancestors of these "robber-baron" families.

All of which goes to show that paradoxes and ironies abound in political life. It is best to acknowledge complexities and contradictions and shifting realities honestly. Too often we on the left lapse into simplistic fantasies, thinking all oppressed groups should just be one big happy family, a big united rainbow front. This doesn't mean we shouldn't work hard to find common ground and shouldn't tone down our disagreements, but we need to analyze the groups that compose our bases of support realistically and attempt deep understanding, not wear rose-colored glasses. For example, African-Americans and some Hispanic communities are indeed the most reliably progressive sectors of the population on domestic economic and foreign policy issues, but many in these groups are far more religious and conservative on moral questions (such as abortion and gay rights) than average middle class white lefties. Churches have long been the most stable and well-organized social-solidarity institutions in black neighborhoods, and the Catholic Church an absolutely essential part of most Hispanic communities.

Women do tend to vote for far more liberal candidates than men do and exhibit more compassion and less machismo in their political views, but they are also the main driving forces of consumer culture and do rally to law and order candidates in large numbers when they perceive a threat to community safety. Some new immigrant groups can be surprisingly conservative, not just in their strict, traditional cultural/familial norms, but on many political issues as well, despite the discrimination and hardships they face, as they are understandably most concerned with material success and a stable economic environment. And the Jewish community in the U.S., long a major source of support and leadership in progressive movements, is far more divided now as the polarized politics of the Middle East (and of U.S. inner cities) have ripped apart old alliances, and as the neo-conservative movement (led initially by Jewish, formerly socialist and Trotskyist intellectuals) has had great success in pulling quite a few Jews to the right.

It is, in fact, almost hallucinatory to see extreme millenarian Christian fundamentalists, the same sorts of people who were the mainstays of rabid anti-Semitism (not to mention intense anti-Catholicism) for hundreds of years, and obsessively anti-Communist, become great defenders of Israel, a state founded by socialists, and of its messianic settlers who depend on massive state hand-outs to survive. The recently emergent dynamic alliance between the frequently Jewish neo-conservative intelligentsia who are arch-supporters of the Likud and are at this moment so influential in U.S. foreign policy, and the Christian right is truly bizarre, since the Book of Revelation-obsessed folks support Israel because their reading of prophecy convinces them a very specific scenario has to transpire in the Holy Land (the gathering of the Jews, the battle of Megiddo) before the Messiah's second coming and the rapture. At that point, of course, the Jews will have to convert to Christianity or be wiped out (or be damned in the hereafter or something). This is ultimately far more anti-Jewish than even the most militant Palestinians' ideology, since even Hamas or Islamic Jihad would love to drive all the Jews away from the region, but don't really care if they thrive elsewhere, and don't predict their total annihilation from the face of the earth by pre-ordained divine fiat.

It may seem surprising that this very strange alliance has gotten so little scrutiny from mainstream media, but if we study the ideological terrain, the reasons become apparent. There are several taboos at play. First, there are so many people in the country at least sympathetic to evangelical Christianity that a close, intense and sustained look at just how incompatible its prophetic apocalypticism is with modern, rational-scientific norms would offend too many (and cause boycotts and commercial losses), and would also go against the grain of American religious tolerance (and let's face it, all religious beliefs seem weird to outsiders). Then there is a taboo about mentioning that segments of the Jewish community exert substantial influence and power, because of the justifiably vivid memories of two millennia of anti-Semitic conspiracy fantasies that ultimately culminated in the Holocaust. This taboo also extends to any mention of the fact that segments of the Jewish community lobby very intensely on behalf of the Israeli right, with an effectiveness far beyond what one would expect given the small size of the Jewish population; that tiny Israel is the biggest recipient of U.S. foreign aid, and so forth. The reasons for these taboos are understandable, but the result is that large swaths of truth are off limits in the public debate.

In any case knowing the terrain means we have to keep our eyes not just on the realities (no matter how jarring and painful) of present political configurations and alignments and their historical roots, but on the trends that are shaping the future. How will the large increase in the Hispanic population and the rise of Asian communities play themselves out politically? How will the continuing shift of the country's center of gravity to the "Sun-belt" play itself out? How will the looming battles over a dwindling water supply and an aging infrastructure play themselves out? Will the new, more overt and unilateralist aggressiveness of the American empire tolerate even less dissent at home if things go awry in one or more of its foreign military adventures? What types of populist and isolationist movements are likely to emerge on the right if the empire's foreign adventures demand too many economic sacrifices at home, and how would we relate to them? Will the Web and other increasingly segmented electronic media continue our culture's fragmentation into an ecosystem of subcultures, sapping the political commons yet further? Or will these media's capacity to spread information (and rumors and lies) instantaneously facilitate resistance and novel forms of social engagement and cultural weirdness? Or all of the above?

I realize trying to keep abreast of such a complex socio-political landscape, understanding its roots in history and seeking to suss out its probable directions, is a very tall order, more demanding than *The Art of War*'s counsel on studying the physical topography of a battleground. But if we don't study, and, ideally, marshal all our wisdom, lucidity and creativity to master the terrain upon which we hope to build a more sustainable and humane civilization, it will become what battlefields have always been for the unprepared, unobservant, overconfident, rigid and rash: a graveyard for all our hopes and ideals.

Notes

Alexis de Tocqueville (1805-1859), a French nobleman, thinker and political figure toured America and wrote the most penetrating and prescient analysis of the young nation: *Democracy in America* (Volume I, 1835 and Volume II, 1840).

Lawrence Durrell, poet and novelist, is most famous for his "Alexandria Quartet" of four novels released between 1957 and 1960.

Weber, Max. *The Protestant Ethic and the Spirit of Capitalism* Talcott Parsons, trans. (G.

Allen & Unwin, Ltd., 1930). The most recent re-edition is by Dover Publications, 2003.

Horatio Alger's (1832-1899) formulaic stories made his name synonymous with "rags to riches." A few titles are: *Luck and Pluck; or, John Oakley's Inheritance* (Loring, 1869); *Ragged Dick; or, Street Life in New York With the Bootblacks* (Loring, 1868); and *Struggling Upward; or, Luke Larkin's Luck* (Porter & Coates, 1890).

Juliet Schor, a brilliant analyst of trends in American life, has written the best book on American overwork: *The Overworked American: the unexpected decline of leisure* (Basic Books, 1991).

There are reams of books about the unintended consequences of the CIA's sponsorship of coups around the world. One of the most famous recent books is: Chalmers Johnson's *Blowback: the costs and consequences of American empire* (Metropolitan Books, 2000). Others include: Kinzer, Stephen. *All the Shah's Men: an American coup and the roots of Middle East terror* (J. Wiley & Sons, 2003); Kinzer, Stephen and Schlesinger, Stephen C. *Bitter Fruit: the untold story of the American coup in Guatemala* (Doubleday, 1982); Kornbluh, Peter. *The Pinochet File: a declassified dossier on atrocity and account-ability* (New Press, 2003); Westerfield, H. Bradford, ed. *Inside CIA's Private World: Declassified Articles from the Agency's Internal Journal, 1955-1992* (Yale University Press, 1997); Blum, William. *Rogue State: A guide to the world's only superpower* (Common Courage Press, 2000); Blum, William. *Killing Hope: U.S. military and CIA interventions since World War II* (Common Courage Press, 2003). And Alfred McCoy's *The Politics of Heroin in Southeast Asia* (Harper Colophon, 1973) is a great classic on the CIA's indi-rect role in the drug traffic.

Margolin, Malcolm. *The Ohlone Way: Indian life in the San Francisco-Monterey Bay Area* (Heyday Books, 1978).

Dennis Martinez, of Chicano and O'odham descent, is the founder of the Indigenous Peoples' Restoration Network. A contract seed collector, vegetation surveyor, eco-forester and restoration consultant, he is an expert on traditional indigenous land management practices.

I list many figures and episodes in the history of the left and environmental move-ments. Most of them are so well known (Emerson, Thoreau, the Abolitionists, Cesar Chavez) I won't elaborate on them here. For more on the battle to save Storm King Mountain, see Talbot, Allan R. *Power along the Hudson; the Storm King case and the birth of environmentalism* (Dutton, 1972); and Cronin, John, and Kennedy, Robert Francis. *The Riverkeepers: two activists fight to reclaim our environment as a basic human right* (Scribner, 1997). For more on the Karen Silkwood case, see Rashke, Richard L. *The Killing of Karen Silkwood: the story behind the Kerr-McGee plutonium case* (Cornell University, 1981); Kohn, Howard. *Who Killed Karen Silkwood?* (Summit Books, 1981); and the movie: *Silkwood* (1983), directed by Mike Nichols.

For more on the saga of Joaqin Murieta, a mythic figure in Chicano lore, see Ridge, John Rollin. *The Life and Adventures of Joaquín Murieta, the Celebrated California Bandit* (University of Oklahoma, 1977); Burns, Walter Noble. *The Robin Hood of El Dorado: the saga of Joaquín Murrieta, famous outlaw of California's age of gold* (University of New Mexico Press, 1999); Thornton, Bruce S. *Searching for Joaquín: myth, Murieta, and history in California* (Encounter Books, 2003); Paz, Ireneo. *Joaquin Murrieta: life and adventures of the celebrated bandit: his exploits in the state of California* Frances P. Belle, trans. (Arte Publica Press, 2001).

For more on the Seminole Wars and chief Osceola, see Koestler-Grack, Rachel A. *Osceola, 1804-1838* (Blue Earth Books, 2003); Wickman, Patricia R. *Osceola's Legacy* (University of Alabama, 1991); Missall, John. *The Seminole Wars: America's longest Indian conflict* (University Press of Florida, 2004); Meltzer, Milton. *Hunted like a Wolf: the story of the Seminole War* (Pineapple Press, 2004).

For more on the "robber baron" era, see the great classic, Matthew Josephson's *The Robber Barons* (Harcourt, Brace, 1934).

Section IV:
What Is to Be Done?

Introduction

"O.K.," I hear the reader who has slogged through this text think (and if you are such a reader, my most profuse thanks and appreciation): "You've been kvetching for pages and pages mostly about what our problems and erroneous assumptions are, so, what do you think we should actually do, smart ass?" Well, my main purpose in writing this polemic was to challenge us to examine more deeply our political reflexes and beliefs and to stimulate reflection and, ideally, discussion. My focus was mostly not on what to think or do but on *how we look* at political landscapes. I never claimed to have any miracle cures for our political ailments, just perhaps a few better leads on some possible diagnoses. But, I do realize it would just be too obnoxious a cop-out not at least to offer a few possible tacks, some suggestions for specific initiatives or approaches after all that critique. So, I will attempt to do that in what follows.

Since I am not pushing any specific party line or program, my suggestions are not geared to what those of us involved one way or another in the broad swath of progressive and environmental movements should or shouldn't believe, but are rather about how to enhance the chances of broadly positive outcomes working within the existing ecosystems of our movements and the wider political panorama as it is. Nearly all the ideas I mention have already been broached or at least hinted at in earlier chapters, so some of this section repeats or recapitulates earlier points. Also, a lot of what I propose is already being done to some extent by different individuals and groups, so frequently I am advocating expanding or better coordinating already existing initiatives.

I'm not making any claims to having figured out universal principles of political strategy applicable everywhere at all times. Most of the ideas I'm advancing are merely suggestions for approaches that strike me as possibly appropriate to the current moment. And, obviously, one's analysis of current socio-political reality will determine whether one finds merit in them or not. Political winds can shift, and like most phenomena, seem to be somewhat cyclical, so the current hyper-reactionary period in the U.S. will pass. But my long-term view is that even when a somewhat more progressive agenda regains favor, the forces of the right and of entrenched corporate power are not about to melt away, and that our struggles with them will be very long and painful, and that they have, by far, the upper hand. So those who are convinced a global people's revolution is imminent or that there are millions upon millions of "cultural-creatives" just waiting for the right political vehicle, and that a new sustainable paradigm is inevitably coming very soon will most likely find my outlook too pessimistic. But if you are at least willing to entertain the possibility that our adversaries are very powerful and unlikely to disappear in the foreseeable future and that we need to get far more creative in our political thinking and behavior if we are to achieve even a modicum of success, perhaps some of what follows will be of interest to you.

Some Recapitulation: Toning Down Internecine Warfare; Pragmatism and Utopianism; Electoral Dilemmas

Political Aesthetics

I urge us first of all to strive for higher standards of accuracy, precision and elegance in our speech and writing. Our arguments are, in my view, frequently quite persuasive. We don't need to exaggerate and over-dramatize. If we can maintain a high level of integrity and truth telling in our discourse, we will, in the long term, do better when we seek to discredit our adversaries as they routinely fudge the facts. I'm not saying one has to be a saint or that some deviousness and even ruthlessness are not on occasion a necessary part of political life. Machiavelli and Hobbes are still read for a reason (and lefties should read them more often). But tactical feints and bluffs are, as in poker, best resorted to infrequently at exquisitely appropriate moments and should not be so dubious as to totally taint one's core values.

As I have argued, though the left does seek to organize the disenfranchised to further their tangible material interests, another of its main historical roles has been to encourage humanity's most generous and enlightened aspirations, and this places it at a disadvantage in most day-in day-out political struggles (and has also, ironically, resulted in some horrific excesses of "the ends justifying the means"). But this role and its burdens should be more consciously understood and accepted, and we should just realize we have no choice but to try to hold ourselves to a higher ethical/aesthetic standard than our opponents. We need to reflect those exalted aspirations we espouse as much as we can in our political lives without being naïve wimps. I realize that is not easy.

And we really have to try to do it with far less arrogant pomposity and smug certainty. Humor, especially self-deprecating humor, is crucial. If you can't genuinely laugh at yourself and see no irony in the human condition, you are most likely a terrifying prospect for a political (or any other) leadership role. We must begin to address the horrifically whiny, self-righteous, even histrionic tone so often associated with the left, including an over-reliance on guilt as an organizing tool and our too frequent demagogic forms of rhetoric. It would also help us to refrain as much as possible from ad hominem attacks, as tempting as they may be. We should be elegantly ferocious in attacking our opponents' positions and actions when it is appropriate, but glib mockery (at least in public) is too facile and not ultimately helpful.

I realize mainstream politics is nearly completely about style and spin, and intellectual lefties have every reason to want to focus on content, not aesthetics. But I'm not talking about superficial aesthetics, rather the quality of soul that radiates from individuals who are speaking from their hearts and experience and are also willing to work hard to discipline themselves to transcend their baser political reflexes. And this same appreciation for aesthetic elegance and vitality should also extend to artifacts of political life such as meetings, marches, demonstrations, rallies, benefits, and so forth. What a wonderful thing it would be to go to a large demonstration free of silly chants and strident speeches, a gathering that seemed more like an assemblage of centered, independent thinkers than the usual group-think pep-rally brimming with angry indignation.

Negotiating Our Divisions

Another big problem that characterizes the left is our seemingly insatiable appetite for savaging each other more than our opponents. Part of this is due to the roots of the modern left in the secular rational movements of the eighteenth and nineteenth centuries. The quest for the intellectually "correct" position on all issues has historically been an obsessive-compulsive disorder of the radical left, splintering movements into smaller and smaller ideologically anal-retentive groupuscules. This is somewhat less true in the post-Soviet era, but these reflexes remain. We would do well to remember Spinoza's arguments against René Descartes' rigid separation of body and mind. Spinoza's insistence that rationality and bodily and emotional states are not separate but part of a linked continuum, a holistic feedback loop, has now been largely vindicated by modern neurology. The radical left is the part of the political spectrum that suffers the most from antiquated Cartesianism. It doesn't need to become anti-intellectual, but it could stand to be a lot less rigidly cerebral and disembodied. Of course that wouldn't change the fact that there are authentic, substantive divisions among us, and I have, in fact, tried to unearth and analyze a whole slew of them in the preceding pages. It is naïve to expect us all to "just get along." If you are absolutely certain other factions are worthless sell-outs or mindless fanatics (and those attitudes are almost the norm), nothing I or anyone else is going to say will change your political approach.

I realize quite often we can't even agree who really belongs in the "we" in the first place. If your sincere analysis convinces you capitalism is inherently evil, it may be hard for you to work with more moderate progressives comfortable with a "mixed economy." If you are passionately certain that irrational superstition and any metaphysical beliefs are the bane of progress, it may be hard for you to work with activists motivated by their religious convictions. Conservationists and affordable housing advocates clash over sprawl and zoning issues in many suburban locales; Indian tribes, often allied with environmentalists, also battle them not infrequently over land use questions. Immigration and population issues have roiled the environmental community. These sorts of deep disagreements aren't going to vanish, and I've actually been arguing we need to explore them more systematically. But unless we are willing to be more fluid and less fundamentalist in our certainties, or at least tactically willing to work with very different people both within the broad left and outside of it toward well-defined common goals, the whole left will remain politically marginal.

I'm arguing it would serve us better to examine more thoroughly what divides us—not to resolve all differences, which is impossible, but so that, once our cards are on the table, we can see those areas on which we authentically agree, and we can build more clearly defined alliances with specific goals. It is counter-productive to overstate the solidity of our coalitions as we have done in recent years with the supposed "red-green" anti-globalization "united front," or with the recent anti Iraq war movement, which certainly brought vast numbers to the streets around the world but was revealed to be far more disparate and weak than it initially seemed once the war began, at least in the U.S.. I'm not at all saying these movements or initiatives had no value, just that overselling our level of support or unity is ultimately self-defeating because it merely demoralizes the novices or most idealistic among us as illusions are dashed again and again. Demonstrations can be useful, but let us use less bombastic rhetoric, make fewer demagogic claims about the depth of support we enjoy, and be more realistic in our strategic thinking.

I urge us to begin at least to tone down some of the brutal ideological battles that have raged among us. One prime example is the war between "identity politics" and class-based organizing advocates. A similar struggle (race vs. class as a primary political fact of American life) tore apart SDS in its late stages during the Vietnam War era. The identity politics issue has been discussed to death on the left, but most of the debate has been rigidly un-dialectical. New ideologies and philosophical and artistic movements always arise to challenge the certainties of the previous paradigm, usually bringing in needed correctives. And they need to be brash and radical to make their points.

But (unless you're a fundamentalist), no ideology is the final word, and each new artistic and philosophical and political "school" has brought valuable insights and later been found to have blind spots. We may reject the lacunae in our parents' ideas, but often we also go back and rediscover older traditions that harbor unexpected relevant lessons for the present. The history of human ideas is a dynamic continuum of inevitably imperfect and partial attempts to decipher reality. Identity politics has been very important in giving voice to groups that were largely excluded from power, and these groups have to fight to be heard and to challenge the status quo, including the old elites of the left. But that doesn't mean we shouldn't also put aside our identities once in a while to find common ground if we can on core economic, social and environmental issues lest we perpetuate the dominance of far more nefarious enemies.

On the intellectual/academic side of the left, some over-enthusiastic American advocates of "deconstruction" have embarked on far too over-arching a rejection of the political values of the Enlightenment. The irony of this is that a close reading of many of the European philosophers who are lionized figures among post-modern academics, such as Jacques Derrida or Jurgen Habermas, reveals that despite their strong critiques of Enlightenment humanism's illusions on the philosophical plane, they still view themselves on some level, at least politically, as heirs of Kant (who was an early advocate of international law and UN type bodies as necessary cures for war) and of the core values of the Enlightenment.

The Enlightenment tradition (and of course a very complex and contradictory mix of ideas is covered by that rubric), like any other, has deep flaws, but it is, politically at least, one indispensable cornerstone of our worldviews, and we can't abandon it. Yes, it's very important that thinkers have come forward to point out its weaknesses and hypocrisies and to add insights from indigenous peoples and other cultures and hitherto disenfranchised groups to the mix of our ideas. And yes, Enlightenment philosophers (including the U.S. founding fathers) may have started as a white guys (with property) only club. But the remedy for that is to strive to correct the deficiencies of their legacy, to fight so the most truly revolutionary, noble ideas about inalienable human rights they put forth live up as much as possible to their universality. To jettison the only real solid ideological foundations for a humane social order applicable in a mass, modern society is a form of political suicide.

And we have these tiresome debates about whether genetics or culture is determinant. How can anyone now deny human behaviors result from a dyadic dance between nature and nurture? By all means, let's study precisely how this constant interplay of genetics, environment and complex cultures creates social traits and phenomena with open minds. It is understandable that "anti-essentialist" feminists are wary of genetic explanations of behavior since dubious science was used for so long to deny women (and ethnic minorities) equal rights, and the critique of science's cultural assumptions and its ties to power by some of these scholars has been very valuable. But to then reflexively resist any genetic or evolutionary-biological explanations for human tendencies or male-female differences is throwing out the baby with the bathwater. Gender may be, on some level, a social construct, and, yes, there may be all sorts of gradations between male and female and inter-sexual people, and so on, but the large preponderance of people are either males or females and there are very big, measurable hormonal and other differences between the genders. Gender may not be an absolute category, but it is definitely describes something real that exists in the physical world.

When some in these schools of thought go overboard and argue that because nature is also a "construct" there is no compelling reason to limit human prerogatives in exploiting and dismantling it, or thoughtlessly genetically modifying any organism we feel like, they have begun to lose themselves in the self-referential hall of mirrors of disembodied intellect. I understand that new ways of looking and new movements of the previously excluded must be excessive in their early stages, and that is as it must inevitably be. But some of these debates are now ready for more fluid, creative thinking, or at least need to be tempered to the extent they hinder any hope of political cooperation between potential allies on many crucial questions. If American left intellectuals want to play a role in real political struggles they will need to rediscover some common sense and some sense of connection to the life of flesh and blood and water and air and dirt outside their "texts."

I hate to use a military analogy, but if the Swiss citizens' army can bring together people from different cantons, ethnicities and linguistic groups, who are free to squabble and mock and disdain each other the rest of the time, into a very efficient force ready to defend their valleys and lakes, we should certainly be able to tone down our internecine tiffs enough to mount some kind of common defense of our own rivers and forests and atmosphere and rights and livelihoods (and yes, you nit-pickers, I know the Swiss are helped by having some one-third of the world's capital, a lot of it of dubious origin, in their banks, but that wasn't the point of the analogy).

Remediating Utopian/Pragmatic Tensions

One very important factor in our divisions and confusions is our lack of clarity about the mix of utopian and pragmatic elements both in our own personal political beliefs and in our movements. As I discussed in an earlier section, all political ideologies combine some aspects of both these poles, but very few of us ever attempt to analyze the dynamic relationship between them. Some sectors of the political landscape are easy to categorize. There are always certain, usually somewhat marginal, political and cultural groups that specialize in promoting obviously utopian ideas or practices, even though at certain unusual historical moments some of these can become very influential and can even grow and mutate into mainstream tendencies. In fact, nearly all of the most important movements in history began as utopian religious or political cults, though for each one that achieves such prominence, thousands of others remain marginal or disappear.

There are all kinds of utopians, right, left and inter-galactic, but the left has historically been a particularly fertile spawning ground and nesting place for them. In any case they are without question an important, if on occasion dangerous, part of the political landscape and a vital source of new ideas. And of course pragmatists involved in the world of electoral and bureaucratic jousting form the mainstream of political life. But a great deal of that life falls somewhere between these obvious poles, and even pragmatists have dreams (and illusions). In fact, nearly all of us have a stew of usually barely examined ideas and assumptions (many of them utopian or dystopian) that underlie our political belief systems.

In my view, this unexplored pragmatic/utopian tension is currently critical because it is being expressed in profound fractures on the left over how to confront the crises of modernity and globalization. On the left neo-Luddites and advocates of local economics form a sort of radical rejection front vis-à-vis globalization while the pragmatists argue globalization is inevitable so we must fight for a more humane version with more environmental and labor safeguards. In this case the sincere left pragmatists may also be dreaming because it's not at all clear globalization in an era dominated by immense transnational corporate empires and dizzyingly rapid capital flows can be made more humane. So far the evidence is that it is exacerbating poverty and worsening wealth disparities badly in the developing world, and to some extent even in the industrialized "North," where the middle class is rapidly losing ground. Most attempts to soften the effects of globalization have been fig leaves. But, while the radical critique may be largely on the mark (and valuable and worth pressing) their camp has no real practical solutions, just utopian alternative models of localized economies, which simply won't replace mega-business on any significant scale in the foreseeable future, barring the advent of a sci-fi post-apocalyptic landscape. An occasional country (such as, recently, Malaysia or Argentina) may resist the IMF on certain policies for a limited period, but at this point no country is in a position to fully escape the global economic architecture without facing a collapse of its currency and, most likely, its social order.

This is a puzzling conundrum: on globalization, the radicals' critique is largely on the money, but their solution is impossible (at least on a sufficient scale in the short to medium term). The "pragmatists" are actually being utopian in their analysis, but it might be better to at least have folks who really want to mitigate the most brutal outcomes of globalization in positions of influence than total social Darwinists, at least until a real shift in global trends might create some openings for other options. Again, I've been arguing this type of tension between radical critics and reformers is a given, but that it might be made to produce more beneficial results if both tendencies were more consciously willing to think of each other as competing, perhaps, but also symbiotic, and more interested in exploring how to enhance that symbiosis (beyond the usual "good cop" role the reformers can play when radicals play the heavies). Of course, it is often tough to decide who are genuine left pragmatists and who are corporate globalizers in sheep's clothing making promises that can't be kept. And I'm not at all advocating radical anti-globalizers stop their protests. Maintaining that pressure is vitally important in slowing down the momentum toward complete mega-corporate domination of the world economy.

In general, pragmatic/utopian positions are very hard to reconcile, and my goal in this book is not to pick sides. But I would like to suggest we try to be more creative and expansive in our thinking without necessarily having to change our core views or global analyses. Is there some way to make headway on at least those common goals we can all agree upon: preserving biodiversity and air and water quality, defending civil liberties and effective social spending programs, limiting the power of corporate elites, avoiding the most problematic military adventures, and so forth? Perhaps we can agree on some ground rules and develop some mechanisms of arbitration for intra-movement disputes during specific campaigns. And radicals should perhaps consider a two-pronged strategy: by all means continue to protest and offer pointed systemic critiques and support local alternatives, but also try to help create more space for sympathetic moderates in positions of influence to temper the ravages of globalization in the medium term.

If we can think of our broad movement as a diverse ecology of species that simultaneously cooperate and compete, but that we are all trying to make more symbiotically efficient and productive (at least for a limited time, to achieve specific goals), we might get better results. We can still find times and places to attempt to rip each other to shreds if we must, but perhaps more privately. And we could perhaps muster just enough discipline to work together on clearly targeted objectives. Let us attempt to find the most productive niche in the political ecosystem for our specific worldviews and skill-sets, and try at least to cut down on the number and the ferocity of our fights with our cousins, especially at those times when our squabbles will be most helpful to our real enemies.

Electoral Dilemmas

The same types of utopian/pragmatic divides and arguments are replicated in U.S. electoral politics over which candidate (if any) to support: the mainstream lesser of two evils, or one who is more closely aligned with our values even if his (and so far it's always a he) chances of victory are nil. And the question of how the left should relate to electoral politics is a particularly thorny one in the U.S. at the moment given the result of the 2000 election.

In a European-style parliamentary system, small party candidacies are far less problematic, as the success of the German Greens illustrates. Though, of course, participating in government brings inevitable compromises and often fractures idealistic movements. It is a bit surreal to see the 1960s street fighter Joschka Fischer now the most popular political figure in Germany, but he is an exceptional case. The democratic left is not accustomed to acceding to power. Nearly all its reflexes are geared to anti-authoritarian, oppositional political stances.

The labor and moderate socialist parties that have in recent decades come to power in many Western European nations have only done so because they moved far to the center. In fact, often, in this age of massive transfers of industrial and agricultural production to low-wage parts of the world and aging populations in Europe, left-leaning governments have felt compelled by global economic realities to push through unpopular measures such as pension cuts, privatizations and reductions in services normally associated with the right. They just try to do it less rabidly and a tad more humanely, if possible. The U.S. too is heading towards a fiscal train wreck with its social security system as the "baby boom" generation reaches retirement, but has not mustered the political will to tackle it.

The same phenomenon is occurring now in other parts of the world, including in Brazil with the government of Lula. While obviously far more progressive on most social questions than its predecessors and more aggressive in championing developing nations' interests vs. the "North," it is, predictably, moving to the center on economic issues and disappointing environmentalists by allowing giant soybean operations to supplant rainforest in parts of the Amazon, and by lifting bans on genetically modified crops. Lula is also sure to be unable to satisfy fully the demands of landless peasant movements. Some of this comes with the logic of governing any nation and being forced to balance competing power bases. We are now, tragically, all embedded in the global economic system, and no country can escape its trends, no matter how well intentioned its governing party of the moment.

The very process of actually getting in a realistic position to come to power electorally in a society with a large middle class will inevitably de-radicalize your politics. The alternative is to serve the function of eternal opposition. And that is certainly a valuable social role. In fact, a vital political ecosystem should always include ideally incorruptible, intelligent utopians who point out the dubiousness of each compromise and keep pointing the way to more perfected moral states. But the best outcome for the left, given the realities of the *rapport de forces* as they stand at the present, might be if we can keep alive a dynamic ecosystem that includes decent left-pragmatists who are able to make some inroads into ruling institutions and can at least mitigate the harm the economic elites can do, and lively utopians who can keep more exalted models alive.

Again, I know I'm beating a dead horse, but the trick to making it work at all is that these various tendencies have somehow to understand that they feed off each other, rather than to incessantly devour each other. It might not be possible though, because even entertaining this sort of ecosystemic view would, especially for many utopians, already constitute an apostasy. And, again, I'm not advocating that radicals roll over. If I were a Brazilian environmentalist I would vigorously oppose the Lula administration's policies on GMOs and lackluster forest protection, for example, but it is also the first left-leaning government there in recent memory.

In any case, especially in light of the rigid two-party system here in the U.S., an over-emphasis on electoral politics may not be the wisest course for more radical American progressives. Concentrating on core issues and specific goals often makes more sense. Tightly focused campaigns such as the Rainforest Action Network's ultimately successful intense pressuring of Mitsubishi, then Home Depot, and then Boise Cascade, all corporate giants and major lumber users, to pledge to stop using old-growth forest wood (and then, most recently, Citigroup to stop funding such projects) can succeed whoever is in power, to cite only one example.

There is, as we have seen, far more chance in the U.S. for a disgruntled right-leaning populist party or figure to get over ten or twenty percent of the national vote than any authentic left-progressive candidate. The base of support for an authentically anti mega-corporation, anti-imperial left candidate is just too thin in the U.S. And even though vanilla environmentalism enjoys much mainstream support (at least as an abstract concept), very few Americans vote for candidates based on their environmental records, and only an extraordinarily horrific eco-catastrophe would alter that.

The most liberal wings of the Democratic Party share some aspects of a progressive agenda, but no candidate who is genuinely concerned with reining in corporate power in a way that would begin to satisfy radicals, or who is unwilling to enforce U.S. military/mercantile hegemony (even if more discreetly) could accede to power or survive long if, by some miracle, he or she did. This won't change in the foreseeable future, barring a massive economic crisis; and even then, the most one could realistically hope for would be that a Rooseveltian figure would emerge to rescue capitalism from its own excesses and rein in the plutocracy, rather than some form of authoritarian right faux-populist. The U.S. is, as I have been arguing, still at its heart, a very conservative nation. There are periods during which more liberal, reformist movements come to the fore, but that usually requires a dire economic situation or a major crisis of institutions, and periods of reaction inevitably follow.

The reality is that conservative business-elite governments are the norm, the "default setting" of U.S. politics. Occasional bursts of reform break through only when the wealth pyramid becomes too dramatically skewed for anyone to ignore, and/or the system has hit some other historical impasse. I don't think the current Bush administration is the norm either. It's the deepest some far right elements have come into the governing elites in the history of the modern U.S., but even when the winds shift and a less hard-right or even more "liberal" administration takes over, it's very unlikely ever to create a political Eden for left-progressives. That said, I would certainly breathe a sigh of relief at even a small turn away from the very dangerous cliques in power at the moment.

Local politics are of course another affair, and there is no reason not to run candidates for office in some small or mid-sized municipalities that have large eco-left constituencies. And if some progressives do decide to launch national third-party electoral efforts, I would at least recommend that they take a page from European left coalitions and attempt to cooperate with left-leaning Democrats race by race. In a parliamentary system there are usually two rounds in an election, with a slew of candidates in the first round and the top vote-getters in a run-off. In European socialist-green coalitions, the top vote-getter on the left in the first round gets all the support of both parties (or more if it's a multi-party coalition) in the second round. This is not possible in the U.S. obviously, but polls could replace first rounds. If polls indicate an election is very close and a divided progressive vote will bring in a right-wing candidate, the left could close ranks behind the most likely left-leaning candidate by a certain date. In that sense it is unfair to blame only the Naderites for Gore's defeat in 2000. The Democrats could have attempted to make more aggressive overtures to the Nader campaign as well, and tried to work out state-by-state tactical agreements.

The Democratic Party is a corrupt and dysfunctional entity, but it is still, at times, the only last-ditch, leaky and precarious dyke that can be used to slow down the assault of the hard right. In any case, a serious attempt to forge a new national political party is one thing, but casting a vote as a form of symbolic protest seems a bit pointless (unless it's truly an artful Dadaist act, as voting for Jello Biafra or Sister Boom-Boom in San Francisco might arguably have been). And, in my view, while I wish it weren't true, an authentic left-progressive party is not a realistic vehicle to accrue increased leverage, let alone accede to power at this stage of U.S. political history.

What is possible, however, is that at some point an angry populist movement could, under the right conditions, gain a great deal of traction, and such a movement would most likely combine right and left, libertarian and anti-corporate elements. If such a movement avoided the racist pitfalls of many previous populist episodes, people on the left would then have to decide how to relate to such a hybrid. And, given the historical decline of the left in the current post Cold War period of savage economic globalization, finding some common ground with disenchanted sectors of the right may be the only way the fractured left can at least slow the rapid advance of corporate capital's global hegemony.

Notes

NEGOTIATING OUR DIVISIONS

For a defense of Spinoza in his disagreement with Descartes over the role of emotions in the light of modern neurology, see *Looking for Spinoza: Joy, Sorrow, and the Feeling Brain* (Harcourt, 2003) by Dr. Antonio Damasio.

For recent political commentary from the philosophers Jacques Derrida and Jurgen Habermas, see *Philosophy in a Time of Terror: Dialogues with Jurgen Habermas and Jacques Derrida* by Giovanna Borradori (University of Chicago, 2003).

REMEDIATING UTOPIAN/PRAGMATIC TENSIONS

For a piece on the "Lula" administration's pro soybean mega-farm land policies in the Amazon, see "Relentless Foe of the Amazon Jungle: Soybeans" by Larry Rohter in the *New York Times* of September 17, 2003.

The 1982 mayoral run of Sister Boom-Boom, a transvestite activist with the Sisters of Perpetual Indulgence collective, which garnered 23,121 votes (more than the Republican candidate) led the San Francisco Board of Supervisors to outlaw unorthodox names from the ballot. Coming on the heels of punk rocker Jello Biafra's famous run, the city fathers feared the Dada factor could overwhelm the local electoral process.

Tactics and Strategy

Right/Left Coalitions

I have argued in this book that right/left divides are not irrelevant but are only one lens through which to attempt to interpret political reality. Recently, on many important questions such as civil liberties and privacy, soft drug decriminalization, corporate control of media, and even globalization and some military interventions, we have seen ad hoc coalitions of groups on the far right and far left of the spectrum (by U.S. mainstream political standards) attempting to stanch initiatives nearly the entire center supported. These have been mostly defensive tactical alliances that are reacting to what they perceive as sudden, dangerous power grabs by government or powerful business interests. The American Civil Liberties Union (ACLU) worked with ultra right political figures with libertarian streaks such as Bob Barr, Dick Armey and Grover Norquist to attempt to resist the post 9/11 rush to give the government sweeping new powers to spy and detain citizens, for example.

A similar coalition (including the far right National Rifle Association!) sprang up out of a groundswell of opposition to new Federal Communications Commission (FCC) rules allowing large media conglomerates' further expansion. Groups that are out of the mainstream on both sides of the spectrum are afraid of being frozen out of media access by a mono-tonal money machine that eschews all controversy and flattens out local and regional differences. The last progressive TV journalist with national gravitas, Bill Moyers, has been, on occasion, featuring voices from the right on these issues on his admirable program, "NOW." Some fiscal conservatives and economic libertarian groups (such as the Cato Institute) are as opposed to "corporate welfare" as many of us on the left. Traditionally, nativist and isolationist wings of the right, as exemplified by a figure such as Pat Buchanan, are often far more skeptical of military adventures than many liberals. And the foes of globalization include a broad range of opinion, from traditional nationalist and culturally conservative rightists to left syndicalists, indigenous peasants and radical environmentalists.

These types of "nightmare coalitions" are very important because the left is weak and divided. In periods of retreat it is imperative at least to slow the enemy's advance until one can regroup one's forces; and finding as many allies as possible (even among other virulent enemies who happen also to be your main adversary-of-the-moment's enemies) might just help keep you alive to fight another day. This can be fraught with risks, however. Some lines have to be drawn. Even a limited association with out and out neo-fascists or racists or fanatical anti-modernists will taint your political future. And most of these alliances have to be very narrowly focused, because the groups involved are for the most part poles apart on nearly all other issues, and can have a joint press conference one day and be viciously attacking each other on another topic the next day. But, still, on a number of crucial issues the centrist, liberal left has simply been AWOL, and the only potential allies are on the right.

Drug War Politics

The "War on Drugs" is one of the most fiscally and morally destructive, wasteful, counter-productive and corrosive policies in human history. It costs billions, erodes civil liberties, destroys millions of lives, including especially those of young blacks and Hispanics here, and of whole indigenous and mestizo populations in regions of Latin America, and serves no purpose but to feed immense international organized crime networks and equally bloated police bureaucracies. There have actually been more noteworthy voices among right and libertarian political figures than among liberals proposing some forms of decriminalization. Pusillanimous Democrats, terrified of any residual politically poisonous association with the counterculture, are unwilling to risk any political capital to remedy this ongoing catastrophe, allowing some non-violent drug offenders to serve longer terms than murderers. Despite the heroic work of Ethan Nadelmann and the Drug Policy Alliance, and its courageous funding by the philanthropist George Soros and a few others, this issue is almost never even raised in national politics. It offers another depressing but fascinating example of U.S. exceptionalism. Nearly all of Western Europe and Canada are gravitating to saner positions on this question, but a rigidly anti-ecstatic puritanical moralism is still a very potent force in American life.

An argument could be made that in the long run it might be worth considering, if such an opportunity arose, supporting a candidate on the right who was sincerely willing to take on this issue on fiscal grounds, even if that politician were anathema to us on other issues. This war is so socially harmful, politically painful trade-offs might be worth entertaining to try to end it. But these are the types of very tough, realpolitik questions we will have to face, issue by issue. In real politics just pushing for your entire agenda incessantly will get you nowhere (unless you're part of a coalition that has assumed power, in which case it's sometimes, and only sometimes, smart to try to push through as much as you can before the winds change). But utopians are, by definition, unable to countenance this type of political horse-trading, and the left is, for better or worse, the part of the political spectrum most colored by utopian aspirations, so I'm not sure it will be able to muster the type of hard-boiled narrow focus it would take to tackle a question as thorny as the War on Drugs.

Brave New World

An emerging issue with immense potential implications is whether our society will allow the genetic enhancement of human beings. This debate to date over genetics in the human realm has mostly been a confusing one over cloning and stem-cell research, but the real core question is whether we will become a technologically eugenic species. There are a handful of critics on the left who are very concerned about the potential dangers of exacerbating social stratification with a sort of consumer-driven eugenics if the well-to-do were able to enhance their children with extra features and advantages, and about the ethical conundrums posed by the utilitarian view of humans implicit therein. So far their only allies are a few religious leaders worried about yet further human hubris in seeking to control every aspect of creation, some holistic biologists worried about radically monkeying with hereditary traits we don't understand; and those few ecologists and environmentalists who realize that if this type of eugenics in the human realm is permitted they will have no ideological leg to stand on to oppose the wholesale genetic alteration of plants and animals.

The bulk of the left and the center is reflexively pro-science and "progress," and the bulk of the religious right with its abortion obsession won't get worked up unless embryos or blastocysts are being terminated, and libertarians tend to view the issue as parents' rights to do what they want with their offspring. So, on an issue which could ultimately be far more determinant of the future shape of the entire species than any other save perhaps nuclear annihilation or biospheric collapse, only a so far tiny, very disparate band of right and left, religious and secular communitarian ethicists is desperately trying to start a debate, and failing badly in the midst of the techno-utopian enthusiasm that may be one of America's most defining traits. Though I suspect it is pointless, I urge more liberals and leftists (and everyone else) to look at this question far more closely, as we are very likely about to cross a genetic Rubicon into a post-human future even sci-fi geeks may wind up being freaked out by.

Secular/Spiritual Reconciliation

I have argued that though progressive religious groups have played a major role in nearly every important social justice movement from Abolitionism to the present, the tone of the left is generally aggressively secular, an inheritance from the militant (and, at the time, very understandable) anti-clericalism of the Enlightenment. There has been a lot of improvement in this area. In the U.S. and many other parts of the world, religious constituencies are just too vast not to be taken into account. The environmental movement, which had all but ignored religious groups until fairly recently, has been actively seeking to work with many denominations. Paul Gorman of the National Religious Partnership for the Environment has been a key figure in this effort, as have Carl Pope of the Sierra Club, and religious leaders as varied as Patriarch Bartholomew of the Eastern Orthodox church and the Dalai Lama. Theologians and scholars in nearly every spiritual tradition have been re-examining their texts and traditions with a "green" lens, a phenomenon well documented by the "Religions of the World and Ecology" conferences and book series put together by the Harvard Divinity School.

In the past religious hierarchies were often closely tied to oppressive feudal and later capitalist and authoritarian social structures, and were a logical target of the left. This is far less true on a systematic basis today when amoral corporate materialism poses far more of a threat to the biosphere and human life than any religion. And there have always been rebellious egalitarian religious movements. Furthermore, the landscape of religious movements is as complex and varied as the political spectrum and runs the gamut from arch-reactionary to radically revolutionary tendencies—from Opus Dei to the martyred Archbishop Romero and liberation theologists among Catholics; from ultra-right Japanese Zen militarists to anti-nuclear pacifists among Buddhists, and so forth. And because nearly every religious tradition emphasizes concern for the poor and compassion, liberal churches have often been the most solid and consistent resisters of economic inequities, and the main opponents of military adventurism.

Some eco-thinkers have laid the blame for our anti-nature attitudes on anthropocentric Judeo-Christian teachings, but while there may be some merit in this argument, it is an oversimplification. Religious traditions can be read and reinterpreted in any number of ways. These debates are interesting and thinkers should of course argue to their hearts' content, but on the level of practical activism, our situation is too desperate for us to be wasting energy in theological nitpicking. Anyway, many forms of secular leftism are quasi theologies, and many eco-activists, myself included, are closet pantheists or at least nature Romantics whose passion could easily be described as spiritual. And whether we want to ensure that we have vital and robust ecosystems for utilitarian reasons or because they are God's creations or because we experience a unique rapture in wild places, let us just agree to focus on tangible ways to fight to prevent their degradation and annihilation and to try to build a sustainable civilization.

Building Other Untraditional Alliances

I keep returning to coalitions, because my reading of our situation is admittedly pessimistic but I'm trying to be a constructive pessimist. Naïve optimism can be far more dangerous because if you overestimate your power and chances of success, you won't take appropriate measures to compensate for your weaknesses, and you'll be far more likely to be picked off and fail. Recently there have been a number of incipient initiatives to bring together groups that were historically at each other's throats to face an immediate problem.

One small example of this is environmentalists and wildlife biologists in the arid western U.S. who have long been battling publicly subsidized cattle grazing on federal land, often a major cause of the degradation of riparian areas and habitat for wild species. In recent years, though, the dizzyingly rapid loss of open spaces and the spread of sprawl and subdivisions throughout the West has become an even more pressing problem. Neither environmentalists nor ranchers want the West completely converted to malls and suburbs, so some of these historical enemies are increasingly finding they might need each other. A flawed ranch might harm wildlife; a mall precludes its very existence. New initiatives to begin buying out ranchers' public land grazing allotments are also arousing interest in both camps. Many of these ranchers are suffering financially and want out of the business anyway.

Meanwhile, pioneering figures such as the watershed expert, polymath genius and wildlife biologist Peter Warshall, Dan Dagget of the Quivira Coalition, and Dave Foreman, co-founder of the Wildlands Project, have been working with ranchers who are willing to reform their grazing practices to look for creative strategies of all kinds to preserve open land and biodiversity. These are not easy alliances. They only involve a few pioneers to date. Most environmentalists and ranchers remain highly skeptical. But it's a model of the types of unusual alliances we will need to build and nurture to slow the devastating onslaught of uncontrolled, shortsighted greed and cornucopianism which will cover our world in golf courses, cement and genetically-altered luminescent landscaping, if we don't put up ferocious and very sophisticated resistance.

Environmentalists have reached out to hunters' groups at times, a very big constituency. Again both groups value open space and wildlands though they can fiercely disagree about predators, off road vehicles and other questions (including gun laws), and animal rights groups obviously view these alliances with horror. But again, sometimes it's better to accept flawed wildlands management in an area if the alternative is the total loss of that wildland. Fishermen's organizations have been key allies to environmentalists, from the battle over Storm King Mountain on the Hudson in the 1960s to current salmon wars and the heroic shrimper Diane Wilson's legendary battles against polluting plants on the Gulf of Mexico. But commercial fishermen are also often our bitter enemies as they oppose limiting their catch or using turtle excluder devices and insist on using destructive drag lines, and so forth, and ocean fisheries are nearly all radically declining or collapsing. Eco-politics are not easy. We wind up being allied with groups at certain times and having to fight them at others. We have to be flexible, and there have been a wide range of unusual alliances, but more concerted efforts to build larger fronts of groups that could be brought to agree on some common broad platforms or positions would be a good idea—as would the development of mechanisms or institutions to mediate in internecine disputes within progressive movements. But that takes us beyond the primarily defensive tactical ad-hoc alliances I've been describing into the realm of longer-term strategy.

Notes

TACTICS AND STRATEGIES

There has been a lot of coverage of the "strange bedfellow" civil liberties-conscious left and libertarian, authority-fearing right coalitions that have emerged to challenge aspects of the post 9/11 "USA Patriot Act," which radically enhanced federal police powers and FCC regulations that would have favored large media conglomerates' expanded ownership of radio stations. See, for example: "Ideologically Broad Coalition Assails FCC Media Plan" by Stephen Labaton in the May 28, 2003 *New York Times*. Prominent hard right political figures involved in these efforts included former Georgia congressman Bob Barr and former Republican congressional majority leader Dick Armey as well as the National Rifle Association (NRA).

DRUG WAR POLITICS

For more on the admirable Drug Policy Alliance and its leader, Ethan Nadelmann, www.drugpolicy.org

SECULAR/SPIRITUAL RECONCILIATION

About Paul Gorman's work, see "Genesis of a Movement: Paul Gorman's quest for a whole-earth religion" by Trebbe Johnson in the spring 1997 *Amicus Journal*. For more on Patriarch Bartholomew, "To have dominion in the earth: The Green Patriarch, head of the Orthodox Church, preaches the doctrine of environmentalism" by Melba Newsome in the Winter 1999 *Amicus Journal*.

For more on secular/spiritual alliances in the environmental movement see "Reaching Beyond Ourselves: It's time to recognize our allies in the faith community" by Carl Pope in the November/December 1998 *Sierra*; and, in that same issue of *Sierra*, "The Second Creation Story: Redefining the bond between religion and ecology" by Trebbe Johnson. See also the entire issue of *Whole Earth*, winter 1997 ("Special Issue: The Earth in Crisis: Religion's New Test of Faith"); and *Wild Earth*, fall 1996 ("Religion and Biodiversity").

For info on the "Religion and Ecology" conferences and the Harvard University Press "Religions of the World and Ecology" book series that emerged from them, see www.hup.harvard.edu/

Opus Dei (Latin for "God's Work") is a somewhat shadowy, secretive, very strict, ultra-conservative lay Roman Catholic organization founded in 1928 by St. Josemaría Escrivá, a Spanish priest. It has ties to rightist movements and its adherents are said to practice self-flagellation.

Archbishop Romero was killed at the altar in 1980 by a right-wing death-squad during the conflict in El Salvador. He has become a legendary figure for many left-leaning Catholic social justice advocates.

BUILDING OTHER UNTRADITIONAL ALLIANCES

For one view of the need for cooperation between environmentalists and ranchers, see Dagget, Dan. *Beyond the Rangeland Conflict: toward a West that works* (Gibbs Smith/Grand Canyon Trust, 1995). See also "Reform on the Range" by Mark Blaine (*Forest* magazine, Fall 2003).

Dave Foreman, one of the founders of the radical group Earth First!, has more recently worked with some of America's most eminent wildlife biologists, including Michael Soulé and Reed Noss, in the Wildlands Project and its journal *Wild Earth*, of which he is the publisher. He is the author or co-author of many books including *Ecodefense*, and *Defending the Earth, Confessions of an Eco-Warrior.*

Diane Wilson is an extraordinary activist: a shrimp-boat captain from Seadrift, Texas, with five children and little formal education who, sometimes alone, took on giant corporate polluters in the Gulf of Mexico with dramatic acts of civil disobedience.

Thinking Strategically:
Vision and Action

Wise defensive tactics are essential to slow your opponents' advance and to prevent them from consolidating their gains so totally that rolling them back later will be impossible. But to increase the chances that you can one day pass to the offensive, and that when you do you will be poised to make substantive progress in advancing your agenda, intelligent strategic planning and development are crucial. This is where the U.S. right excelled with its creation of networks of think tanks and its development of innovative communications methods starting in the late 1960s. We on the left will not be able to match the financial resources available to the institutions of the right, as they are closely tied to business elites whose interests they largely advance. Centrist to moderate Democrats are just starting to regroup and take a page from the right, to create their own more aggressive think tanks (such as John Podesta's new American Majority Institute) and even media outlets, and some of these people can raise cash from certain sectors of the economy where there are some mon-eyed liberals (entertainment, high-tech, trial lawyers, and so forth), but their efforts are unlikely to match those of the right. Meanwhile more radical progressives will have to make up in imagination what they will lack in funding, not unlike independent filmmakers.

Strategic thinking and language needs to be bolder and more visionary than tactical discourse. A strategic approach needs to be more tenacious, to point to a desired goal, to stay on message and keep on pushing because it is trying to create long-term momentum. Tactical battles require more compromise, more ability to change tack. But the purpose of strategic vision is to push the envelope and to provide inspiring models of what is possible that will over time prove to be attractors of energy. Far too often left/progressives don't understand the difference between these two modes of engagement. Radicals are also very often notoriously unwilling to put any parts of their agendas on the back burner to focus on specific outcomes.

There is also a whole sector of "new-age" and hipster-artist types and cyber-psychedelic enthusiasts of various stripes who constitute a not insignificant portion of those with eco-left worldviews, but many of these folks tend to be enamored of fuzzy, mythic visions of a coming green utopia, and are also simultaneously, conversely and ironically, prone to paranoid conspiracy theories. To a mainstream reader these people may sound farcical, and one might wonder why I even mention them, but actually they are an important sub-cultural stratum from which many interesting and influential ideas and inventions have sprung. They include major figures in the computing elites, in the arts, and the like, and they are no weirder than other American subcultures from Pentecostals to NASCAR afficionados to ballerinas to rappers to bikers. That said, while many of the mytho-poetic visions that emanate from this part of the culture can be creative or harmless or entertaining, some of them can also dissipate resources and energy that more rigorous initiatives could desperately use.

Strategic initiatives require institutions. Given American political realities, my view is that we could use a range of think-tanks or groups with very focused, specific goals, i.e., drug policy reform; sweeping wildlands policy changes; a radical shift to "alternative energy" and benign, non-toxic technologies; a rethinking of globalization; a multi-polar rather than imperial foreign policy; a less skewed wealth pyramid; reining in corporate domination of political life; studying the right; and so forth. There are already a number of worthy organizations working on these and other issues, but they need more support, and the better the coordination and harmonization of the efforts of groups working in specific areas, the better the chances of not wasting precious resources and dissipating energy. The think-tanks that do exist on the left tend to be quite small, under-funded, not well integrated into the whole left/progressive ecosystem (let alone the larger political landscape), and often a little too culty or under the sway of one or a handful of frequently inflexible founders.

Groups that have a broader, over-arching social vision, if it's a compelling one, also serve a vital function. They can inspire people with models of what a more desirable world would look like, and that is exceedingly important, as far too often we are so busy desperately playing defense and criticizing the powers that be that we fail to articulate what we are *for*. We would do well to be bolder and more willing to take on, in a very tangible way, the aesthetic/cultural dimensions of life. What type of society do we want? Do we have any say over its shape, over what our towns and farms and forests will look like? What if we want more small shops and farms and fewer chain stores and industrial ag operations, less traffic in our cities, and more open space and parks and wildlands? Why would those things be unattainable or out of our control?

We are told in one breath the "invisible hand" of the economy makes the loss of manufacturing jobs, the malling, the Wal-Marting, and the fast-fooding of the world impossible to halt, as though zoning and trade policy were forces of nature, outside of human control. And in the next breath we are told we are the greatest people in the history of the world who can achieve whatever we set our minds to. We can send people to the Moon, decode the human genome, and (supposedly) bring "democracy" to the Middle East, but deciding what we want our buildings, daily lives, our communities and our environment to look like is simply impossible. Those who raise these types of issues are accused of elitism, but this hollow charge shouldn't frighten anyone. Giant farms and fast-food corporations are good at cloaking themselves in a populist mantle, but behind those smokescreens they make juicy targets. These cultural/aesthetic questions are vital, so groups that take on this broader panorama of issues, if they do it deftly, are playing a crucial role in the ecosystem of resistance. It is not just "elitists" who are upset at the growing sterility of the landscape and global aesthetic homogenization.

But, nonetheless, to achieve concrete results in the political, as opposed to the cultural, sphere, narrowly targeted campaigns are required. There are many people who might support a radical change in environmental policies but not drug decriminalization or a reduction in the military budget; or those who might support some drug policy reforms but who also support large corporations and an imperial foreign policy; or those who oppose foreign military interventions but don't want any increases in peaceful foreign aid either. Since my analysis is that authentic eco-left/progressives are, and will remain for a long time, an occasionally influential but ultimately small minority in U.S. politics, the best way for us to achieve what we view as desirable socio-political outcomes is to build coalitions around very specific objectives and to garner as much support for each objective, separately, as possible. If we insist everyone should agree with all our positions, we will all be left standing alone in separate rooms.

This requires a type of a-la-carte segmentation that goes against the grain for many radical lefties who are attached to their entire menu of positions. It is rare, for example, to attend an anti-war demonstration without being subjected to a torrent of speakers reciting a long laundry-list litany of their pet issues (usually with self-righteous rage), which, even if some of us agree with some of them, invariably irritate, alienate and confuse the masses of more mainstream folk present—whose support is, obviously, the most crucial. If we can't muster the discipline to cordon off our various political desires from each other and to work with a wide range of groups across political divides on precise topics, we won't accomplish very much.

To revitalize the left/progressive/enviro-ecosystem we need to be both, as an internal martial artist or be-bop musician would understand, more disciplined and more fluid. We have to find ways to divide labor and to pick those focused niches where we can, as individuals or groups, do the most good. When useful we can come together in broad coalitions. Conversely we should stay out of each other's way when appropriate. We need to strengthen the worthy institutions already up and running and try to avoid redundancies. On the drug front, for example, it seems to me that the Drug Policy Alliance is an admirable vehicle that could serve as a primary coordinator or core intellectual resource for efforts in that sphere. On the environmental front, which is a much vaster landscape of myriad large and small groups, better inter-group coordination, more aggressive horse-trading and outreach to non-traditional potential allies, and perhaps some broad, simple and clear platforms most groups could agree upon on specific issues could perhaps help build national momentum to reform policies on clean water, air and wildland protection. Again, the radicals can remain radical, the moderates moderate, if they can all remember that despite ideally healthy internal tensions, we're all part of a large front that wants to move forward, rather than tribes of rabid self-devouring Hobbesian cannibals.

Building Visionary Attractors

Tactical battles include retreats and compromises that inevitably come with the territory, but in formulating long-term strategic targets one can be daring in delineating the ultimate goal. The idea is to articulate a clear vision of what we're working toward and then to seek to plot out a bold but realistic and grounded (pardon the expression) "road map" in order to get there. One example of a visionary strategic effort is that of the small conservation biology organization, The Wildlands Project, which is advocating connecting as many of the isolated "islands" of wildlife habitat as possible with green "corridors" and animal-friendly road crossings, through land purchases, easements, government policy at all levels, and the like, so the North American landscape can be "re-wilded." This vision of ultimately linking the continent's wildlands from Mexico to the Yukon, Baja California to the Bering Sea and Florida to Newfoundland and the Hudson Bay is a seemingly utopian idea, but it stands on solid scientific and spiritual/aesthetic ground and is the type of bold, inspiring, large yet very focused vision that can resonate in the public imagination.

Though a lot of the attention of conservationists is usually focused on the extensive public lands of the West, the Northeast is a region where, for a variety of largely accidental historical reasons and the vision of some nineteenth and early twentieth century patrician preservationists, forests have begun to rebound. Many species from wild turkeys to moose are returning to wider swaths of their traditional ranges, and the attainment of a balance between a huge human population and vibrant and connected, restored wildlands is actually imaginable and attainable. And a few groups are starting to advance this vision. But somehow connecting the woods of Quebec and Ontario with Baxter State Park in Maine; the Green Mountains of Vermont and the Whites in New Hampshire; the Adirondacks, Catskills and Berkshires; the Massachusetts to New Jersey Highlands; and even perhaps the Alleghenies and, later, the Southern Appalachians; and bringing back wolves; while not impossible, will run up against immense human population pressures. Still, it is an extraordinarily inspiring and hopeful possibility that is worth the enormous collective effort it would require to midwife.

A region that included one of the densest and most urbanized human populations on the planet and immense, connected swaths of healthy forest and plentiful and diverse wildlife would be an incredibly hopeful model to offer the rest of the world. Throw in a sustained transition to benign technologies and energy sources; anti-sprawl and open-space preservation initiatives; pesticide phase-outs; more urban parks and "fresh air programs" for inner-city youth; stricter air and water quality laws, support to preserve small farmers; further boost farmers' markets and CSAs; and encourage sustainable wood-lot operations, specialty furniture makers, and so forth; and, over time, the Hudson River and Connecticut River valleys and the whole east of North America could be transformed into a sort of Ecotopia.

Of course, this dream would require thousands of aggressive campaigns throughout the region; private and public initiatives of all types at local, county, state, regional and federal and international levels; thousands of land conservancy and easement negotiations; academic conferences; protests and ballot initiatives. But only an over-arching vision can create the attractor, the pull from the future that can inspire the type of massive efforts from countless people over several generations that could bring this type of scenario (in some form) into being.

Besides a great, inspiring, even intoxicating idea, a sweeping vision of this type generally requires a few key, passionate, charismatic figures who devote their entire lives to convincing a wide range of people that the dream is within reach. And it requires behind them a core group of nimble and egoless organizers who can act as tireless unseen architects, harmonizers, coordinators, diplomats, cheerleaders and therapists. We need the bold visions to inspire us, but we also need the wisdom of sages, the savvy of street fighters, the patience of saints, the resilience to survive repeated crushing disappointments, and a firm grasp of the reality principle. And since no one can contain all those qualities, it is best to each find our most productive niche. Unfortunately too often street-fighters think they are philosophers and vice-versa, so attempts at honest self-evaluation should be pre-requisites for activists, but lucky and rare is the movement in which the right people find the right place to best express their gifts.

Another example of a nascent impulse with an inspiring and compelling vision is what some are calling the "Ecological Medicine" movement. This movement posits that, given the incessant onslaught and build-up of new chemicals and pollutants (which now turn up in everyone's blood and tissues all over the earth), contemporary medicine cannot ignore environmental health as a key factor in the health of individuals. Pioneered by groups such as the Healthcare Without Harm coalition and individuals such as the brilliant thinker on science and law, Carolyn Raffensperger, as well as medical figures such as pediatricians Drs. Philip Landrigan and Mike McCally at Mount Sinai in New York and Ted Schettler in Boston, this movement engages a wide range of core philosophical/ethical/legal issues, including the "Precautionary Principle," the rights of children to be born free of toxins; and racism and class discrimination (the placement of the most toxic facilities in poor communities, especially minority ones, i.e., the "environmental justice" movement). Tactically it encompasses anti-corporate activism; lawsuits; legislative initiatives; direct action protests; and the substitution of polluting technologies with more benign alternatives.

Obviously this covers a lot of ground, and encompasses many people working in very different places in radically different milieus to whom it is not always apparent that they are directly linked to the other struggles—and there is no way or reason to attempt to unify fully such varied initiatives. But the realization that all their efforts are part of a new paradigm, of new ways of looking at human health's relationship to the environment's health, of assigning responsibility for toxic technologies' impacts, and of designing the whole human enterprise, can be a powerful boost to their various projects. This is a very young, still inchoate movement, but it has enormous potential to galvanize opinion because, in a society plagued by cancer and autoimmune disease epidemics, it strikes very close to the bone of self-interest. When people hear that no mother's milk on the planet is free of traces of hundreds of novel chemicals with unknown long-term effects, they begin to take notice.

But this movement too will need far more communication between its very disparate wings. Healthcare Without Harm has been a very good model for that type of coordination and coalition building. Its chosen mission was to reform the medical system's own toxic habits (a not inconsiderable source of mercury and other toxins in its incineration of PVC IV tubing, in mercury thermometers, and so forth), an area in which it has had admirable success. A larger "Ecological Medicine" movement will need core groups to provide broader coordination and some even more daring, sweeping visions such as the idea of a "Marshall Plan" to substitute toxic technologies with more benign ones. This could be a powerful, mythic attractor. Americans are enamored of technological innovation, and many young idealists are passionate about the environment. The idea of a collective, society-wide effort to transform our technologies and lead the world to a more enlightened "green" future, if promoted cleverly, could inspire a new generation of youth the way the space program and the Peace Corps and the Civil Rights movement did in the 1960s. Instead of seeming to be Luddite scolds, we could attempt to harness the very powerful techno-utopian and idealistic strains in American culture and canalize them in less destructive pathways. Obviously, there would be a lot of potential for "green washing" and cynical corporate behavior as well as government corruption in such programs, but that's no reason not to try such a tack.

These are just a few examples of nascent, visionary ideas that have great potential to become deeply influential because they deal with very tangible, concrete areas of life that are viscerally important to people—health, air, water, forests and streams—and offer mythic, inspiring solutions to dire problems. There are quite a few other movements I could mention, from anti-globalization to organic farming, but how successful any of them will ultimately be will depend to a large extent on how effectively their essence can be communicated to the public in the face of vicious counter-attacks and sly disinformation campaigns by vested interests.

Notes

THINKING STRATEGICALLY

For an article on former Clinton chief-of-staff John Podesta's attempt to create a Democratic think tank, see "Democrats, Seeing Dominance of Conservatives' Message, Form Group to Fight It" by Katharine Q. Seelye in the *New York Times*, June 5, 2003.

The Heinrich Boll Foundation (a think-tank affiliated with the German Green Party) has done interesting work looking at how policy can be formulated so that potentially destabilizing new technologies can be put to benign uses. See, for example "The Good Life: New technologies in the service of human and natural development" (www.boell.org).

For more on Wal-Mart's devastating impact, see: Quinn, Bill. *How Wal-Mart is Destroying America (and the World) and What You Can Do About It* (Ten Speed Press, 2000); and "Stores Follow Wal-Mart's Lead in Labor," by Greg Schneider and Dina ElBoghdady in the *Washington Post*, November 6, 2003; Greenhouse, Steven. "Illegally In U.S., And Never a Day Off At Wal-Mart" in *The New York Times*, November 5, 2003; Harold Meyerson, "Wal-Mart Nation" in *The American Prospect* vol. 15 no. 1, January 1, 2004; and a segment on the show *Now with Bill Moyers* on PBS: "Wal-Mart and the World" shown December 19, 2003. See also http://www.walmartwatch.com/wal/

BUILDING VISIONARY ATTRACTORS

For more on the visionary idea of "re-wilding" more of the Northeast U.S. and creating wildlife corridors between the existing "islands" of wildlands to recreate vibrant ecosystems in the midst of such high population density, see the inspiring *Wilderness Comes Home: Rewilding the Northeast* Christopher McGrory Klyza ed., (Middlebury College Press, 2001). Some recent related articles: "Group Buying Land to Link 2 Big Parks" by Debra West (*New York Times*, July 1, 2003); "A Wildlife Corridor, Green but Imperiled" by James Gorman (*New York Times*, July 8, 2003); "The Sierra Club and Environmental Allies Release Wild Highlands Map" in Winter 2002 *Sierra Atlantic*. Quite a few groups are working in this area, including the Vermont-based, Forest Watch (www.forestwatch.org) and the aforementioned Wildlands Project (www.wildlandsproject.org). The Center for Land and People and the Trust for Public Land (www.tpl.org) do great work and have a great series of books. The most recent is a collection: *Coming to Land in a Troubled World* (TPL, 2003). There are far too many conservation groups out west to name them all but one cool little group doing similar work in Montana is American Wildlands (www.wildlands.org), and a great group in Utah is the Southern Utah Wilderness Alliance (www.suwa.org).

CSA stands for "Community Supported Agriculture," a movement that began in Japan and Switzerland and spread to the U.S. in the 1980s, especially, initially, in the Biodynamic Agriculture community. It involves arrangements between groups of urban buyers and small farmers in which the farmer receives money for his crop before harvest season (when he/she needs it most) from the group and then delivers food to the group as it's harvested. This method cuts out the middleman and helps get vibrant produce to consumers, helps keep small organic farms afloat, and creates ties between city and country. A pioneering group setting up CSAs in New York is Just Food (www.justfood.org).

For more on "Ecological Medicine" see: *Ecological Medicine: Healing the Earth, Healing Ourselves* Kenny Ausubel ed. with J.P. Harpignies (Sierra Club Books, 2004). The most important coalition in this movement is Healthcare Without Harm (www.noharm.org), and Drs. Philip Landrigan and Mike McCally are director and co-director of The Center for Children's Health and the Environment at Mount Sinai School of Medicine in NYC.

For more on the "Environmental Justice" movement in the U.S.: *Confronting Environmental Racism: Voices from the Grassroots* Robert Bullard ed. (South End Press, 1993); *Deeper Shades of Green: The rise of blue-collar and minority environmentalism in America* by Jim Schwab (Sierra Club Books, 1994); and *Environmental Justice: Issues, Policies and Solutions* Bunyan Bryant, ed. (Island Press, 1995).

Communication Breakdown

It is quite apparent to everyone that in the U.S at least, the right has been winning the communications war. The immediate, universal adoption of the term "War on Terror" by U.S. media (instead of treating it as an international criminal matter) is only the latest example. Often, once one has lost the initial battle over language, the "war" is already over. There are a number of reasons for the success of the right besides media ownership patterns. First, the traditional left has been in a period of historical decline since the collapse of Communism. Free-market ideologies are currently in the driver's seat, and the right has the confidence and chutzpah that come with sensing it's your historical moment. These are just the winds of history, and they can shift, but no one can know when or exactly which way. One has to accept reality and adopt strategies that fit the times. Second, as has been discussed, some conservatives, after the loss of their standard-bearer Barry Goldwater in the 1964 election, decided to build networks to plan and execute a long-term strategy to bring themselves to power and went ahead and accomplished their goal. They had the advantage of access to rich sources of funding and to the best public relations, advertising and spin-doctor specialists in the land. They were intensely motivated by their revulsion at the counterculture and its "betrayal" over Vietnam, and by their sense that the moral decay of the society had to be reversed and America's omnipotence restored. Their efforts also benefited from the inattention of the center and liberals who just didn't take them seriously enough until it was too late, as well as from lucky breaks. Without the Iran hostage situation, for example, Carter might have defeated Reagan in 1980.

The ideological hard right is not a majority, however, and needs coalitions to govern. These coalitions have proved fractious and hard to maintain at different junctures in the past, but they have improved their discipline and cohesion and their patience and are more formidable for it. They will not always succeed politically, but they have managed to push the entire political debate quite far to the right. They have also become very good at disguising and soft-pedaling those aspects of their agendas that go far beyond mainstream opinion, except when they're among the faithful. They have been very deft at radically reducing funding for popular programs and redistributing wealth to the rich and deflecting the blame onto local governments, which become the brunt of popular rage, for example. They have become masters of stealth, subterfuge and the masking of their goals. They were perfectly willing to come up with any excuses that would convince the public to go to war in Iraq, for example, because their real reasons would not have done the trick.

The right has also mastered communications techniques specifically adapted to our short attention span, sound-byte era. They use hypnotic slogans they repeat incessantly; design photo-ops and public political spectacles (i.e., Bush Jr. landing on the aircraft carrier) that would have impressed Joseph Goebbels and Leni Riefenstahl; and are utterly ruthless in their willingness to distort and obfuscate facts, and to accuse their adversaries of treason. And they do this cleverly, in that they pick figureheads who exude amiable, good-natured, relaxed faux populism which charms the largely apolitical mainstream voter, and let a specialized phalanx of rabid attack dogs do the dirty work.

A few liberals and lefties can be tough political fighters too, but in general lefties find it hard to compete on this level. They often come off as more cerebral and cosmopolitan. The right has been good at making the left always seem a bit alien, a bit too egg-heady, a bit un-American, and at keeping it on the defensive. The right ideologues just seem more tenacious and tough and willing to do nearly anything to achieve their political aims at this point in history. This was evident in the battle over the Florida vote that brought Bush to power in 2000. One could sense those in the Gore camp weren't willing to risk bringing down the republic, but those on the other side would not have hesitated. They have the religious fervor of true believers. They're proud to be the wild-eyed guys in the rumble with the broken bottles and rusty razors who just look too crazy to fuck with.

The center left and liberals are generally unwilling to play the populist economic card, which, in periods of heightened income disparities, would be the only tack that if done properly could give them some real traction. Their timidity is especially inexcusable in that globalization is threatening to radically reduce and impoverish the middle class as more and more white (and not just blue) collar jobs are being farmed out to low-wage nations. But the center left and liberals don't dare resist because they are also tied to big corporate interests, and they are scared of being accused of "class war" demagoguery, a taboo in U.S. political discourse. As Noam Chomsky has pointed out, in the media every group in American society (women, workers, minorities, the elderly, and so forth) gets called a "special interest" even though, collectively, they constitute most of the population. The only exception is business, which is never referred to that way. Business is the norm. So, at the moment, mainstream "left" politicians don't generally really offer a gutsy enough alternative to inspire strong feelings even among people who would logically be supporters. As long as "left" politicians don't dare push an aggressive agenda of sane economic populism, the right will get away with their very clever faux cultural populism masking their elitist economic policies.

A core component of the right's ideology is "small government" (except for a huge military), and they tap into people's quite understandable antipathy for intrusive and impersonal government bureaucracies. The left has mostly failed to convince people that giant corporations are as powerful, even more intrusive and virtually unaccountable institutions, and that, sadly, often only government can offer a counterweight to their power and abuses. But progressives could tap into people's anti-bureaucratic impulses and distrust of politicians by driving home that yes, government is a big problem because it has been taken over largely by corrupt big moneyed interests. In the U.S. a successful economic populist reformer would have to be an outsider running against the unholy marriage of government and mega-business, and for everyday people, to restore balance and fairness, and couldn't appear to be a traditional liberal critiquing big business but simply proposing new government initiatives. That's just the reality of the

American political landscape.

Progressives are going to have to decide to pick a few core issues they are very clear about and for which they are willing to fight tooth and nail, and find ways to enunciate these issues simply, clearly and compellingly. This doesn't mean stooping to the level of the rabid right. We can devise clever slogans, but they should express truths we believe in, not distortions; and we can be tough and funny and hold our ground and more, but we do not need to emulate the hit-men (and women) of the right. During some of the pre-Iraq war demonstrations in the U.S., it was clear the very internet-savvy, sophisticated and impressive cadre of young activists who had been among the main organizers and coordinators of the best of the demonstrations were attempting to borrow a page from the "staying on message" sloganeering of the right, by all repeating the same catch-words on every interview show. They had devised a feel-good phrase that would capture the patriotic bona fides of the protesters, something like: "We support our troops, that's why we want to bring them home." One can understand the impulse to borrow a page from Karl Rove's successful "cliché of the week" technique, but one has to be careful not to become a caricature/mirror of your opponent.

Obviously, there are different styles of discourse that are appropriate for different fora. There is a need for refined, sophisticated, detailed analysis at the "policy wonk" level and in academic and intellectual circles, and for specific language in scientific, legal and other realms. In the political arena of mass opinion, messages have to be expressed in simpler, clearer terms, but it's still important not to approach that task with an attitude of condescension toward those with whom one is attempting to communicate. Yes, let's tailor our speech according to our audience—ethnically, regionally, professionally—but as honest attempts to communicate, not as transparent, clumsy stabs at manipulation. It is tough to grab and to hold attention without stooping to the level of our huckster culture or of our Machiavellian adversaries, but perhaps we can emulate the spirit of the most clever blues or country songs that manage to express profound truths with simple, catchy phrases.

The right's coalition is vulnerable on a number of fronts. Americans have consistently, to the puzzlement and chagrin of socialists, resisted appeals to working class solidarity, as the dream of upward mobility and possible affluence defines the national character (whatever the statistical reality), but they are also obsessed with fairness. And the current exacerbation of wealth inequities, the loss of jobs to low-wage countries, regressive taxation, corporate scandals and worsening public services create an opening for an aggressive, steadfast advocate of fairness. And these issues are not hard to explain. Corporate greed, unfair tax codes, the tainting of the political process by big money: these are realities people understand. But a political figure would have to have the stamina to stake out a well thought-out version of economic populism and stay with it through perhaps several election cycles without flinching until an alignment of propitious conditions could lead to success. Tenacity and steadfastness are crucial. But the fact that corporate influence and money are so pervasive in politics explains why no major Democrats have the nerve to hammer home the close ties of the administration to Enron, Halliburton, (not to mention some Bin Laden relatives!) and so on, with any verve and consistency. People in glass houses are afraid to throw stones, even if their glass houses are smaller than their opponents'.

The movement to reduce the influence of big money in politics has floundered. A bizarre tradition of American jurisprudence began with the weird (and murky) 1886 Santa Clara County vs. Southern Pacific Railroad Supreme Court ruling, which gave corporations some of the same rights as individuals (without the responsibilities), based on the 14th Amendment, which was originally intended to protect the rights of former slaves! Since then rulings have come close to equating commercial speech and political speech, and have decided that money and political donations are a form of "speech" protected by the 1st Amendment. Conversely, high-level political bribery seems almost impossible to prove even when businessmen pay enormous sums just to lunch with leaders and "advise" them on pending legislation that just happens to affect their profits.

But a larger point could be made that corporate behemoths have become so powerful and influential that we need a separation of corporations and the state as formal as the separation of church and state.

Sweetheart deals and revolving doors between government bureaucracies and lobbyists for major industries are the norm. People understand this, but they are cynical about the idea that anything can be done about it. To a certain extent they are right in that, forgive the Marxist truism, legal remedies can't change fundamental power alignments.

Corporate interests are dominant; the society's institutions will reflect that dominance. I don't think an out and out leftist politician could break that hold. But a reasonable-sounding, amiable economic populist who argued that capitalism is good and fine but that our society has gotten out of balance and that the little guy doesn't have a chance could go a long way. The Wal-Marts and Con-Agras and Cargills don't let the small merchant and farmer survive. Big businesses are fine, this politician (I envision a folksy war veteran, former farmer, independent Governor from, say, Iowa) could argue, but, gosh, we need more balance, more choice. Why, these giant pig farms stinking up my county just are not right. And when I call the bank or Sears, gee whiz, why am I talking to someone in Bangalore or Indonesia (or in prison) who makes one-tenth what an American would earn, about my account or my washing machine.

Big money has too much influence, he would continue. Today we need someone just like the Roosevelts who toned down big business for its own good to save it from itself. We need to have a nation with downtowns and small stores as well as big malls, and a political system where not only the big guys get their way because they can pay to play. I think this type of pitch from an independent populist could build a powerful reform movement because it would appeal to many small business owners and small town conservative voters as well as to the anti-corporate left. It wouldn't bring a socialist utopia, but it could perhaps push corporate interests back a bit.

These types of sane populist arguments can be expanded to cover issues involving privatization of the commons and globalization. We will need to rebound from our losses to the surging forces of privatization, to wage a fiercer battle to define what constitutes public space, from public lands to the air waves, to air and water and some food resources, and to put them off limits. This doesn't mean some hitherto public spheres have not on occasion become more efficient in private hands or benefited from competition, but people can understand viscerally why something as fundamental as water, for example, needs to be a public good. People everywhere can also understand that food self-sufficiency is critical. A nation or region that has to import its food is highly vulnerable in a crisis and perennially dependent, so a world with only a few giant food exporters and a huge mono-crop agribusiness sector controlled by a handful of immense cartels is a dangerous and unstable world. "Free trade" for TVs or vacuum cleaners is one thing, but food and water are certainly in a different category. We need to formulate these arguments clearly and on the gut level (that is, air, water and the air waves belong to all of us; no nation should be at risk of being denied food). And we must re-conquer domains such as prisons and public schools and forest service sectors that should never have been privatized. Here in the U.S., despite anti-government populist strains, there is also a strong reservoir of mythic sympathy for the idea of noble public service, from the WPA to the Peace Corps to Americorps to volunteer fire departments. That tradition must be reclaimed and revitalized.

On the environmental front, barring an extraordinary eco-catastrophe, "green" issues alone won't propel a candidate to victory, but an otherwise popular candidate who took an aggressively pro-environment stance once he/she was in office and stuck to it unapologetically would, in my view, gain stature as a result. Of course, that administration would have to be willing to stand up to disinformation and propaganda assaults from the corporate interests who have the most to lose, willing to steadfastly refute accusations of sacrificing jobs to protect weeds and minnows and so on, but a tough, no-nonsense willingness to state that the environment comes first and act accordingly, could pay off politically (depending, of course, on the gestalt of the political situation and the overall level of support of the President at the time).

Public lands for recreation are immensely popular. A leader who stepped forward with a vision to expand and protect them and to repeal obscene remnants of the robber-baron era (such as the 1872 mining act that basically gives away public resources to mining companies and lets them destroy the land), could come off as a great historical figure. A strong, catchy campaign about taking our public lands, which all

Americans own, back from the irresponsible and the greedy, could suceed if well orchestrated. The West has changed and the mining and ranching lobbies, while still locally dominant in some places, are in historical decline. It would be a bruising battle, but a tough-enough leader could do it and benefit politically. People admire someone with a vision who sticks to it. It would take a fortuitous set of circumstances, however, for such a person to be able to accede to power and to pull it off.

The environmental health movement is also something that has the potential to galvanize public interest. Activists have to be ready with well-coordinated, aggressive communication campaigns to pounce on any major breaking news story that highlights the health impacts of toxics, and to drive home that we need systemic, not just localized, changes in our approach to our entire industrial and agricultural systems. Asthma, cancer, clusters of birth defects, chemical and oil spills—these are things people understand and fear. So far, the health-industrial complex has been adept, in very American fashion, at making all health problems seem personal or familial/genetic (as has been the case with crime: conservative academics have managed to make it highly unfashionable in the U.S. to point out that there's any link between poverty and crime). But there is just too much evidence out there linking health problems and the increasing amounts of toxics and hormone-mimicking chemicals in the environment. The powerful idea of the "Precautionary Principle" which basically states that it is better to be safe than sorry when you're talking about health and life and new technologies is gaining acceptance in Europe and Japan and terrifies American corporations, which like to market first and worry later. Here too there are clear and simple, easy-to-understand ways to explain this to the public and put polluters on the defensive, if we are willing to push hard and not back down. The manufacturers of chemicals will use every form of intimidation and dirty trick and slander (as they did with Rachel Carson), but they can be put on the defensive because their greed and lack of concern are easy to make transparent, and topics like children's exposures to pesticides and asthma rates give them nightmares. Let's try to make sure they never get any sleep.

In all these cases, we need to be able to formulate clear, simple slogans and catch phrases that have visceral resonance, and to stick with them with patience and tenacity. But we must not deceive or use Orwellian obfuscation as the right does (i.e., the inheritance tax becomes the "death tax;" polluting industries trade groups take on green-sounding names; efforts to repeal clean air protection becomes the "Clear Skies" Initiative, and so forth.) Our cases are strong. We can tell the truth. To revitalize the progressive ecosystem we need to strengthen our existing institutions and divide and coordinate their work more effectively, merge redundant ones, create new ones where needed, mediate our disagreements more civilly, and be willing to build broad coalitions around very specific goals. But we will need to study our opponents far most astutely first.

Notes

Joseph Goebbels was Hitler's propaganda minister and Leni Riefenstahl was "Hitler's favorite filmmaker," most famous for *Triumph of the Will* (1934), her propaganda masterpiece that contains a lot of incredible footage of the Nazis' Nuremberg rallies.

For more on the Florida 2000 vote, see Greg Palast's *The Best Democracy Money Can Buy: an investigative reporter exposes the truth about globalization, corporate cons, and high-finance fraudsters* (Plume, 2003).

Noam Chomsky is a renowned linguist and the most persistent of all American critics of U.S. foreign policy.

For more on Karl Rove, master strategist of the right, see the scary Moore, James and Slater, Wayne. *Bush's Brain: How Karl Rove Made George W. Bush Presidential* (Wiley, 2003).

For more on the weird 1886 case that began to give the rights of personhood to corporations and the tragic history of American jurisprudence regarding corporations, see: Hartmann, Thom. *Unequal Protection: the rise of corporate dominance and the theft of human rights* (Rodale, 2002); Stiller, Richard. *Broken Promises: the strange history of the fourteenth amendment* (Random House, 1972); Nace, Ted. *Gangs of America: the rise of corporate power and the disabling of democracy* (Berrett-Koehler, 2003); and Korten, David C. *When Corporations Rule the World* (Berrett-Koehler, 2001).

For a critique of global water privatization, see "Blue Gold: The Global Water Crisis and the Commodification of the World's Water Supply", by Maude Barlow (an International Forum on Globalization paper, 1999. www.ifg.org).

For a good counterpoint to and refutation of the now prevalent "broken windows" theory of crime, enamored by right wing sociologists, politicians and police officials, see: Sampson, R.J., Stephen w. Raudenbush, and Felton Earls. "Neighborhoods and violent crime: A multilevel study of collective efficacy" (in *Science* 277, Aug. 15, 1997) which shows community cohesion and cooperation are key factors in limiting crime. Also: Sampson, Robert J. and Steve Raudenbush. " Systematic Social Observation of Public Spaces: A New Look at Disorder in Urban Neighborhoods" in *American Journal of Sociology* 105: 603-651, 1999.

For more on the Precautionary Principle: Harremoës, Poul, ed. The *precautionary principle in the 20th century: late lessons from early warnings* (Earthscan Publications, 2002); and Raffensperger, Carolyn and Tickner, Joel, ed. *Protecting public health & the environment: implementing the precautionary principle* (Island Press, 1999).

Dividing the Right

There are individual scholars and groups on the left that track the right in different ways, including the Southern Poverty Law Center which (among other missions) tracks far right extremists, and Jean Hardisty's Political Research Associates; but they are few and far between, and the average progressive is woefully ignorant about the opposition. Since I discussed the right in my section on the importance of "knowing" one's adversaries, I won't rehash my entire analysis here, except to stress that we need to divide and weaken the right's coalition to enjoy some political success, and that in order to do that we must develop an exquisite understanding of the various groups and tendencies that compose it.

The U.S.' right is a unique phenomenon. The hard right of the spectrum is far more based on various religious fundamentalisms and a distrust of federal authority here than in Europe where the hard right tends to be more composed of secular ultra-nationalists and neo-fascists (and a few feudal/monarchist relics). There are, of course, religious conservatives throughout Europe, especially in Russia, Serbia, perhaps Greece, residually in Italy, and the like, but they are nowhere as numerous or organized as here. And there just isn't the same prevalence of deep-seated wildly anarcho-individualist anti-government attitudes as there are in the U.S.. Business classes on the center right are as interested in profit everywhere, and big European and Japanese and Malaysian-based multinationals are obviously as eager to pilfer the globe's resources as their American counterparts and just as willing to bribe and pressure to gain advantage. But European and Japanese capitalist elites are more reconciled to the stability provided by welfare states, social pacts with organized labor, and strong central governments. Of course these elites prefer lower taxes on themselves, but they are more accepting of the general shape of their own societies and their "social contracts" than the far more politically aggressive U.S. business classes, which contain quite a few fanatical utopian free marketers. It is astonishing to Europeans, for example, that a disciple of Ayn Rand could be the head of the U.S. Federal Reserve (Alan Greenspan).

The two main pillars of American conservatism, the economic libertarians and the religious communitarians, are radically different cultural species, but they have come to understand that they can use each other to further their respective goals. In a few cases recently, cleavages have surfaced. As I mentioned, on FCC regulations that would have encouraged further consolidation of the media, some sectors within these two tendencies were at odds. The religious folks don't all trust big business, especially big-city entertainment media, which many view as vulgar, amoral, cynical profiteers. And some of them respond to economic populism when they feel the big money guys are being too greedy and the average person is suffering. On an issue such as drug policy, a few libertarians are willing to point out the waste of resources and tax dollars, and so forth. So, there are times these two pillars of the right will not be in lock step. But, by and large, progressives will not have much luck winning over folks in either of these two constituencies, except, as we have seen, on very specific issues. There may be clever ways to encourage discord between them though.

Also there are many sub-categories within these two larger tendencies, and some hold more promise than others as potential allies on some questions. For example, there is a subset of radical social as well as economic libertarians, and these people can be reliable partners on civil liberties encroachments or drug policy reform, while remaining our opponents on economic questions such as taxes or on government social or environmental initiatives, i.e., on any notion of a commons. There are also some evangelical Christians with strong environmental concerns because they view the natural world as God's creation, and they differ radically from the apocalypse-obsessed who view environmental collapse as another hopeful indicator of the coming "End Times." It is important for there to be progressives who specialize in studying the subtle distinctions among the various right-wing and evangelical groups and maintaining communication with a wide range of usual opponents to probe to see which of them might be willing to join in on resisting this bill or supporting this initiative. That has been happening more, but too often it has been limited to inside the Washington "Beltway" horse trading between DC-based advocacy groups. We need to encourage and increase these outreach efforts at the regional and local grassroots level as well.

Most important, though, are a variety of other constituencies which often vote Republican but are less ideologically "hard core." In my opinion, one of the most important of these is the small business community, a pillar of the Republican Party, electorally, organizationally and financially. Small business people are most interested in low taxation and fewer government regulations (including environmental ones), and they resent labor laws that force them to have to pay onerous medical premiums for employees or that give employees more rights. It is easy to see where they clash with a left agenda. That said, their interests and those of big corporations do not invariably dovetail. The average opening of a new Wal-Mart leads to the death of 100 small retail businesses. The center-left would benefit greatly from a detailed study of the small business community and should try to develop a strategy to drive a wedge between small and large business interests. Progressives can't jettison employees, a core constituency, but there may be ways of offering small businesses creative aid programs, tax reforms, streamlined regulations in many areas, and the like, and to sell them on the fact that too many corporations are shipping capital and manufacturing jobs overseas and avoiding their fair share of taxes, raising the burden on smaller enterprise.

The majority of this group will not change its voting patterns overnight, but an intelligent program of outreach and perhaps the creation of a more moderate national small business group with creative ideas could siphon off enough support to hurt the Republicans in close races. And I'm confident a very good case can honestly be made that current policies are generally not favorable to small enterprise, and that a progressive agenda could include support for measures to help small businesses and farms. The key might be to develop policies that really focus on helping the smallest businesses, those that hire dozens to two hundred at most employees, and separating them from larger enterprises that hire several hundred and up, especially as regards onerous healthcare costs and overly complex regulations.

The right has long been studying the electoral landscape and long ago tailored strategies to win over first the Deep South white vote, then the blue-collar, Catholic men who used to vote Democratic ("Reagan Democrats") in swing "rust belt" states, and even a few unions. More recently they have made inroads into the Jewish vote, and are now targeting married women and middle-class Hispanics, among others. The electoral left needs to get far more daring in its strategies, but rather than with Clintonesque/DLC cynicism, with genuine creativity to bring new constituencies aboard by fashioning initiatives to help them on some fronts without screwing the weak and disenfranchised for political mileage. Obviously, most electoral outcomes depend on how the bulk of fairly apolitical "swing voters" lean, and many unpredictable factors—scandals, accidents, attacks, foreign policy fiascos, economic cycles, ends of historical periods, new cultural phenomena—can suddenly become determinant, so no strategy guarantees success. But progressives don't have many options, and they don't have that much to lose by shedding some mental shackles and broadening their horizons a bit.

Even if the current administration were sent packing as a result of its astonishing megalomaniacal arrogance and sheer incompetence, if the desert quagmire it has plunged into continues to be as unforgiving as it currently seems, and a more center-left (by U.S. standards) government succeeded it in the next election, the core socio-political landscape wouldn't change that much in the near term (though eventually demographic changes are likely to radically reshape the nation). To achieve the type of profound, more lasting transformations that would begin to take us toward a more sustainable and life-affirming civilization, we need to study deeply the highly complex social and ideological currents that shape our world, and marshal all our political skills to somehow try and nudge enough of those currents in a desirable direction.

Notes

I mention two groups on the left of the spectrum that study the right: The Southern Poverty Law Center (http://www.splcenter.org/) tracks potentially violent far right groups among many other of its long-lived civil rights activities. It was one of the only groups warning of potential trouble just before the Oklahoma City bombing. Jean Hardisty's Political Research Associates (http://www.publiceye.org/) is a much smaller endeavor studying the political landscape of the right. Jean is the author of: *Mobilizing Resentment: Conservative Resurgence from the John Birch Society to the Promise Keepers.*

For more on Alan Greenspan (Chairman of the U.S. Federal Reserve Bank) and his relationship to the ultra economically libertarian circles around the writer Ayn Rand, see Tuccille, Jerome. *Alan Shrugged: the life and times of Alan Greenspan, the world's most powerful banker* (Wiley, 2002); Martin, Justin. *Greenspan: the man behind money* (Perseus Pub, 2001); and Jeff Walker's *The Ayn Rand Cult* (Open Court, 1999).

DLC stands for the Democratic Leadership Council, the centrist-right wing of the Democratic Party establishment that includes Bill Clinton and many of the remaining southern Democrats.

Historical Compromises?

(Disclaimer: In what follows, I am about to throw up a few trial balloons that fill me with trepidation, because the topics they relate to are so emotionally charged and politically sensitive, and the very idea of compromising on some of these issues will make some people in my camp want to boil me alive. I am not certain about any of these proposals. I am advancing them as exploratory probes, topics of discussion, thought experiments, not as an advocate. But I do believe some creative brainstorming is essential to get out of some of the ruts we are in.)

The Threatened Welfare State

While there are still small groups of radical anti-capitalists on the left, even former Communist parties now accept some version of the free-market. Capitalism is a fact of life for the foreseeable future, whether we like it or not. The right/left divide these days on economic issues is defined by how reined-in corporations' prerogatives and the market should be. As I have mentioned, globalization and savagely competitive international capitalism are putting intense pressure on the perks of workers and the middle class in "Northern" economies, weakening unions, and forcing governments to trim their welfare states. Until recently there had been a de-facto entente with the U.S., which permitted post-WWII Western Europe and Japan to give their working classes far more job security, better pensions and medical coverage, longer vacations and better early educational opportunities and day-care for their children, compared to the more socially Darwinian U.S. In exchange they would defer to the U.S. on major foreign policy questions, support it in the Cold War, and live under its military umbrella. The money they saved on military expenditures could go into social spending, to show the world capitalist workers could prosper more than their Communist brethren, and to maintain social peace. And the American economy, despite its enormous military expenditures, was so dynamic after the war, and enough privileged sectors of the American working class in some manufacturing industries were receiving high enough salaries in the 1950s and 1960s—a golden age of wealth equity and upward mobility by historical American standards—that a vital left-leaning labor movement in the states was not a risk. But with the end of the Cold War and the globalization frenzy, these ententes are breaking down. Multi-national capital is not facing a global socialist competitor. It is the only game in town; it no longer needs to maintain a humane veneer. It wants low wages and high productivity and is in a position to get exactly what it wants. Some Europeans are chafing at U.S. hegemony, and many U.S. workers are starting to notice they have to work two to three jobs without sleep to stay afloat.

To compound the problem, Europe and Japan now have very low birth rates and declining populations, a good thing environmentally but not easy to negotiate in a global system based on an economic model geared to constant growth. So these countries, and the U.S. and some other nations as well, are all facing aging populations, threats to the solvency of their pension and social security schemes and medical systems, declining median family incomes; and erosions of their middle classes and social safety nets. Obviously one function of the left in a reactionary period such as this is to fight to preserve as many of the social gains won by hard battles over the last two hundred years as possible.

But one also has to be realistic. We can't pretend the global economy is other than it is. Yes, we can bemoan it and rail against it and advocate other models, but we're in it. Yes, we should fight unfair global trade agreements tooth and nail, demand that corporate elites pay a fairer share of taxes, and so forth, but governments don't have that much room to maneuver. If an anti-IMF leader comes to power in a developing country, a flight of capital and CIA destabilization teams throw that society into turmoil (as someone like Michael Manley in

Jamaica, to name one of many, discovered in the 1970s). If a richer country tries to curtail corporate abuses, companies and investors can also move facilities and capital elsewhere, exacting a high price.

I'm not at all saying we shouldn't continue fighting and resisting and advocating a totally different value system and economic model, but (and this is just a thought experiment) it might also be worth considering that instead of always fighting desperate defensive skirmishes, the left might not offer some historical compromises. For example, the pension and social security funds of most Western nations are certain to be changed as they do face insolvency given demographic patterns. We have seen recent strikes in Germany, France and Brazil fail to deter those governments from taking steps to require later retirement ages or otherwise curtail benefits, and two of those governments were of the "left," one with Greens in the ruling coalition. What if, instead of holding out and striking, and invariably losing, unions went to their center-left governments and said: "We all understand these systems have to be made solvent and sustainable. We will work with you to make painful but inevitable reforms, but we want concessions in other domains such as halting privatization of certain social spheres, solemn written guarantees that core areas of the welfare state are sacrosanct, a new social contract for the new era." I realize this sounds wimpy and pessimistic, but if the global winds are blowing against you, it might be wise to be clever to lose as little as possible. Sometimes if you try to hold on to everything, you lose far more.

I can hear the teeth of many of my former comrades grinding as they read the passage above. Some might argue persuasively that the only way to hold on to some gains is to be as militant as possible. That is often true, and, as I've said, a healthy left political ecosystem should always include vivacious radicals exerting pressure on more moderate elements to keep them honest. But one has to be attuned to the real economic and technological trends at work in the world, Marx himself would no doubt remind us. I am not at all suggesting we cave in on all fronts or stop pressing to slow down radically the globalization juggernaut or to reduce the power of large corporations and neuter their political access. I'm just suggesting that if you see something inevitably approaching, it can be wise to get in the process early and try to shape it, rather than resisting it totally, losing and having to swallow the consequences. The first strategy can strengthen your political stature and support so that you'll be in a stronger position to go on the offensive again when the political weather shifts, the second leaves you weaker than ever. And right now, these battles are all being lost anyway as some unions, seeing the writing on the wall, have invariably broken ranks in each of these struggles, and the holdouts have been left defeated and increasingly impotent.

Abortion, Education and the Religious Right

I know I'm really going to regret even attempting to discuss these questions, but the cultural clash with the religious right in the U.S., especially over abortion and now gay rights, has sucked up so much energy and created such stalemates and blockages in the nation's political life, that it has to be possible to at least brainstorm about some possible ways to take some tentative stabs at lessening the impasse. There is obviously no easy way out because we are dealing with two basically irreconcilable worldviews (and yes I know there are Catholic pacifists and some others on the left who oppose abortions, and I respect them, but they're not big players in this battle). Most of us on the left (myself included) are completely unwilling to restrict a woman's access to abortion, and, rightly in my opinion, view this is as non-negotiable. Those on the other side sincerely view it as killing, which, on some level, it may be. But nearly all political decisions—who gets food aid or immigration papers or asylum; which drugs or toxic chemicals or sexual acts are legal or illegal; which wars will be fought; which towns will be evacuated for a highway—portion out pain and premature death to some and not others. In a sense, violence, coercion and the distribution of death underlie all socio-political decisions. Anyway, we lefties find it bafflingly contradictory that many of the same folks who oppose abortion also oppose sex education or contraception and say they are "pro-life" but support wars and the death penalty, and seem unconcerned with feeding or housing the embryos when they grow up; but there's no point in re-hashing these endlessly repeated arguments.

The average person is understandably squeamish about abortion. The mammalian instinct to protect the young of one's species extends to some degree to embryonic life. Most people realize abortion needs to be legal and available, but they don't like being reminded about it, and they don't feel comfortable defending it too forcefully. Abortions are very traumatic experiences for women, so even the many women who have had them have mixed emotions about them. This permits the religious right to go against the majority consensus and achieve some tactical victories on occasion.

In a sense the country has reached a sort of historic stalemate. Abortion will remain legal, but it will be difficult to find providers in conservative parts of the country. Poor women will have trouble getting access to or affording them, and the right will keep cleverly fraying around the edges, making some types of procedures illegal; making it hard on doctors who perform them, and so forth, but without being able to roll back the clock fully. An enormous amount of energy goes into this conflict as picketers harass abortion clinics and the current administration tries to pack the federal courts with deeply religious anti-abortion judges, and liberals are resisting as best they can. The cynical business elites, low tax enthusiasts and muscular unilateralist neo-conservatives in the Republican party who don't care about this issue need the zealots in the anti-abortion ranks as electoral foot sol-diers, so they're willing to throw them just enough bones to keep them on the team, but they don't want them to succeed too well or the right could lose too much mainstream support at the polls.

One interesting aspect of this battle is that on issues of sexual free-doms, abortion and now gay rights, progressives have made great gains over the last few decades because they have appealed to libertarian val-ues: individuals' rights to choose what to do with their own bodies. The movement to give adults the right to medically assisted suicide is also making some headway. The religious-right's radically communi-tarian morality goes against some very strong libertarian streaks in American culture. But those same types of individualistic, libertarian attitudes can also make many supporters of the right to an abortion unwilling to pay taxes to help poor women here or abroad get them or get contraception, for example. And taking a libertarian tack can then make it a little trickier to make communitarian arguments on other issues such as environmental regulations or on limiting genetic enhancement.

I have argued that the religious right is an integral part of the American political landscape and is not about to vanish. Its influence in the corridors of power is currently at a zenith; that is not likely to last indefinitely, but they will be players nationally and strong factors in many regions of the country. And so I have to ask myself: "If I'm a progressive who believes in tolerance and respect for other cultures, shouldn't I also muster some tolerance for American evangelicals, especially since they're a permanent feature of the mix?" After all, many of the other groups I am surrounded by here in Brooklyn, from Rastafarians to ultra-orthodox Jews to stockbrokers to wise guys, are just about as culturally alien to me as are the evangelicals.

One problem is of course that these evangelicals are not content to organize their own communities but are intent on imposing their morality on the rest of us, and we have to resist. But they of course experience that as our morality being imposed on them, because they are very numerous and view themselves as the real heartland Americans and the whole nation as their turf. They are not just willing to run their own enclaves as the Amish or Hassidim usually do and grudgingly accept a secular state and public commons as neutral ground. They keep pushing their agenda at every level from school boards to the Supreme Court. Still, I somehow feel that we should exhibit the willingness to create tolerance and space in the commons for them as much as we do for other culturally unique groups, as long as it doesn't put our core values and rights at risk.

Here I'm going, again, to indulge in some experimental brainstorming. Many of us on the left were sympathetic to the conscientious objector status afforded pacifists when there was a military draft. This was an exception created for ideological reasons, an example of a secular state's flexibility. We on the left are also often sympathetic to pacifist activists who withhold and put in escrow the portion of their taxes that would go to military spending, though this is obviously illegal, and it sets a risky precedent: the anti-abortion right makes similar arguments when it balks at spending tax dollars on abortion or on family planning programs overseas that might include abortions.

This is where some sort of painful historical compromise (at least a temporary one until perhaps these people's relative numbers and their clout might decline over the decades) might be worth fantasizing about. What if anti-abortionists were promised no federal tax money would go to funding abortions at home or abroad (each state could decide its own policies), but that abortion would forever remain legal. Liberal U.S. administrations could work out backroom agreements with the Europeans about funding the World Health Organization's (WHO) and other contraceptive initiatives in poorer nations so, symbolically, at least, the U.S. didn't directly provide funds. Right-wing administrations are not providing those funds anyway. Progressives and women's groups would need to raise money to replace federal funds for domestic abortion providing institutions such as Planned Parenthood, a daunting task; but if we really believe abortion is a crucial right, we should be able to support our own institutions and sustain viable networks of family planning clinics, and more progressive state governments would provide support.

I'm not sure the scenario I just described is necessarily a good idea. I realize it could concede too much or be interpreted as weakness and only encourage more aggressive assaults from the cultural right, and could institutionalize poor women's lack of access to abortions, especially in "bible belt" areas. That said, those things are occurring anyway. It is possible that a minority of the cultural right is also exhausted by this endless war, and that some sort of grand gesture of historical compromise on the part of the left on this issue, while it would never satisfy the core of the zealots on the right, could take just enough wind out of the anti-abortion movement's sails to make it a less potent, more marginalized force, and liberate enormous amounts of our own political energy. I realize the price would be very high. Anyway, whether my speculations on this are half-baked or not, it is worth trying to think outside the usual parameters of our reactive politics on this issue, or we're going to be stuck in the same trenches on this front for a very long time.

Another example of a smaller cultural compromise would be that religious clubs could meet in public school facilities after school hours, as long as all groups had equal access (including gays, neo-pagans, atheists, and the like). I believe in a secular, neutral commons, reject any school prayers, and so forth, but see no harm in acknowledging that various religious groups are part of the community and deserve equal shots at public space. I don't see that as a violation of the separation of church and state. This is a small matter, though such cases do make it to the Supreme Court. Many public schools now accommodate home-schooled children, letting them use libraries, labs, participate in group-sports and so on. Some of these kids are Christians, others not. I think that's admirable flexibility on the part of the system. Yes, sadly perhaps, we need fairly uniform rules in a mass society, but a healthy multi-ethnic, multi-cultural, multi-perspectival social landscape should also exhibit a lot of creative flexibility to accommodate difference. And that's one aspect of our culture that has shown a lot of progress and is very positive.

The larger point I'm trying to make is that it is important for progressives to examine their own attitudes. Most lefties, for example, were not very concerned by the massacre of the Branch Davidians in Waco. Whatever one thought of these people's beliefs, these were human beings and the authorities were brutally repressive in that action. The same is true of China's treatment of the Falun Gong sect. Sure these people are fanatics of a sort, but so are many of us. We either believe in human rights and due process, or not. We need to strive to practice what we preach in terms of tolerance, and to find ways of accommodating passionate Christians as much as we can without compromising our own core values. They won't make it easy. Trying to be tolerant of the intolerant is one hell of a challenge, and I'm not naïve enough to think our battles with them will end any time soon, but even small compromises can, at times, radically alter a situation.

I realize now might not be the best time to offer compromises, as we are fighting tooth and nail not to lose completely previous gains in this reactionary period. But when the winds shift and we are in a more advantageous position, it might behoove us to make some bold gestures instead of pressing our advantage so forcefully that we simply make the next swing of the pendulum even worse as the bitter enemy regroups and emerges even more clever and more determined. If we were totally certain the evangelical right was a fading anachronism that was bound to weaken in the near future, perhaps a no-holds barred strategy would make sense, but that is wishful thinking. They are going to be around for a long time, and in my opinion we have got to become cleverer at isolating the most rabid elements from some of their support-base by varying our tactics.

Environmental Compromises?

This following idea is not mine, and I can't support it because I'm too passionate a lover of wildlands, but it does offer another example of the type of historic compromise I've been discussing. A pro-environmentalist scholar at Yale named Daniel Esty floated (very nervously) the idea of a historic compromise on U.S. energy policy. The environmental community would allow drilling in the Arctic National Wildlife Refuge, which it has been bitterly resisting, but first, only with very strict safeguards (winter drilling only to avoid as much harm to wildlife as possible, and so forth); and second, in exchange for a massive change in environmental policies, which would include serious funding for alternative energy; serious, mandated improvements in vehicle efficiency, committing to better-than-Kyoto carbon emissions goals, and the like.

Now there's no chance the current U.S. administration would ever consider accepting such a proposal, and there's no way most environmentalists at this juncture could go for it without infuriating their supporters, so it's not going to happen, though drilling may happen because, if things go badly, we may simply lose the battle and get nothing in return. But I mention it because one way or another we're making trade-offs all the time. Even most environmentalists drive cars and heat their houses. The fuel is coming from a sacrifice area somewhere. We advocate alternative energy and the phase-out of the petroleum era, but even utopian scenarios (and right now we're in a very dystopian one with no real sign of major changes in direction) describe a transition over decades.

A willingness to make some sort of bold, realistic compromises on the environment might make sense if we were confident it was a genuine social environmental compact, in which the various sectors of the society were genuinely and sincerely coming to a historic agreement, recognizing the severity of the environmental situation, working toward transitions to less toxic and sustainable technologies, with agreed upon goals and benchmarks. In that sort of situation some painful sacrifices might be worth considering. One could perhaps imagine a few European countries achieving that sort of social cohesion, but most of the world, especially we here in the cheap-gas addicted U.S. are so far from such a possibility that this type of speculation is likely to remain just that for the foreseeable future.

And wilderness protection is one area where "compromise" can be absurd because we've lost so much of it. If only five percent of your old growth forest is left, what's a reasonable compromise? To cut only half? Then you're down to two-point-five percent? What's a reasonable compromise then? There comes a point (and we're beyond it in most cases) where the only sane position is absolute protection to save what is left, and the burning desire to restore more so that we have robust, vital ecosystems where we can go admire in humility the self-organizing power of the natural world, not slowly dying islands of the wild, fading museums of biodiversity where we go to mourn the decline of nature's vitality, and weep.

Notes

Yale eco-scholar/researcher Daniel Esty's ideas about the Arctic National Wildlife Refuge were discussed in: Kristof, Nicholas D. "Casting a Cold Eye on Arctic Oil," an Op-ed piece in *The New York Times*, Sept. 10, 2003. A list of Esty's publications can be found at: http://www.yale.edu/epcenter/front/EstyPubsSubject.html.

Some Closing Questions

It is impossible to know the political future, but leaders and activists have no choice but to hypothesize about possible scenarios to devise strategies. As I look at the current socio-political landscape and geopolitical tensions and ponder the future in attempting to think about the potential role of the broad left and of environmental movements, a slew of disturbing questions in three fundamental areas leap out at me. I don't know the answers to these questions, and they are depressing, but they are the types of questions we must reflect upon intensely and honestly if we hope to make political gains. I passionately hope far more intelligent people than I will find ways to begin answering some of them and lead us out of this dark period.

1. How quickly will environmental degradation affect specific regions, industries, ecosystems, and global climate? Are humans intrinsically incapable of avoiding the overuse and depletion of whatever resources are available, as the collapse of many earlier civilizations suggests; in other words, is the human attention span just too short-term to tackle large-scale, global problems that would require concerted efforts and radical changes in behavior? Will we just see the highly adaptive human species keep adjusting to an ever-more impoverished biosphere, and each new generation with no tangible memory of a richer world simply accept the world it finds itself in, no matter how bleak their lives might seem to us? So is the environmental movement's role merely to slow the rate of decline and preserve as many species as possible in museum-like preserves and fight for somewhat cleaner air and water, despite the inevitable impoverishment and toxification of the biosphere? Is the race to a post-human, cyborgian, gene-altered era inevitable? Or is there some realistic hope that we can actually attempt to build a far-more sustainable civilization? Why does sanity seem so hopelessly utopian?

2. What is the fate of the American Empire? Is it as dominant and powerful as it appears or are there signs within it of potential weakness and decline, especially in the foreign ownership of so much of its ever-expanding debt, its technology transfer and loss of manufacturing capacity to Asia, and its increased wealth stratification? Can political movements that don't support the hegemony of the empire they are embedded in ever have any chance of shaking the impression that they are treasonous or disloyal, especially in a uniquely reflexively patriotic, militarily fetishistic culture? And can they therefore never achieve substantive political traction, unless they ally themselves with nativist isolationists whose opposition to military adventures stems from an entirely different ideology? How intense will political repression of dissidents of all stripes become if the empire suffers setbacks or more internal attacks and its ruling elites begin to feel vulnerable?

3. Is the progressive left as marginal and largely irrelevant as it currently seems to be in the core centrifugal/centripetal dynamic battle generated by globalization, that between the leveling forces of modernity and the resistance of anti-modern traditions and cultures? And if not, how can it achieve enough traction to offer viable "third way" alternatives in the midst of such intense polarization?

Notes

On the future of biodiversity and ecosystems, see "What is Sustainability Anyway?" by Thomas Prugh and Erik Assadourian in *World-Watch* magazine, September/October 2003; and Lester Brown's "Against Rising Temperatures…Time May be Running Out" in *New York Press*, September 10-16, 2003. On Empire, see: "A Trap of Their Own Making" by Anatol Lieven in the *London Review of Books*, May 8, 2003.

J.P. HARPIGNIES, a radical "new left" student activist in the late 1960s and early 1970s in the U.S. and Europe, has been involved with many environmental causes. A former program director at the New York Open Center and contributing editor to its magazine *Lapis*, he is an associate producer of the annual *Bioneers* environmental conference as well as a program consultant and conference producer for other organizations. He is the author of *Double Helix Hubris* (Cool Grove, 1997), a polemical critique of genetic manipulation, and co-editor (with Kenny Ausubel) of the first two titles in the Bioneers book series *Ecological Medicine* and *Nature's Operating Instructions* (Sierra Club Books, 2004). He is also a long-time instructor of Taijiquan and is based in Brooklyn, NYC.

The complete Spuyten Duyvil title list is available at
http://www.spuytenduyvil.net

Printed in Dunstable, United Kingdom